ALL ABOUT
STAINED
GLASS

For My Mother

ALL ABOUT
STAINED
GLASS

BY NANCY WALKE

TAB TAB BOOKS Inc.

BLUE RIDGE SUMMIT, PA. 17214

FIRST EDITION

FIRST PRINTING

Copyright © 1982 by TAB BOOKS Inc.

Printed in the United States of America

Library of Congress Cataloging in Publication Data

Walke, Nancy.
 All about stained glass.

 Bibliography: p.
 Includes index.
 1. Glass craft. I. Title.
TT298.W34   748.5′028   81-18270
ISBN 0-8306-0075-2   AACR2
ISBN 0-8306-1103-7 (pbk.)

Contents

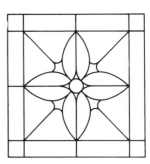

Introduction

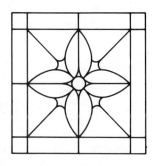

I have never known anyone who could not appreciate the beauty and artistry of stained glass, though few admirers really appreciate the amount of time and degree of craftsmanship that go into creating it. When I began working in glass, I understood some of the complexities of the craft and believed that it would be impossible for me to master. And, indeed, although many people work in stained and leaded glass, not so many can claim the term craftsman, and fewer still have truly mastered the art. To do either requires time, experience, and application.

But everyone must begin somewhere, and that is what this book is all about. Whatever your age, background, or artistic training, you can learn how to make leaded stained-glass objects.

Everything you need to know to begin is covered, including all about tools and materials required, seting up a work space, and where to find design sources. Each step of making leaded glass is covered in detail from pattern making and glass cutting, to leading, soldering, glazing, bracing the work, and final installation. Though most of the instruction deals with leaded glass, an entire chapter is devoted to the copper-foil technique. Safety precautions, answers to most frequently asked questions, and how to make repairs are also covered. Once you have gained some experience you will want to try some of the more advanced three-dimensional projects, such as boxes and lamps.

The instructions and techniques covered have been culled from my experiences in making, experimenting with, and teaching stained glass. Doubtless there are other ways of doing things; you may even discover a few of your own.

There is so much that goes into a book of this sort. For my own research and work, of course, the information has been readily available, but an amazing amount of input also came from my coworkers, friends, and other professionals, without whose contributions this book would not have been possible.

Gary Ecker, my friend and coworker at Stephen's Stained Glass in Riverside, California, was a primary source of technical information and an inspiration to me.

Kim Bruttomesso, my original instructor and a dear friend, supplied encouragement and ideas during times when I was floudering, and I can never thank her enough.

George Siposs, an author many times over, took all the photos except where otherwise noted and was instrumental in the book's initial creation and in teaching me the technical aspects of writing.

I'd also like to thank Michele Burgess, whose terrific job of retyping this manuscript has made everyone's job infinitely easier, especially mine.

Although there are many dozens of others who have contributed to this effort, it would be impossible to name each and every one, so I'll just say "thank you" to all.

Lastly, I would like to express my deepest gratitude to my parents, who have encouraged (or put up with) my itch to write and have also been recipients of many of my earlier glass works, most of which I would like to destroy. However, their eyes never saw the flaws in the glass, or in me. Their support over the years has brought this book to fruition.

Chapter 1
Glass

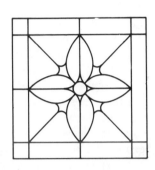

The exact origin of the use of colored glass in windows is still obscure today, although it is believed that crude versions of the craft were in existence during the early Egyptian empires. The Greeks used glass as a replacement for marble in mosaic work. Later on, in Rome, the use of copper, bronze, and lead framing brought into being the formal beginnings of the glass craftsman.

For many centuries thereafter, stained glass enjoyed great popularity, although it was nearly always installed in churches and cathedrals. The colored glass lent itself well to a meditative mood, and to the portrayal of religious figures and stories for a religious but often illiterate congregation.

In St. Denis, France, Abbot Suger pioneered the Gothic movement in architecture and stained glass alike. Glass was used to enhance and complement the arched Gothic building style and was an integral part of the structure.

During the fifteenth century, architecture began a decline, and overrefinement and commercialism took over the glass trade. Painters used glass as if it were a canvas; stained glass of the next few centuries suffered badly. Old techniques were lost as windows became almost entirely painted, with lead used solely to hold them together. During the sixteenth century, the Reformation also proved disastrous for stained glass. Queen Elizabeth ordered the removal or destruction of many shrines and religious artifacts, including painted glass windows. Stained glass became a lost art.

In the 1800s America saw a revival in stained glass. John La Farge, credited with the invention of opalescent glass, greatly popularized its use in stained-glass windows. A contemporary of La Farge, Louis Comfort Tiffany became perhaps the most well-known personage in the history of glass crafting. Tiffany was a restless, artistic man who dabbled brilliantly in several fields of art. Because he could not obtain the glass he envisioned would bring his windows to life, he opened his own glass works and began experimenting with the opalescent glass of the day. He patented Favrile, a type of glass with a beautiful iridescent quality that he in turn used to create his exquisite works. His designs were very realistic and ornate in the art nouveau trend of the day.

Tiffany also invented and popularized the use of copper foil to hold the pieces of glass together. Without the use of a more delicate framework than was possible with lead, Tiffany's lamps, some containing thousands of small pieces of glass, would have been not feasible and perhaps impossible.

A long road has been traveled from the roots of the glass craft to the present state of the art. Glass artists are testing and stretching the boundaries and discovering that there are very few limitations in this versatile medium. Much of the contemporary work being done is exciting and innovative.

Traditional styles also have a secure place in today's world. With the new techniques and better tools available, craftsmen are producing stained glass that rivals medieval work. Stained glass in general is enjoying a popularity unsurpassed previously. It is seen everywhere and is universally admired. May it always continue.

This book is about what is technically called leaded glass, not stained glass. *Staining glass* is a process by which special glass stains are painted onto clear or colored antique glass, which is then fired in a kiln to fuse the color right into the glass. Staining glass is the method used mostly in cathedral and other church windows where you will notice that details and shading (such as in faces and garments) are extremely precise and lifelike. These effects could not have been achieved with leaded glass alone.

Leaded glass is the technique of joining together pieces of colored glass with lead. The glass is colored as it's made. It is not, as some believe, painted on later, or dipped in some kind of dye.

Stained glass has become such a popular misnomer for what is actually leaded glass that there is no point in arguing the difference. The two terms are commonly, as here, used interchangeably.

Glass is made from silica sand mixed with other oxides that aid the melting and combining process. Different colors of glass are produced by adding chemicals, minerals, and oxides to the mixture. The addition of cobalt and copper oxide produce blues; iron and manganese produce orange hues; gold oxides are used in making red glass, which accounts for its comparatively high price. The ingredients are melted together until molten. It is then blown or poured and rolled by machine to the finished form. After forming, it must be carefully and slowly annealed or cooled. This is done in an annealing oven where controlled heat is reduced gradually over a period of many hours until normal room temperature is reached. This is a crucial stage in glassmaking because, if the glass cools too quickly, internal stresses are formed and weaken the glass. Because of poor annealing, glass may break by itself—an entire sheet shattering while being carried is not unheard of.

There are many different types of glass used for leaded glass, and they fall into two broad categories—hand-blown and machine-rolled.

Hand-blown glass is manually formed into cylinders about two feet long. When it is removed from the blow-pipe, the ends are cut off and the crystal is split down one side. From there it goes back into the furnace, where a milder heat allows the glass to become pliable; it is then flattened into a sheet.

Machine-rolled glass is mixed and heated to the molten stage; the glass is then pressed out between large rollers. Sometimes it is then embossed with special stamps and designs to add pattern to the glass. Of the machine-made glasses, there are a considerable variety from which to choose.

As you learn more about glass working, you will also learn more about glass. It happens almost like osmosis, from hanging around glass stores and pawing through scrap bins and pressing your nose against a piece of sky blue antique glass that delightfully colors the world beyond.

There is some mysterious and sometimes confusing lingo that you should know. Different glasses are often referred to simply by the name of the company which makes them, i.e., Wismach, Kokomo, or Spectrum. Most of this usage is confined to opalescents, probably because there is such a wide variety of them. Don't let this throw you; you'll be name-dropping with the rest of them in no time. There is also some confusion about the correct term for the various textured glass. Deep ridges on the back of the glass are correctly called *granite back,* but you will hear ripple back, wavy, and "those funny little ridges." Glass, especially opalescents, with no texture on the back are *slate-back* glasses, but may be called flat-back, smooth, hard, or "without the ridges."

Don't forget that there is also a place for plain window glass in your work. It is cheap, readily available, and good to use in backgrounds when you don't want to detract from the focal point of your piece. On the other hand, many elaborate and large pieces have been executed in nothing but plain window glass, with stunning results.

CATHEDRAL GLASS

Cathedral glass comes in wide range of colors and textures. Although most professionals seem to use it quite sparingly, it can be used effectively in large areas, especially as background or filler in combination with other types of glass. Most windows made entirely of cathedral glass tend to have a European look, but few look downright bad. Because it is rolled, it does not vary in thickness as does antique glass; cathedral glass is usually a uniform one-eighth inch thick and cuts well.

Many factors in the annealing glass process affect its ability to be cut cleanly and evenly; there are, therefor, no hard and fast rules about how a particular glass will cut. So when I mention the "cutability" of a particular kind of glass, keep in mind that I am speaking in general terms. If I say it is easy, I mean it's easy about 90 percent of the time.

Cathedral glass is recognized by a hammered finish on one side, although there are other designs, such as small wavy lines, ridges, or abstract patterns stamped into the glass. It is about the cheapest and most widely available colored glass.

ANTIQUE GLASS

Antique glass is so named for its method of manufacture, not for its age as is sometimes assumed. It is hand-blown in a manner not unlike early glass. Antique glass is seldom of uniform thickness; its hand-blown character gives it a number of irregularities and impurities that enhance the glass.

Antique glass has tiny bubbles and striations. The tiny bubbles, or seeds, created by forcing air into the glass, catch and refract light. Striations (very fine, thin lines running through the glass) are caused by placing the blown cylinder into a device called a porcupine, which has very fine "teeth," and then rotating the cylinder.

Antiques offer the purest and most brilliant colors, and they come in a wide range of hues and shades. For the most part, they are the easiest to cut. Unfortunately, they are also the most expensive. All antique glass is made in Europe—mostly in France, Germany, and England—except for Blenko antique, a truly beautiful glass made in West Virginia. This, and the fact that it is hand-blown, no doubt accounts for its expense, but often it's well worth it.

A new glass worth mentioning is called *simulated antique*. It gives much the same striated and delicate does true antique glass. Of course, nothing can truly compare with the real thing, but this, being a rolled glass, is of an even thickness throughout and cuts like butter—two noticeable advantages. The color range is small and mostly pastels. It is considerably less expensive than antique.

OPALESCENT GLASS AND STREAKIES

Opalescent glass is quite different from cathedral and antique glass because it does not let light through to the extent that other glasses do. While opalescent glass is by no means opaque, it does act more to diffuse light and bring out its own color and effects. It is seldom one-color, usually at least two, and quite often more. The colors are swirled and streaked through the sheet. The result is a striking effect of subdued colors with whorls of marbled opacity.

Because of its density, it can almost stand alone, without the aid of natural or artificial light, although preferably it should be placed where the light can bring out its own special beauty. In picture frames and mirror edgings it does not go flat as do the other glasses and so is quite effective.

It is also the type of glass used predominantly in lamp shades. It is colorful when the lamp is not lighted and does not create "hot spots" or areas of blinding glare from the lighted bulb as do transparent or semitransparent glasses.

Opalescent glass ranges from "reasonable" to "difficult" to cut. It is medium priced and averages about $5 per square foot.

Streakies are similar to opalescents in that they, too, combine one or more colors in a bold streak across the sheet. Because this glass is fairly transparent, however, they are quite impressive when used in a window.

FLASHED GLASS

This is a hand-blown glass that is made by putting one color over another in very thin layer, usually done by dipping the hand-blown cylinder into the color. It is most common for this to be done on clear antiques, although occasionally colored antique glass is also flashed. You can tell flashed glass by holding it up to the light and looking at the edge; you will be able to see the base layer of glass and the thin layer of color on one side. Flashed glass is used primarily for etching because the top-most layer of color can be removed, exposing the base color below and leaving the surrounding area in a complementary tint.

SLAB GLASS

Slab glass, also known as *Dalles de verre,* is about one inch thick and comes in rectangular slabs. Because of its thickness and irregular edges, it is cut with a special wedge and is not much used by hobbyists. It cannot be leaded and is most frequently used in mosaic work.

BEVELED GLASS

This is a special treatment, and describes edges that are cut to an angle or slant. It is perhaps one of the most elegant glass treatments possible. Done on plate glass of varying thicknesses, the beveled edge acts as a prism that reflects light like a jewel. Beveling is somewhat a lost art these days, though there are still a few craftsmen doing it despite the high cost of beveling machines, which can cost as much as $50,000, and the many hours of labor involved in each piece. Beveled glass can usually be bought or ordered through a stained-glass shop. Be prepared to pay dearly. Often, though, that extra touch is well worth the cost. Beveled glass is especially fine in traditionally designed windows, although by no means is this limited.

FACETED GLASS

Gems and jewels are small, uniform pieces of faceted glass. They come in many shapes and sizes and as many colors. Often used in old traditional windows, they are now finding their way into contemporary designs. Again, the only limitation is your imagination.

Rondels are circles of spun or pressed glass that somewhat resemble bottle bottoms. They come in an assortment of colors and are usually 3 to 5 inches in diameter, although there are larger and smaller ones.

OTHER ADORNMENTS

Anything that can be leaded or foiled can be used leaded-glass designs. Shells, flat rocks, even plates have been used. I have seen entire lamps made from small abalone shells (and lots of solder!) and windows that incorporate flat slices of Australian agate to give a gorgeous translucent effect.

Some artists prefer to work with only one type of glass; there are those who will use nothing but German antique and those who make windows out of opalescents and nothing else. Personally, I feel that this limits both the artist and his potential for producing, so I recommend that you experiment with different kinds of glass, using it in different ways and designs. Not all of the results will look great, but you will learn more about the different glasses and how each can be used most effectively.

Most glass is sold to hobbyists in square pieces 10 to 12 inches on a side. If you need more than a couple of square feet for a project, it is usually wiser to have the glass shop cut a piece to your dimensions from one of their stock sheets. This will save you money be eliminating unnecessary scrap.

GLASS AND SAFETY

There is no need to be overly concerned about the possibility of cutting yourself while handling glass. Caution is the keyword. Don't stick your hand into a box or bag of glass and don't run your hand along the edge. Don't lean on your work table with your elbows or attempt to brush it off with your hands. Small glass chips can be the nastiest.

Do keep a box of adhesive bandages nearby. It isn't necessary to wear gloves; they are clumsy and will only hinder you. You may wear safety glasses; they are recommended but are not needed if you are careful while cutting and grozing the glass.

Most beginners will not handle large sheets of glass; but should you do so, always carry the glass vertically, gripping it by both edges with your hands and holding it to the side of your body. Never carry glass flat, under your arm, or above your head. Do not carry stacked pieces of glass, thinking to save an extra trip. If there is a fracture in the glass or it has a lot of internal stresses, it just may shatter of its own accord. If you are holding it correctly, it will fall to the floor. If not, it may fall on you!

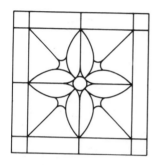

Chapter 2
Lead

Lead forms the skeletal structure in most stained glass. It is formed by an extrusion process. Bascially, this means that melted lead, usually mixed with some tin and sometimes zinc for added strength and resistance to oxidation, is poured into cylindrical molds. When they cool, the solid lead cylinders are placed in an extruding machine that forces the lead into steel dies to shape it. It is then cut into lengths about 2 meters long and placed in long, thin boxes where it can lie flat for shipment or storage.

CAMES

The proper name for the kind of lead used in stained-glass work is *came* (pronounced just as it is spelled), and it is sometimes sold by the term *calme*, which is the old spelling of the word. It is sold in lengths of about 2 meters. The average price of a 2-meter length is between $1 and $2, although it may be slightly more for border lead and the wider varieties. Lead came is probably one of the smallest expenses you will encounter (comparatively speaking, that is); and that's good, because it will surprise you how fast a couple of meters of lead will vanish!

Lead serves as a strengthening factor in glass works as well as designating the space and form of design.

There are three parts of lead came, as shown in Fig. 2-1. Came is always measured across the face of the lead. The channel is usually of a standard width and does not vary significantly. The

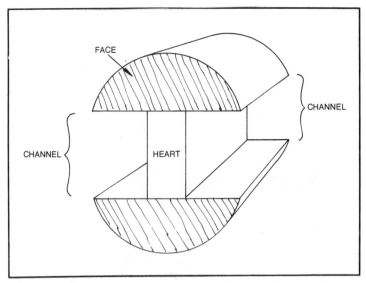

Fig. 2-1. Cross section of H came. Lead is measured across the face.

heart of the lead divides one piece of glass from another; the face overlaps the glass on both sides. The heart is usually several millimeters across. This, as you will see later, is an important measurement. There are many different sizes and shapes of lead, and all have their own uses.

Lead came comes in different styles. *H leads*, so named because their cross section resembles the letter *H*, are primarily used in the interior design of stained-glass work. They are available with channel spacings ranging from 3 mm to 2.5 cm and with round faces and flat faces (Fig. 2-2). Though hobbyists generally consider round-faced came to be more attractive and use it more frequently, flat-faced came is often used in large pieces requiring added strength.

U came, shaped like a squared off *U*, comes in several different sizes, measured from the heart of the lead to the outside edge, not across the back surface (Fig. 2-3). It is used as the border on the outer edges, usually for free-hanging panels. It is also called *border lead*, although there are other types of lead used in borders and the term may be confusing. The small, 3 mm U lead is sometimes used as a border on other glass objects such as lamps, boxes, or small window decorations.

Another type of widely used border lead is *Y came* or "special window border." This lead, like its name, is shaped in the form of a

Fig. 2-2. Flat and round H came, so called because in cross section it resembles the letter *H*.

Y (Fig. 2-3) and is used primarily when the leaded glass is designed to go into a frame or window sash.

There is varying opinion on which lead you should use in the beginning. Some say that you should use a wider H lead, usually 5 or 6 mm, in the first project or two. In my own classes, I have students use 3 mm lead, which is thin but not the thinnest available. There are advantages to both methods. Mainly, the difference is this: the wider the lead, the more mistakes you can cover; likewise, thinner lead means fewer concealed mistakes.

When I was learning, I was grateful indeed for a few extra millimeters with which I could cover my erratic, first cutting

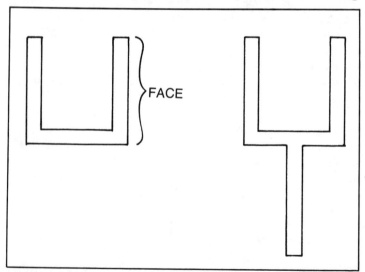

Fig. 2-3. U came and Y came.

attempts. With hindsight, however, I feel that it is really better in the long run to start with the thinner lead—at least after the first project or two—so that you learn to cut as well as you can. It takes much longer to learn to cut correctly when you know you can hide your mistakes with lead. Also, in small panels, which you will be doing in your first efforts, anything much wider than 4 mm looks heavy. For some reason, the majority of my students do just fine with a smaller lead; somehow, they don't have that many mistakes to hide!

Stretching

Regardless of its size, all lead must be stretched just before it is to be used, and not before.

You usually buy lead in 2-meter strands that resemble spaghetti. By stretching the lead before using it, you return to it some of its original tensile strength and at the same time remove all of the kinks and bends. This latter point is important because lead that has been bent and twisted is very difficult to use: the kinks don't ever really disappear. When you buy your lead, keep it as straight as possible until you are ready to use it. It may be folded in half once, but avoid folding, mutilating, twisting, or rolling it further. Lead is stretched with a lead vise or lead grabber (although there are more unorthodox methods), explained in Chapter 4.

Storage

If lead is stored for any length of time where it is exposed to the open air a coating of oxidation will form. Dampness increases the chance of oxidation, so it is important for lead to be stored correctly. The best way is to store it flat in a long narrow box similar to the one it was shipped in. These boxes are about 15 cm high, 30.5 cm across, and 2 m long. You can sometimes obtain them from a large stained-glass supply store, or you can build your own. Divide the box into compartments, if you wish, for different sizes of lead. If stored in such a container with newspaper tucked over it, your lead should be fairly safe from oxidation.

Small packets of dry silica gel and other drying agents are available in some outlets. Place them on top of the lead but under the newspaper to absorb moisture and give extra protection against oxidation.

Obviously, not everyone can spare two meters of living space. If you have no area where such a box can be stored; you can store it on a hook of hang it over an empty spool that is nailed to the wall (do not wrap the lead on the spool). Try to keep the lengths as straight and unmangled as possible. Wrap them in newspaper, too, by interleaving the paper over and under the lead lengths.

If neither of these solutions will do, cut the lead lengths in half (before they are stretched) and tape them securely to a yardstick or other flat board of similar size. Again, wrap them in newspaper. It is not necessary to stretch the lead before taping it.

Cleaning

If your lead looks dull, or if the solder won't flow on it, it has probably oxidized. Brush each lead joint with a small wire brush a few times. This will remove the oxidation so that the solder will adhere. Confine your scrubbing to the joint, as it scrapes the lead and you will have lots of little scratches on areas not covered by solder otherwise.

Purchasing Considerations

Buy as much lead as you will need to complete your project. Too often it happens that someone gets halfway through a project and runs out of lead, so he takes a little piece of it back to the shop where he bought it and, guess what? The store may be out of stock or it may be on order and delivery could take several weeks. With larger, more established glass shops you may never encounter this problem but small, shoestring-budget suppliers cannot always keep up with their stock or may buy their lead from whichever company has the best price at the moment. Don't try to match a lead you bought at one store with another store's offerings. They can hardly ever be matched successfully. The results of changing your lead in the middle of a piece can range from mildly dissatisfying to disastrous. If it is a panel in which one size of lead is used throughout, even a slight difference will be noticed. That is not to say you should not consider mixing (purposely, though, not by accident) your leads to give your work added interest. Emphasize or deemphasized areas by using different-sized leads. For instance, in the foreground you may want certain things to stand out, and a heavier lead blending to a smaller lead in the background will give the piece a more subtly professional look. For small, delicate lines, you would hardly use a lead that all but obliterates the piece of glass it holds.

Lead is a versatile and pleasing substance to work with, all in all. Its pliability accents and brings to glass working the ideal balance of line and color; yet it is amazing in the strength it affords the finished work.

LEAD FUMES

From time to time the question of lead poisoning arises and causes a flurry in the ranks of professionals and hobbyists alike. Lead fumes are not the most pleasant aroma to waft through the air, but it would probably take a huge amount to constitute a case of lead poisoning. Even those of us who solder lead every day for many hours do not worry unduly about it, and I would advise you to do the same. There are, however, some precautions that should be routinely observed:

1. Work in a well ventilated area. If you have a small fan, set it up on your table (although this sometimes affects the actual soldering process by cooling the iron); and open a window or door, but have some kind of air circulating.

2. Don't inhale any more than necessary. By this I mean, don't hang right on top of your iron so that the fumes have nowhere else to go but up your nose.

3. Wash your hands before eating or drinking. This is a simple rule but, amazingly, people still must be reminded.

4. If you have open cuts on your hands. bandage them.

5. Wear a mask. These are available from small surgical types to elaborate gas masks with hoses and tubes running all over the place. If you observe the above precautions, you shouldn't need a mask. They, like gloves, are more cumbersome than helpful; but if you will lose sleep worrying about lead poisoning, go ahead and wear one.

ZINC CAMES AND REINFORCEMENT BARS

Zinc came is a specialized type of came used where all available strength is needed. Very long narrow designs or large panels in which there are many long pieces quite often employ zinc came in combination with lead or by itself. Many windows have zinc around the borders and are leaded within the interior. This makes a surprising difference in the amount of rigidity the finished window has.

Zinc came is also available in the same shapes, *U, H* and *Y*, as lead came and in nearly the same variety of sizes (again, measured across the face). It usually comes in lengths of 2 to 2½ meters. Some shops may cut it to size or you may have to purchase the entire length. It generally costs two to three times the price of a similar lead came.

Zinc does not take well to bending; therefore, it is used primarily in long straight runs only or as borders. Since it cannot be cut with a lead knife, it must be sawed. A small hacksaw works fine; but a jeweler's saw is even better, especially for the thinner came.

When soldering, zinc presents no unusual problems. It can be soldered to itself or to lead with the same flux you use in your lead work.

Brace bars or *reinforcement rods* are steel rods with a galvanized coating that resists rust and enables them to be soldered to lead. Buy only galvanized steel!

The flat bar is used most widely and comes in varying widths, usually a centimeter or so across and 3 millimeters in width. Round bars are available, but these cannot be bent to conform with a curved design.

Brace bars are used on designs that exceed one meter square and on smaller pieces that will be installed in a place where there is unusual stress, such as in doors. They are soldered directly to the seaded glass (on the back), stretching from border lead to border lead. The truly professional method of bracing a window is to bend the bar (with hammer, vise, and muscle) to follow the leading in the design. Many old windows, and far too many new ones, are braced straight across; the bar is then extremely visible as a thick, dark line running through and sometimes just plain ruining the design. More about bracing and bracing techniques is given in Chapter 11.

Chapter 3
Design

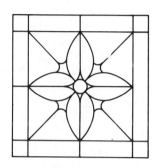

Basically, design is breaking up space or arranging lines, forms, and color within an area. The design of your stained glass project will most often determine whether it "works." The best craftsmanship in the world will not hide a bad design, but a good design can sometimes compensate for flaws in workmanship, providing the flaws are not so obvious that they are immediately noticeable.

LINEWORK

The first element of design—line—is most important in planning your project. Look at one of the many designs in this book. How do you feel about it? Is it pleasing? Are the lines balanced and in harmony or do they seem to come out of nowhere and go nowhere? Look for lines that are stiff and awkward in an otherwise flowing pattern, or extraneous lines that serve no purpose. In stained glass work, the preliminary line drawing can usually stand alone as a total creation. One should feel in it a sense of satisfaction and balance.

An obvious source of design is other people's glass work. While you may draw upon another artist's work as inspiration in your own designing, don't copy it exactly. An original anything is respected more than a copy. It is good to foster your own ideas and your own sense of creation. Your first efforts may be a little rough, but practice brings improvement. Take your time making your own design. Draw it and then set it aside. When you return to it in a few days, see what your first reaction is. Rework it if necessary.

If you cannot draw, you might buy one of the many books of stained glass designs available. Many glass companies offer full-size patterns already drawn up, and quite a few of them are really beautiful and make exciting glass works. You will, at least, be choosing your own glass and colors. But don't rely on premade designs exclusively; making your own original designs is a very satisfying part of the craft too. If you find a design you really like, you can probably alter it sufficiently to make it yours. Make it bigger or smaller, eliminate a bird or add a flower. Change some lines or add a border.

When looking at designs or patterns for stained glass, remember that some lines are there because they have to be. Some shapes cannot be cut in glass, and others present some difficulty even for the experienced craftsman. For this reason, lines (eventually to be made in lead) sometimes make a break in the design where there would not be one in, say, a painting. Unfortunately cutting glass is not like cutting paper. Glass tends to break in areas of stress. Although there are ways to make difficult cuts successfully, they will only prove frustrating at first.

As you design for stained glass, you will always have in the back of your mind the question, "Can this be cut in glass?" The answer is usually yes, with some modifications. For example, you cannot cut a donut shape in glass, but it can be treated as a design element that can be broken up in a number of ways that *can* be cut. The idea, of course, is to do as much as possible during the design stage to eliminate such problem cuts. Or redesign them in such a way that the breaks seem integral to the whole.

For other sources of designs take a look around you. Some fine glass works have been made from the most ordinary ideas: telephones, pots and pans, doors, a dripping faucet, a bowl of fruit, cars, a stack of books. Nature is an abundant inspiration: shells, trees, old stumps, flowers, fences, birds. The list could go on and on. Once you get accustomed to observing the environment, you'll find yourself full of ideas and thinking about how you could represent them in glass.

There is almost no limit to the source of design ideas. Designs on wallpaper, towels, fabrics, tilework, posters, book jackets, postcards, and china offer quite a variety. I keep a file of pictures taken from magazines for those times when I need a little inspiration or a different view of a flower.

Following are some things that you should keep in mind as you design.

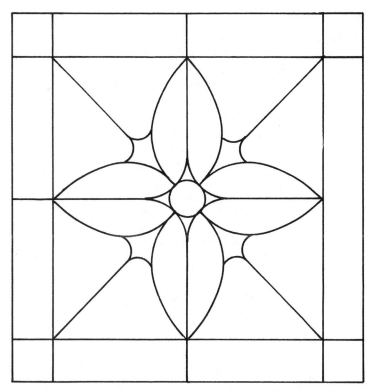

Fig. 3-1. The symmetry of this design creates a kaleidoscopic effect that dazzles the eye without calling undue attention to itself.

Try to avoid or eliminate points in the design where there are many lines coming together in one place. When recreated with lead cames, these points will usually end up looking sloppy because there will be a large gob of lead and solder.

For your first few designs, avoid very long narrow pieces, long points, excessively wavy lines and deep concave curves. Especially avoid inside right angles. Glass tends to break in a straight line, and it is nearly impossible, even for a professional to successfully cut a sharp or right inside angle. Chapter 7 describes other difficult cuts.

Avoid adding lines for the mere sake of being able to cut and lead a particular piece. Lead lines should be an integral part of the whole and should be a unifying element in the design. For instance, if the main interest point is soft, fluid line, it would be senseless to connect the background together with stick-straight lines (Fig. 3-2). Doing so would cause the eye to focus on the background instead of on the central design, and would create a feeling of disharmony.

It is often helpful to experiment. Draw as many different lines as you can think of—jagged lines; curved, rolling lines; etc. Experiment with forms; superimpose one image upon another. Study the designs in this chapter to start off.

Take your time. Many potential problems can be solved here; it is much easier to erase a line or add one on paper than it is to do so in glass. For your first project, begin with a small panel about 30 cm square. Limit yourself to six or eight pieces in all, thereby keeping both cost and temper down.

Don't expect a lot from your first try. It takes a little time to become acquainted not only with glass and how it breaks but with the technical aspects of leading and soldering. Remember that designing is the first step and, being so, the hardest.

COLOR

Color is the essence of stained glass. It is what gives it life and vitality. Throughout the day, a stained glass window will be constantly changing as the sun changes its position and the flow of light

Fig. 3-2. Straight angular lines framing fluid curved ones disrupt the continuity of this design.

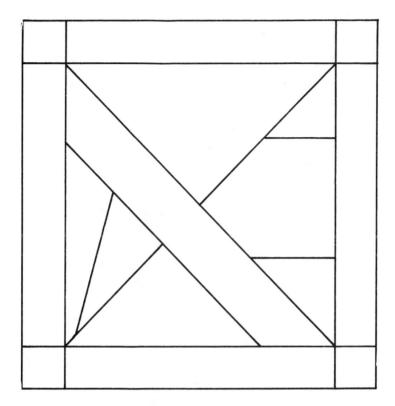

Fig. 3-3. Symmetry and balance, the essence of simplicity, characterize this theme.

intensifies or decreases. Variations in light cause some colors to become stronger, others to recede.

Colors are also important for their psychological impact. Oranges and yellows are cheerful colors; reds are exciting and sometimes violent; greens are restful. Greens, blues, and blue-greens are cool colors; reds, yellows, and oranges are considered warm tones. Cool colors will have a tendency to recede, warm colors stand out. Deciding what colors to use and how to use them is one of the most difficult steps and is apt to take a considerable amount of time before you feel that you have exactly what you want.

There are several methods of choosing colors to produce a harmonious effect. One is to use a monochromatic color layout—a single color that is used in varying shades and intensities. Another is to use complementary colors: shades of orange with shades of blue, shades of green with shades of red, or shades of purple with shades of yellow.

You can choose glass by holding up combinations of different color samples to the light to see which combinations look good together and which do not. It is essential to use some source of light when choosing colors. All glass looks drastically different when held to light than it does on the rack.

When choosing color combinations, consider, too, the amount of space any given color will occupy. A bright red might be just the thing for a small accent, but it would probably be a big mistake if you have a large area to fill, unless you want the window to be dominated by red.

I often have colors in mind before I begin to design. Sometimes this works well for instance, when you are trying to blend with or pick up accents in a particular room. You can design around one particular piece of glass with which you have become en-

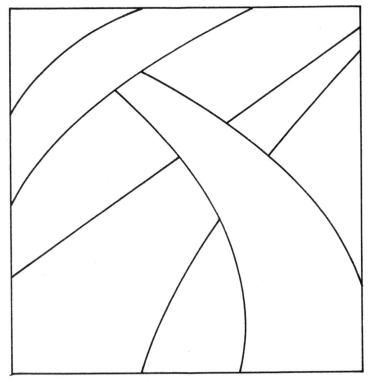

Fig. 3-4. Curves suggest depth. You could choose harmonious or contrasting colored glass as long as visual balance is maintained.

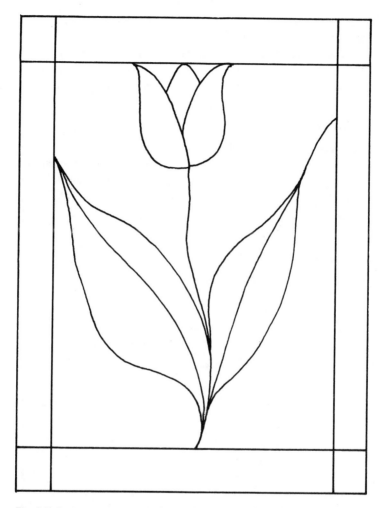

Fig. 3-5. A simple element such as this flower can be used to create very effective lighting effects with only two or three colors.

chanted. This may dictate to some degree what other colors will have to be used if the design is to have balance.

More often than I care to think about, people will want every color of the rainbow in their work. If your window *is* a rainbow, fine, but this can otherwise have disastrous effects. Your window can become so busy with color that the design is lost completely, or else some colors, such as reds and oranges, will overpower the rest and appear to be big blobs of color. Stained glass at its best is a subtle and balanced web of color and line; at its worst it can become downright gaudy.

A lightbox, described in Chapter 5 will sometimes be handy. I say sometimes because lightboxes are lit by fluorescent light that does not give a true representation of glass colors. Some people swear by them, but unless you must choose your colors in a windowless cellar, there is no doubt that natural light is best. However, when you work with large pieces of glass, it is often quite awkward to try to hold more than two up together. A lightbox will prove valuable for such occasions and for when many pieces

Fig. 3-6. A harmonious blending of greens and reds can make this into a striking panel, but be careful to avoid overuse of any one shade of red.

Fig. 3-7. Straight vertical lines and gentle encompassing curves create a gracefulness that can be captured through a judicious selection of colors.

must be matched. Just remember that the glass colors will seem somewhat flatter than they would in sunlight.

One way to work out a successful color scheme, especially if you are working with three or more colors, is to draw out your design on tracing paper (if it is large, draw it small but to scale); then on an overlay of tissue paper, color in the various colors you want to use. Make several overlays trying different combinations. Although you won't be able to match some pencil or crayon colors exactly in glass, and you won't be able to duplicate the effect of transmitted light, this method does work well enough to give you a more solid idea of what colors will look good together.

Then visit a glass shop and see what your colors look like together in glass. Take your time and don't give up.

Keep in mind as you select colors that few objects are made up of one color alone. A tree of sky or almost anything you can think of is composed of many colors and shadings. To attempt to represent

23

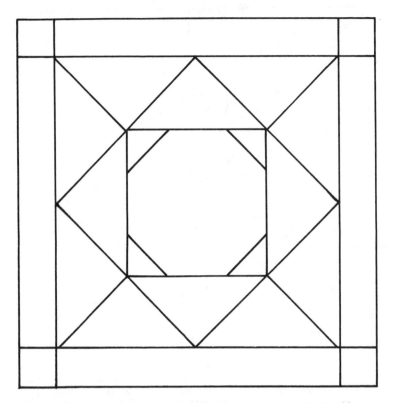

Fig. 3-8. This montage of triangles creates the illusion of depth without sacrificing symmetry. Experiment with colors to avoid the possibility of having one element attract the eye more than others.

this aspect in your glass is important and gives leaded glass an added dimension. Try to blend shades so that they don't give the effect of lumps of color stuck together.

There is such a wide range of colors available that it is possible to use two or even three shades of green for the leaves of a plant. (In general, don't use more than three shades of a color or the object being created will look too "busy.") This is a technique used by professional glass studios to give a more realistic look to their stained glass. But don't overdo it!

There is a personal aspect to glass that should also be mentioned. Some colors look fine to nearly everyone, there are just as many that have a more limited appeal. This is true also of different people's color selections. What Arthur thinks is the perfect combination, Melvin might well find revolting! Dealing with color is also

24

dealing with people and their particular likes or dislikes, their emotions and frustrations.

If this sounds a bit esoteric, stop and think about your own reactions to particular colors. I'm willing to bet that there is at least one color, and probably more, that you dislike. There is one that makes you feel good or cheerful or sad. Thus, when you are selecting colors, your choice is inevitably biased by your personal feelings. This is good because, through it, your creative work becomes even more an extension of *you*. Assuming that you are making something for yourself, then, let some of this sense of feeling guide you with color choice. If it pleases no one else, it will still please you.

You may find, after working in glass for a while, that you tend to use a sort of surefire "formula," commonly known as a rut. You've gotten in a "rut" when, for example, greens and browns and golds looked so good together in the last five designs that they

Fig. 3-9. The rising-sun theme is simple. Use greens, reds, and golds, and try variations that do not disrupt the balance.

Fig. 3-10. Use a variation of this simple plant structure to show off several shades of green that go well together.

seem to just show up in every current project. This is not necessarily bad, but if you reach this point, you should step back and take a good look at what you're doing. It's easy to repeat color in various combinations and designs, but eventually it becomes stultifying and you may find yourself becoming bored with the whole process. Experimentation is vital to creativity, and also to keeping a fresh and interested approach to the craft itself.

A striking abstract design done in brilliant antiques can have the same sort of breathtaking effect as an elaborate traditional design that makes use of subtle and meditative opalescents. So allow yourself a free hand and eye when you pick your glass. Try something different if you've become bored with red and yellow. Some ideas will turn out beautifully, and some will flop to a greater or lesser degree. But you learn from those mishaps perhaps even more than from the ones you are proud to display, and learning continuously and willingly is a large measure of what it's really all about.

Chapter 4
Tools and Materials

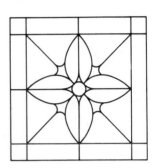

In any craft, whether it's building houses or creating stained-glass windows, good tools are essential and generally prove well worth the investment. They will save you time, money, and your temper—all valuable commodities.

Some items that you will need can be improvised or made, although you will probably find that the small amount of money saved in doing so is almost insignificant.

The following list will be everything you need in addition to glass and lead came. For most items you can settle for average quality; those marked with an asterisk are the ones for which you should buy the best quality. An explanation of each tool and its function is given on the following pages. The tools are listed in the order in which they will be required.

Cartoon paper	Lead knife*
Pattern paper	Cutting wax
Straight edge	Lathekin
T-square	Lead vise
Pencils	Lead nails
Felt-tip marker	Soldering iron
Pattern shears*	Solder
Cutter(s)	Flux for Soldering
Glazing compound	Cutting oil
Chinese whiting	Glass pliers*
Glazing brushes	Grozing pliers*
Patina	Grindstone

*Buy the best-quality available.

If you were to go to your local stained-glass store and buy one of everything you need, assuming you purchase average-to lower-grade tools, you could expect to spend approximately $60. This is just about everything, except glass and lead. If you were to buy the best-quality tools available, the bill could conceivably be as high as $80. Some people launch themselves with the very basics and get away for a mere $20 to $30. It is noteworthy to add, though, that they eventually wander back to buy additional tools and end up with all of the tools listed above.

PAPER

Cartoon paper and *pattern paper* are used in the first stages of the design process. A cartoon is the initial design drawn to its correct size (the size that the finished glass work will be) and ready for a pattern to be made from it. Cartoon paper can be pretty much any paper that's not too thin; butcher paper works the best, but plain white (unglazed) shelf-lining paper may be used, as might anything else large enough to accommodate your design.

From this cartoon make two copies, one on the same kind of paper, which is called the *pattern,* and one on a heavier paper, (not quite as heavy as cardboard) called a *working copy.* The pattern is made on a thin cardboard, not as heavy as poster board, but more like the cover of a paper notebook. Most stained glass suppliers sell pattern paper or can tell you where you can purchase large pieces.

For pattern making, there are several tools that would be good to have because they will save you time. They may already be around your house, or you may have to purchase them. You should have a good *straightedge.* This is not your garden-variety ruler or yardstick—these are often warped just enough to alter your pattern and, in the end, your glass design. A metal 1-meter straightedge or yardstick is a good investment and can be purchased at a blueprint store and at some stationers.

A tool that is invaluable is a *T-square.* Again, buy one of metal unless you can afford a good wood one (they start at about $80). Metal ones can be bought at building supply outlets for $5 to $8. To use one, simply place the T-square on your cartoon paper and draw along the two inside edges. You now have a perfect right angle. Work from this to extend your lines, if necessary.

When you finish drawing the perimeter lines, check each corner with the square to make sure they are square. Don't think that ½ centimeter off makes no difference—it will make a vast difference by the time you get to leading your design.

You'll also need *pencils* and a dark *felt-tip marker* of good quality. A set of pastels, crayons, or various-colored flet-tip pens is helpful in laying out your colors.

PATTERN SHEARS

The person who invented this handy-dandy tool was brilliant. Pattern shears are three-bladed scissors (Fig. 4-1) having two blades on the bottom and a single blade on top. The top blade slices down between the two lower ones; as it does, it extracts a strip of paper about 2 mm wide. This measurement is the allowance made for the heart of the lead to pass between the two pieces of glass. The shears themselves seem quite mysterious, and it is somewhat difficult to envision their function without performing it yourself.

Suppose you were making a window that measures about 30 cm square. You have cut your glass to each pattern piece and you are ready to begin leading. You put the first piece of glass in, then the lead, then the next piece of glass, and so on. Do you know what's wrong here? Right! Each time you set a piece of lead in, you are gaining 2 mm, which means your window will "grow" on you. It will grow right out of the space you had intended it to fit. Even if you were intending to hang it in a window instead of fitting into one,

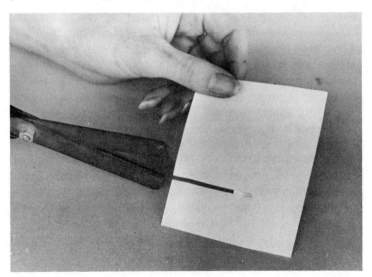

Fig. 4-1. Pattern shears.

you can be sure that you will have very uneven edges. As you can see, you must have pattern shears if you are serious about glass.

When I started in glass, pattern shears cost $26. These were the imported ones—the only ones really—and they were made from a high-quality steel that kept an edge well. They are now available for about $20, and are as good as they always were. There is also now on the market a good pair of Korean shears that cost about half the price of the others.

There are alternatives, if you do not want to spend the money on pattern shears. One is to use two single-edge razor blades taped together with a 2-mm shim between them. Allegedly, this method is used widely, but when I tried it, it seemed as if one or the other of the blades kept slipping up or down, and it was just plain difficult to maneuver such a small instrument smoothly along the lines of a pattern and still maintain an even enough pressure to cut well.

Another alternative is simply to cut along one side of your line and then go back and cut on the other so that, in effect, you are cutting out the heart allowance. This is fine if you can remember which side of the line you have already cut on in your 60-piece pattern.

GLASS CUTTERS

No glass cutter actually "cuts" glass. A glass cutter is an instrument with a handle, and an axle on one end. The axle holds a small steel wheel that makes a small groove in the glass as it turns. This creates a fracture in the glass. When you apply the right amount of pressure in the right place, the fracture begins to "run" and the glass will separate, ideally on the scored line.

In the medieval days of glass crafting, a heated iron was placed at the edge of the glass to start a fracture. It was then drawn along the glass in the desired shape. This run would follow the heat as it set up the line of stress in the glass. This seems rather a hit-or-miss affair, but some of the world's finest windows were cut in this manner. Some day lasers may make glass cutting as easy as cutting paper. Fortunately, we are not in the Dark Ages, and the tools now available make cutting glass fairly simple and foolproof.

Glass cutters come in wide array of sizes and types for a wide array of uses. For stained glass work however, you need concern yourself with only a few, and your choice of the right one for you is determined primarily by the type of glass you will be cutting and to a lesser extent by personal preference.

Cutters are numbered according to the size and hardness of the steel wheel. For most cuts you will want a No. 2 or No. 9. The *Fletcher Terry* company makes the glass cutter most widely used for stained glass, and the price is more than reasonable—usually less than $1.50. The cutters you will find in the five-and-dime store are not meant for stained glass; they are for the handyman.

Your glass cutter will be one of your most valuable tools, so get a good one. Also, do not use one that has been lying in the junk drawer for a year or which was found in Uncle Bernie's toolbox. Their histories are questionable, to say the least. Glass cutters also should not be shared between two (or, heaven forbid, more) aspiring craftsmen because, while you may score a line perfectly, your partner may be gouging his out, damaging the wheel irretrievable and, likewise, your next cut.

Basically, then, here are the glass cutters and their particular uses.

Fletcher No. 2 is used for single- and double-strength window glass, mirror, cathedral glass, and most antique glass. These are the softer glasses.

Fletcher No. 7 is color-coded with a blue band on the handle and has a harder wheel for cutting harder glasses—all opalescents and the harder antiques. Red and orange antique glass are usually extremely hard and takes a No. 7. This glass cutter is most useful for cutting straight lines or very gentle curves.

For pattern cutting, you will want a *Fletcher No. 9*. It has a harder wheel that is smaller than the one found on a No. 7 and that allows easier cutting of curves and pattern lines. It has a green band.

As you can see from Fig. 4-2, the cutter has a rather slender body, with the wheel on one end and a solid ball on the other. The ball is sometimes used for tapping the score line. Some people might find it difficult to keep a good grip on the metal handle. If you do, you might try wrapping the handle with masking tape; this affords a better grip.

Diamantor cutters (see Fig. 4-2) are made in Germany and are friendly looking cutters with bright green wooden handles. They have no ball on the end and fit very well in the hand. These are one of my favorites. Regrettably, they come only in the No. 2 size, so do not use them for opalescent glasses and those that require No. 7 or No. 9 cutters. A *carbide cutter* is what you might call an all-purpose cutter. Made of silicon carbide, they last considerably

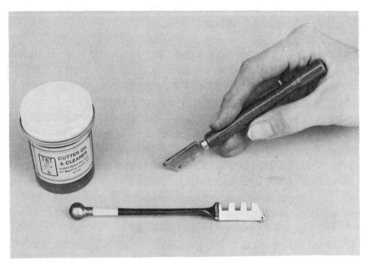

Fig. 4-2. Fletcher cutter (metal with ball on the end), Diamantor cutter, and cutting oil/cleaner.

longer than the others, usually four to six times longer than regular glass cutters. They cost about $6. The carbide cutter looks quite similar to the Fletcher cutter, so it is wise to mark it unless you are using a carbide exclusively. You could do this by wrapping a bit of tape around the shaft.

One of the newer developments on the glass-cutter scene is the *self-oiling cutter* (Fig. 4-3). This is an ingenious device that lubricates itself as it cuts. Figure 4-4 shows a diagram of the internal workings of this cutter, which draws oil down through the shaft from a self-contained reservoir. The oil is released through a very small wick in the head, which allows the oil to be let out as the wheel scores the glass. To fill the reservoir with oil, the screw cap is removed from the end and the oil is put in with an eyedropper or similar device. Trying to pour the oil directly into the reservoir will mean more oil on the table than in the cutter.

Once the oil is in, the screw cap is replaced. When the screw cap is fastened securely, a normal flow of oil will come out. To allow more oil to be released, unfasten the screw top two or three turns to the left. Do this when cutting a thicker or harder glass.

Test the oil flow by running the cutter across a piece of paper; you will see the fine trail it leaves in its wake. If no oil seems to be coming out, check to make sure it is filled. If that is not the problem, remove the head by unfastening the small screw. The end

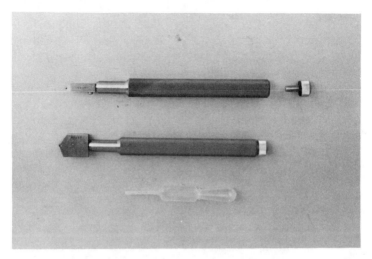

Fig. 4-3. Self-oiling cutter with oil filler. The cutter at the top has a smaller head used for pattern cutting.

of the wick should be visible. If it is not, or if it is mashed up, straighten it out gently. Use a very soft touch; if you pull the wick out, you cannot put it back in.

An oil mixed with kerosene is the only oil that should be used with a self-oiling cutter. This cleans the wheel and prevents it from gumming up.

Like carbide cutters, self-oiling cutters may be used on all glass. The large head is a bit awkward for cutting to a pattern, however, and so should be used only for straight cuts. They have two interchangeable heads, a large one and a small narrow one. This latter is better if you are cutting to a pattern. To change the heads, simply remove the screw, take one head off, and replace it with the one of your choice.

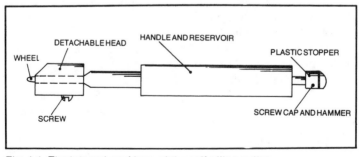

Fig. 4-4. The internal workings of the self-oiling cutter.

Some people feel these cutters are somewhat bulky and difficult to maneuver, but there are just as many who will use nothing else. They cost up to $20, and the second head is usually about another $10.

Circles can be cut with a regular glass cutter to a pattern or freehand, but there are gadgets that makes it easier. Fletcher Terry makes a *circle cutter* (called a *lens cutter*) designed to cut small circles from 1 to 13 cm in diameter (Fig. 4-5). The diameter is chosen and set by adjusting the length of the bar. The handle is then turned and the wheel inscribes the score line on the glass. Lines must be then scored from the circle's perimeter to the edge of the glass so that the outer glass can be broken away in pieces leaving the circle intact.

Another type of circle cutter designed for cutting larger circles, is called a *beam-compass cutter* (Fig. 4-5). It resembles a beam compass with a cutting wheel on the end of the beam. It is positioned on the glass and held in place by a suction cup on the bottom of the base. The circle is then scored and broken out as with the lens cutter.

To get the maximum use out of your glass cutters, they should be properly cared for. To begin with, all cutters need lubrication before each score they make (with the exception of the self-oiling cutter). Household oil or 3-in-1 is oil is fine, although a combination of oil and kerosene (about half and half) is better. Kerosene cleans the wheel of dust, small glass particles, and other debris, and the oil lubricates the axle and wheel of the cutter.

Without proper oiling, you can ruin a new cutter in one score. The recommended way to store a cutter to ensure that the wheel stays clean and lubricated is to stand it in a small jar or glass with a small pad of fine steel wool on the bottom. Fill the jar with ½ centimeter or so of the oil/kerosene mixture. A cutter can be stored in such a manner indefinitely. In this way, when you are cutting glass, it is simple and convenient to dip the cutter in oil before each score is made.

Dropping glass cutters on a hard surface or using them for anything other than cutting glass is unthinkable. If they are dropped on a cement floor, for instance, it is quite likely that the wheel will be a nicked or flattened and become unusable. Sometimes these defects are not readily visible, and the only way to detect them is by seeing how the cutters cut glass.

You tell when a cutter is ready to be scrapped by how it cuts. There is no real visible sign or any set time limit. If the cutter

Fig. 4-5. Fletcher Terry's lens cutter (top), and a beam-compass cutter (foreground) are used for cutting circles.

scores (which most do, bad or not) but the glass refuses to break on the score line several times, the cutter is probably shot—this is assuming you have taken care to oil it conscientiously and have not dropped it, and you've had it for a reasonable length of time. After you have been cutting glass for a while, you will be able to tell more easily when a cutter is going bad. In the beginning it's best to replace the cutter whenever you are in doubt about whether or not it's worn out. Sharpening glass cutters is not really worth the time and effort involved. It can be done but requires a white Arkansas stone and infinite patience. A cutter resharpened in this manner does not keep on edge well or for long and is more frustrating than economical. Buy a new one.

GLASS PLIERS

Glass pliers are used for breaking away glass that is awkward or difficult to break by other methods. Figure 4-6 shows two different glass pliers. They serve the same purpose but vary in size, weight, and jaw width. Glass pliers do not have serrated inner jaws as are found on household pliers, and the latter do not substitute well for the real thing. The jaws of glass pliers meet only at the end. This allows them to grip and break out small pieces the hand cannot reach. They serve to apply an even pressure, enough to fracture the score line and start a run in the glass. They aren't to be used with a lot of pressure or force, as this will simply shatter the glass.

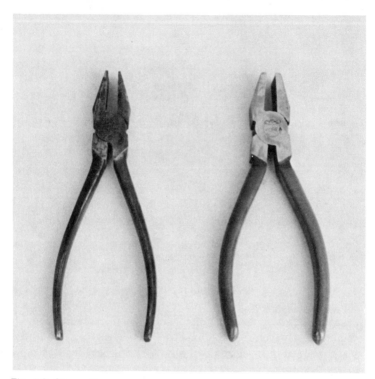

Fig. 4-6. Glass pliers.

Small pliers work best for me; they have a comfortable weight and fit well in the hand. The width of the jaw is small enough to work easily; wider nosed pliers become hard to maneuver.

The wider, almost splay-nosed pliers shown in Fig. 4-7 are also called glass pliers, although they are actually closer to running pliers, which are discussed below. The very large pair in Fig. 4-7 are called *plate pliers* and are used primarily for plate glass, which finds little use in stained glass work. However, I have found that they are quite handy for breaking out large shapes in glass and for separating long narrow strips. The smaller pair in Fig. 4-7 can be used in the same manner as regular glass pliers, but they seem to me to be better adapted to straight cuts and strips.

Running pliers have an unusual curved jaw (Fig. 4-8). They work on the fulcrum principle, with the convex curve of the lower jaw acting as the fulcrum against the concave upper jaw. These pliers are used only for cutting long, thin strips out of glass. This is one of the hardest shapes to break successfully, although it may

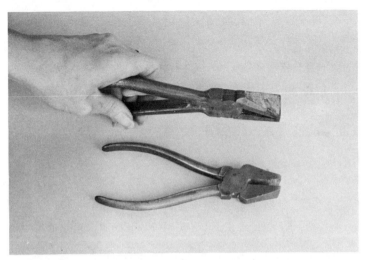

Fig. 4-7. Large glass pliers, also called breaking pliers.

seem very simple. Because of the pressure set up in such a narrow area, the glass has a tendency to run off of the score line. Running pliers make it possible to get the cut right nearly every time.

To use them, you must set a small screw gauge on top of the pliers. After you have scored the straight cut, line up the score line with the line on the upper jaw of the pliers. This will be in the center. When this is done, turn the screw gently until the pliers are holding the glass lightly but without any sliding. Squeeze the handles of the pliers firmly and you will see the glass run the length of the score.

Unless you will be cutting large quantities of glass strips, your initial investment need not include running pliers. They are good to know about, though, and so have been presented here.

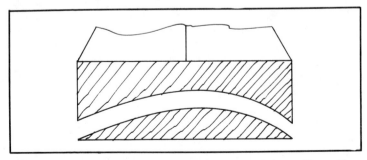

Fig. 4-8. Front view of the jaw of running pliers, which is used for cutting long, thin strips of glass.

You should plan to get glass pliers, however. They are invaluable. You can expect to pay anywhere from $5 to $10. Again, the higher-priced tools are of better quality, but the less expensive ones will suffice.

To keep your pliers in good working condition, keep the axles well oiled so that they do not become stiff. A drop or two of oil now and then will take care of this. Work it in by opening and closing the plier handles for a few minutes. The jaws should not drop open when you hold the pliers by one handle, but neither should they be so tight as to make it necessary to use both hands to pull open each time.

If you are using your pliers well and often, you may occasionally need to regrind the ends of the jaws. With heavy use, they sometimes become slightly rounded. Keeping them flat and even will keep their breaking ability accurate and clean. A small grinder is best used for this, but be careful not to grind away more than a fraction. And be certain that the jaws meet flush with each other at the tip.

GROZING PLIERS

Grozing pliers are one of my favorite tools and, oddly enough, the one I put off buying for longer than I care to think. These are smaller, narrower, and lighter than glass pliers and have a slightly curved upper jaw that meets the lower jaw at the very tip of the pliers (Fig. 4-9). The jaws are lined on both inside edges with small serrations or ridges (Fig. 4-10).

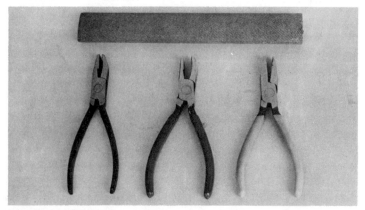

Fig. 4-9. Three different grozing pliers for smoothing rough glass edges. At the top of the picture is a Carborundum stone that is also occasionally used to smooth glass edges.

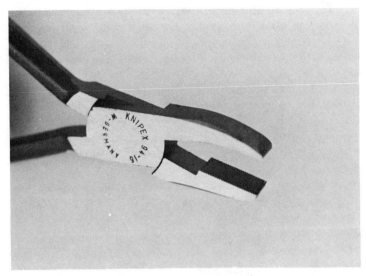

Fig. 4-10. Close-up of grozing teeth.

Grozing is, basically, chewing away at any rough edges of the glass, smoothing out small areas, and sometimes almost carving difficult shapes and cuts from the glass—and this is the function of grozing pliers. They should not be used for breaking glass, because this not only dulls the pliers bite but quite often simply mashes the glass to bits—you will usually end up losing the entire piece. Likewise, I should mention that only the mildest grozing should be done with glass pliers—just an edge smoothed off here or there—because the flat jaw doesn't gently chew away the glass; it will simply shatter the piece. Grozing with your glass pliers will also round and dull the inner edge of the jaw.

It will take a bit of practice before you can groze naturally and easily, but once you have learned how, you will be surprised at how much this tool can simplify your work.

GRINDSTONE

Also shown in Fig. 4-9 is a Carborundum stone, a long, narrow, lightweight stone that is covered with small diagonal-running ridges. It, too, is used to smooth the edges of glass, although its use is not recommended as a substitute for grozing pliers. It is used for the small nubs of glass that refuse to come away with the pliers or for a once-over-lightly on a piece that has small slivers along the edge.

The stone must be used properly, or you will be putting more nicks in your glass than you can take out. Like a file, it can only work effectively on the forward stroke; don't scrub back and forth with it on the glass. Use a light touch and forward strokes at a slight angle to the edge of the glass, not straight across. Don't drag it backward across the glass, as this will probably take some fair-sized chunks out of the glass. Use the grozing pliers for grozing; a stone is just for a little cleanup here and there.

There are other tools that can debur glass. Some people use sandpaper to sand each edge perfectly smooth, while others buy special glass grinding machines or use a small belt sander. This is fine, although time-consuming, especially if you are working in the copper-foil method in which the snuggest fit possible is desired. For most projects, however, and especially lead work, a pair of grozing pliers and perhaps a Carborundum stone is all you should need. Sanding and grinding are tedious, and for the most part pointless.

There is always an inclination to rely heavily on grozing as a corrective measure to poor cutting. You're better off to work on your cutting technique if this is the case. It's not that difficult with a little practice and will be much more satisfying than spending your time evening out the edges of the glass by hand.

LEAD KNIVES

These tools seem to appear in such a variety of sizes and shapes as to be very confusing. They are also the most often-improvised tool, although substitutes usually end up to be quite unsuitable for lead work. A lead knife will have a curved blade and a wooden handle (Fig. 4-11). It very much resembles a linoleum knife except for the fact that a linoleum knife is sharpened along the inner edge of its blade, while a lead knife is sharpened along the outer curve. There is a difference in the width of the blade also. The lead knife has a thinner, gradually tapered (toward the edge) blade.

Figure 4-11 shows three different kinds of lead knives. The bottom knife is an imported tool, which is my own personal preference. The second knife is made in the United States with good-quality steel and is also a fine knife. You'll notice the difference in the shape of the blade. They both serve the purpose well. Use whichever feels most comfortable to you. The handles of both of the knives are weighted and useful for tapping glass into place in the lead channel and as handy little hammers for pounding in lead nails as you're working.

Fig. 4-11. Lead knives and cutting wax. The knife at the top is made from an ordinary putty knife and is not recommended for stained-glass use.

The uppermost "knife" in Fig. 4-11 is one of the most frequently seen impersonators. It is actually a simple putty knife on which the blade has been broken off, curved slightly, and had an edge put on it. I have also seen this same idea with the end of the handle set into a small block of lead to give it the weight it lacks. These sorts of knives and others, such as linoleum knives sharpened on the outer blade, X-Acto knives, razor blades, and even kitchen knives, have made their appearance in my classes from time to time, and they seem to eventually disappear, being ultimately replaced with a proper tool.

A good lead knife may cost $6 to $12; there really is no sense in scrimping here. The function of a lead knife is to cut lead, which is not as easy as it sounds. There is a technique to cutting came, which are discussed more fully in Chapter 8. Suffice it to say that lead is pliable and crushes easily. It is a bear to straighten once this happens. A lead knife is a tool specifically designed for its purpose with the proper size and width of blade and a handle that has many talents.

Lead knives do occasionally get dull, although sharpening will be kept to a minimum if you buy the best knife available. Don't use the household or kitchen knife sharpener for this job. Lead knives are sharpened on circular whet stones. Use a semicircular motion, keeping the knife at an angle almost perpendicular to the stone. A light oil should be used for lubrication. Don't vary the angle at which you hold the knife as you sharpen it; too much of this will ruin the edge entirely.

If you can, take your knife to a professional and have the blade hollow-ground. This tapers it to a very fine, keen edge that lasts for quite a while and makes a smoother cut.

CUTTING WAX

Cutting wax (Fig. 4-11) is one of those little luxuries that is not absolutely necessary but that makes the job easier and more enjoyable. You will need a piece about 7½ cm square and 2 or 3 cm thick. To use the wax, simply drag the sharp edge of your lead knife through the wax as if you were cutting it, but, of course, don't go all the way through the wax. Rewax the blade whenever you feel it's necessary; I usually do it every ten cuts or so.

Casting wax is the ideal wax to use because it is very sticky and stays on the blade longer than other waxes. It is sold in small cakes about 7 or 8 cm square, as well as in larger amounts. Alternatives to casting wax—such as paraffin, slab candle wax, beeswax, and old candles—may be used, but you will have to use them more frequently. The more brittle waxes such as paraffin and some candle waxes crumble and make a mess.

Cutting wax is also handy to wax the end of your lathekin.

LATHEKIN

When lead is stretched, the channels of the came often close up slightly, making it necessary to reopen them so the glass will fit in easily. This is the task that the lathekin (Fig. 4-12) performs. It is a very simple tool.

There are thick metal lathekins for opening the larger cames and a thin metal one for the smaller leads, but I prefer wooden lathekins. They are cheap (about $.30) and after considerable use become smooth and rounded. Lathekins ideally should be made from hard wood, but most are made from regular pine. They are easy to make, and if you have a whittling urge (or a wood shop in your garage), you can turn out a dozen. One woman I know filched one of her small son's blocks and fashioned her lathekin from it.

The rounded edge of the lathekin should be narrow enough to fit easily into the lead channel. If it is too wide, it will bend the face of the lead out too far, which makes for a bumpy-looking finish.

To use the lathekin, simply start at one end of the lead, insert the lathekin into the channel, and draw it backward (toward you) so

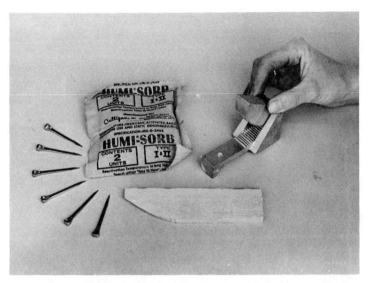

Fig. 4-12. Lead nails, a package of silicon gel, wood lathekin, and metal lead vise.

that the lead is opened up. Or push it forward through the channel; it makes no difference. If you are leading with H came, open both sides. As mentioned earlier, running the tip of the lathekin through cutting wax makes it slide easily through the channel.

Lathekins do wear out eventually, so replace them when they begin to splinter and chip. At that point, their demise is usually close at hand. They are so inexpensive that it does not make sense *not* to discard them.

Lathekins are also used as a buffer between the hammer and glass when you tap pieces in, and as you go along, you will find half a dozen other uses for them in your glass work.

LEAD VISE

A *lead vise,* also called a *lead grabber* or *lead stretcher,* is used to stretch lead came before it is used (Fig. 4-12). A lead vise is simply a small vise with a swinging jaw on the top and a flat jaw on the bottom. Both are lined with small teeth. The vise holds the lead securely while you stretch it. Lead vises cost about $5.

The bottom jaw of the lead vise extends to the rear where there is a small grip that can be hooked over a sturdy table or low shelf when the vise is to be used. It is best to screw the vise on the end of a long work table (there is a hole for this purpose on the vise)

43

if you have the space. If it cannot be permanently installed some-where, have someone hold the vise against the table edge or shelf. Otherwise, when you pull the lead, you are quite likely to get hit in the head by a flying vise.

All lead must be stretched, and it should be done immediately before it is used. Before you stretch lead, straighten out any bends or large kinks in it. Then to stretch the lead, open the lead vise and put one end of the came (about 4 cm) in it. Close the jaws of the vise securely. (This is best done on a long table) Now grasp the other end of the came with a pair of pliers and pull slightly until the came is taut. By doing this you should be able to tell whether the lead is tight in the vise. If it is, simply give a sharp tug on the pliers. With thin leads, you will feel the piece "give." If it only gives a little, give one more pull. Do not overstretch your lead; it should not be stretched more than 4 or 5 cm. Overstretching will weaken the came considerably. The same applies to stretching lead more than once.

You will know the came is stretched by the feel of it more than by anything else. Beginners often ask "How do I know if I stretched it enough?" It is a distinct give in the lead, which you will feed as you stretch it, that will tell you it's done. Try it a few times and you'll see. Heavier leads are a bit harder to stretch because some of them are so thick or heavy that they hardly seem to stretch at all. For these (mostly border leads and thick, flat cames), you need only get as much stretch out of them as is possible in a couple of steady pulls.

To remove the lead from the vise, simply open the jaws and remove it. You can cut the lead in half to facilitate handling; but whether you cut it or not, keep it as straight and free of bends as possible after it has been stretched.

The lead vise is the fastest and most reliable method of stretching lead, but questions always seem to arise about alterna-tive ways of doing things. There are a few other ways to stretch lead came: in a regular vise, by hand, and with a door (you read right). Stretching your lead in a door is somewhat primitive, but it does get the job done. Open the door slightly and put one end of the lead between the door slightly and put one end of the lead between the door jamb and the hinged side of the door. Close the door tightly. With a pair of pliers, grasp the other end and stretch the lead. Open the door and remove the lead. This is a very slow process for any amount of lead cames. It also tends to leave little dark marks and somtimes grooves on the door jamb. If the door fits tightly in the door jamb, the lead may be severed by the tight fit, a fact you probably won't discover until you pull on the lead. So brace yourself and be sure that the china cabinet is not directly behind you. If none of these problem faze you, you can save yourself money, but is it really worth it?

A regular vise can be used, but it has many of the same hazards. It is slow, since you must open and shut the vise by hand each time. It, too, may sever the lead and send you flying.

Then there is two-person by-hand method, probably the least successful method of all. You will need a friend for this one. Each of you must have a set of pliers with which to grasp the ends of the came. Then it's just an adult version of tug of war. You won't be able to tell how much the lead is stretched or if it has been at all. Another version of this method, used for short pieces of came, is to step on one end of the lead and with pliers to pull the other end.

Whatever method you employ, always use a pair of pliers to grip the end you are holding. This not only affords a nonslip grip on the lead but wastes less of the came. Holding it by hand will take up more lead to get a really good grasp, if you can get one at all. Do not use your glass pliers or grozing pliers for this.

Cut off the ends that have been marred by the pliers, vise, or door. They cannot be used because they will either be mashed beyond recognition or will bear the indentations of the teeth. Don't get too carried away with your pulling. Brace yourself and make sure there is nothing dangerous or breakable behind you. It is not unheard of to start stretching a length of lead and be sent flying.

LEAD NAILS

Lead nails are actually not made for lead at all; they're really *farrier nails* or *horseshoe nails* (Fig. 4-12). They are, however, ideal for lead work because they are flat rather than round and have a slim taper.

It is important to use the proper kind of nails for leading your work. Finishing nails, carpet tacks, pushpins, and T-pins should not be used (although pushpins are sometimes useful for copper-foil work, discussed later). The flat surface of a farrier nail fits right up against the lead without leaving little grooves and other unsightly scars left by round nails. Since they must be driven in and pulled out numerous times, the tapered body of the farrier nails is simply more convenient.

Leading nails are tapped into the work board just far enough to hold the lead or glass in place. They are removed each time a new piece of either lead or glass is inserted. If you need a tack hammer to extract them; you are nailing them in too far. The pointed tip of the horseshoe nail adapts well to being repeatedly hammered in and removed by hand.

If they are used often, the tips of the nails occasionally start to bend slightly. If you continue to use them in this condition, they will not hold your pieces tightly and will eventually bend beyond retrieval, thus becoming useless. A nail whose tip is beginning to bend should be straightened with a pair of ordinary pliers. This may seem silly for a simple nail, but there are a couple of reasons for doing this. Sometimes it is difficult to obtain horseshoe nails, and, also, there is no point in discarding something that can be fixed easily and quickly.

SOLDERING IRONS

This is one of the nitty-gritty items you cannot do without. It is also one you may already have, though you should be sure it is suitable for glass working.

Two sizes of irons are shown in Fig. 4-13. One is a *Weller 125-watt* unit; the other is a *Weller 80-watt* version. Both are useful for certain jobs, and it is nice to have a choice. You will probably want to invest in just one iron, however, so choose the best size for you.

For most beginning glass crafters, the 80-watt iron is an ideal tool. It heats up readily and maintains a fairly constant heat. It is also lightweight and easy to control. Your first soldering experience is quite often somewhat frantic as you try to get an even flow of solder on the joints without burning up the lead. Beginners tend to hover on one area in an effort to get it just right while their soldering iron is heating up beyond control. With a small iron, this is still a problem, but less so than setting a heavy, hot iron on the joint and having it go straight through to the glass.

The larger iron is best for soldering heavier cames and large panels with lots of lead joints to cover. It does not cool down as rapidly as the smaller iron and must be moved from one joint to the next fairly rapidly to maintain a controllable heat. As long as the soldering iron is in motion and soldering, the tip can be kept at a temperature hot enough to melt solder yet cool enough not to melt the lead. This does take, however, a considerable amount of practice and feeling for the work itself.

In my classes I recommend the 80-watt iron, although I learned to solder with a 160-watt iron. I remember it being heavy

Fig. 4-13. Weller 125-watt and Weller 80-watt irons, solder flux, flux brush, and file used for filing copper-soldering iron tips.

and awkward and, I might add, that my first window bore a number of strange-looking holes and gaps.

There may come a time when you "outgrow" your small iron. This may be when it finally wears out or when you have graduated to making larger projects and find that you need a more constant heat to cover large areas. When this time comes, you might consider buying a larger iron. By then you will already have had enough experience with soldering, and it should be no problem for you to feel secure in handling the extra heat.

One of the most frequently asked questions is whether a soldering gun is a suitable replacement for an iron. It seems that many people have them around. Whenever someone asks me a question like this concerning any tool, I tell them to go ahead and try it but that it usually proves unsatisfactory. This is definitely true regarding soldering equipment. Soldering guns do not maintain a constant heat and make messy joints. While it is possible to become adept in the use of a soldering gun for lead work, considering the extra time and effort involved, it is not worth the hassle. A serious craftsman will use the proper tools; a soldering gun is a telltale sign of the amateur.

Blowtorches, small soldering irons designed for electrical circuitry, very large irons (above about 175 watts), and welding

47

equipment likewise will not be suitable for stained glass work. An 80-watt iron is about the lowest wattage you should consider using.

All soldering irons should have a stand on which to lean while they are hot. Most come with a small metal stand, but you can make your own with some lightweight sheet metal. A pair of pliers opened so that the iron can rest between the spread handles will do in a pinch.

Wood has a nice smell when it burns, but fires have their place, and it is definitely *not* on your work table. Hot irons, like small children, should not be left unattended. They should always be replaced on their stand, whether heating up, cooling down, or in use.

Look where you are reaching when going for a hot iron. More than one person has grabbed the shaft instead of the handle and been left with memorable but unpleasant experience, not to mention a scar.

With proper care, your soldering iron should last you for quite a while. A word of caution here. A soldering iron is a delicate instrument. It should not be banged on tables, used as a hammer, or dropped. Sudden impact can terminally ruin the heating unit and make a new iron useless. Perhaps the most frequent problem encountered is the periodic erosion of the soldering tip.

Irons are made with two kinds of tips: copper tips and iron-clad tips.

Soldering-Iron Tips

Copper tips, being a soft metal, will eventually become pitted and slightly concave. Two conditions can speed this process. One is application of solder directly to the iron rather than to the work. The other is to neglect the tip as you are soldering by not periodically wiping it off on a damp sponge to remove the dirt and flux that accumulates on the tip. The use of corrosive fluxes or chemicals doesn't help either. Continuing to use a soldering iron with a damaged tip will affect not only the iron by further erosion of the copper tip, but it will also impede the process of soldering and make for rough and uneven joints.

A copper tip may be filed and retinned to return it to a usable state. This can be done numerous times if need be without damage to the iron. To file the tip, let the iron heat slightly. With a flat file, file the tip down smooth, being careful to conform to the original shape of the tip. Remove all pitted areas and ridges, using a forward stroke of the file. Dragging the file backward clogs the ridges and makes the file less effective.

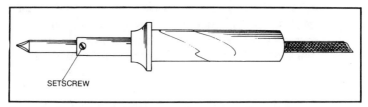

Fig. 4-14. To replace soldering-iron tips, remove the setscrew.

Most irons are tinned when you buy them. This means that a thin coating of solder has been applied to the tip of the iron. Each time you file a copper tip you must also retin it. To retin a tip put a small amount (a few drops) of flux into a cup-shaped piece of tinfoil and melt some solder in with it. Move the hot tip around in this mixture until all of the tip surface is covered with solder. It should be silver and shiny. If the solder does not adhere to the iron, let the iron cool slightly and repeat the process; it should take. When this process is complete, you are ready to start soldering again.

After a copper tip has been filed and tinned many times, it is wise to replace the tip. Soldering tips are cheap—no more than a couple of dollars. To remove the old tip, remove the setscrew that holds the tip in the shaft of the iron (Fig. 4-14) and then simply take the old tip out, put in the new one, and replace the screw. Occasionally, you will find that the screw has frozen in the iron and will not come out. This is due to the constant expansion and contraction of the iron as it heats and cools. You may be able to work it loose with a considerable amount of effort, but usually you must either have the setscrew drilled out or replace the entire iron.

Iron-clad tips have a core of highly conductive copper that is iron-plated. They last much longer than copper tips and do not need to be filed and tinned. Iron-clad tips should never be filed as this will remove the alloy coating and ruin the tip. To clean the tip, it's best to wipe it off on a damp sponge while the iron is hot. This should remove the dirt and grime and restore the tip to a usable condition.

It doesn't really make that much difference which kind of tip your iron has, as long as you know what it is. Iron-clad tips are more expensive than copper tips, although the iron you buy will probably have a copper tip.

On/Off Switches and Rheostats

These are two devices designed to control the amount of heat a soldering iron puts out. Both are fairly simple to install or use.

An *on/off switch* is a small self-enclosed switch spliced into the cord of the iron, usually about 25 cm or so from the end of the handle. This lets you click the iron off when it starts to get too hot without unplugging it from the wall. If you must have this sense of control, the on/off switch is small, cheap, and a better bet than the rheostat.

A *rheostat,* at first glance, appears to be the beginner's saving grace. It is a small box with a control knob, a plug-in outlet, and usually a small pilot light of some sort. The iron is plugged into the box, which is in turn plugged into the wall. From there on, it's like your regular light dimmer, except that instead of regulating light, the rheostat regulates the heat of the iron. It goes from very low (useless for soldering) to full blast, which lets the iron heat to its full capacity. In between, you will find the setting that operates the iron at the "ideal" output. Any light dimmer will operate any soldering iron.

The rheostat is fine for small works. Once you begin working with larger windows, however, this is what you will find happening. You solder a few joints at the right setting. Then your iron begins to cool down from use, so you turn the rheostat up a bit and continue soldering until the iron again begins to cool off, at which point you again move the heat up. This will go on until you find you are using the iron at its highest setting, which means that the rheostat is no longer in control . . . you are.

If rheostats were cheap to make or buy, I would say this is of no consequence, but they are not. In addition they become a crutch. You may burn a few leads in the beginning, but you'll be better off learning to get along without this device. You'll have more confidence in yourself in the long run.

FLUX

The only soldering flux useful for stained glass work is *oleic acid.* This is most commonly in liquid-form, having a rather oily look and feel to it. It falls between being a corrosive flux and a noncorrosive flux. Use only oleic acid on lead work.

Oleic acid may be used for copper-foil technique but better results are obtained with a more corrosive flux. Some stained glass stores mix their own and sell it simply as "copper-foil flux." A recipe for one type of this mixture is given in Chapter 15.

SOLDER

Solder comes as bar solder and as wire solder. What you will want is 2 mm wire solder, which is usually sold in 1-pound quantitites, coiled neatly to make its use more convenient (see Fig. 4-13).

Make sure that you buy solid-core solder, not rosin-core, which has its own fluxing agent already in it that makes up the core of the wire. This flux is not satisfactory for stained glass. It is sticky and oozes from the solder joints long after you've finished, messing up the glass and in general being a real nuisance.

You will find two solder compositions used in stained glass work: 60/40 and 50/50. These numbers refer to the proportions of tin and lead in the solder. The most expensive metal used—tin—is given first, so a 60/40 solder consists of 60 percent tin and 40 percent lead; 50/50 solder has equal amounts of both.

Because 60/40 has a higher percentage of tin, it melts at a slightly lower temperature. A 60/40 solder melts at 188° C; 50/50 solder melts at 212° C. This difference is slight, so the two are really equally suited for glass work. Some people are fanatic about using 60/40 or 50/50 exclusively, but so much concern is questionable. Use what you can buy, as long as it is *only* 60/40 or 50/50 solid-core solder.

GLAZING COMPOUND

After your stained-glass design is completed and has been soldered on both sides, it must be glazed, or puttied; to seal all the gaps between the lead and the glass and make the window airtight and waterproof. Glazing compound is used for this purpose. Some people prefer to mix their own glazing compound. A recipe for this is given in Chapter 10. I find it easier and more convenient to buy materials that require the least amount of mixing.

DAP glazing putty (Fig. 4-15) comes in cans of various sizes. It is a thick putty and must be thinned with paint thinner or turpentine; either one will do. Buy the gray putty if you can find it; otherwise you will have to color it, too. For some reason hardware stores seldom carry gray putty, but most stained glass stores do. If you can only find white putty, you will need some powdered or paste lamp black (found at art stores) or a tube of burnt umber oil paint. Add this to the mixture as you are thinning it to obtain an even color of medium to dark gray. This will blend in with the color of the lead and will not stand out as plainly as would white putty.

Mix glazing compound with paint thinner until you get a pudding-like consistency, free of lumps. Add to this about a cup of Chinese whiting. This will make the putty set faster and harder. If, by doing this, the mixture becomes too stiff and difficult to work with, add a bit more paint thinner.

Fig. 4-15. Glazing compound, Chinese whiting, and glazing brushes.

CHINESE WHITING

Chinese whiting is a fine white powder used to absorb excess putty, dirt, and oils from the glass during the glazing process. Casting plaster may also be used with good results. Sometimes sawdust is recommended for this final stage, but actually, it is far from ideal, as sawdust collects under the lead and embeds itself in the putty, leaving small protrusions that make the edges of the lead look uneven. It is also harder to find, these days—unless you happen to have your own woodworking shop. Even so, whiting or plaster will give much better results.

This sealant is applied with a brush. A small scrub brush and a large scrub brush should be adequate.

PATINA

Patina is a liquid solution used to darken solder or soldered joints. It removes the shiny silver color of new solder and gives it an antiqued look. The patina pictured in Fig. 4-16 turns solder a dull gun-metal gray to black, depending on the strength of the solution, the length of time it is left on, and the amount of buffing done afterward. To apply, you can use a cloth, although a small sponge cut into quarters makes application more controllable.

Dab the solution onto the solder and allow it to work for a moment, then rub it with a dry cloth. If it is still not dark enough, repeat the process. If it is too dark, you might try buffing it with a

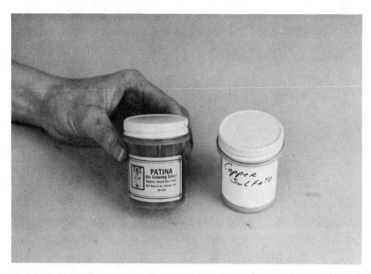

Fig. 4-16. Patina, used to darken solder and give it an antique look, and copper sulfate crystals, which solder a copper coloring.

dry cloth for a few minutes. It may or may not lighten, but it usually does. Patina is hard to clean from glass, so it is recommended that you try to get the liquid only on the solder and not let too much get onto the glass itself, although some is unavoidable.

Copper sulfate crystals, also shown in Fig. 4-16, are also used to color solder. These must be mixed to a liquid solution. It gives the solder a copper color. This is not desirable in leaded work but is used widely in copper-foil work. The proportions and use of this substance are discussed in Chapter 10.

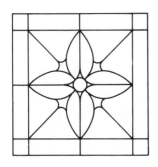

Chapter 5
Work Space

Whatever your working arrangements might be, there are a few standards to be met. Get as much space as you possibly can and put it to maximum service.

You will need, first and foremost, large table. A 4 by-8-ft (122-by-244-cm) work table is ideal—one with a surface of plywood that is a couple of centimeters thick. A height of about a meter seems to be the best for "standing" operations. It should be high enough so that you do not have to stoop over and low enough so you do not feel that you are constantly stretching. The tabletop should be level, and the legs or framework must be solid. This workbench will take a good deal of abuse, and a rickety table will not last long.

The work surface can serve both as a *glass-cutting table* and a *construction table* for assembling, soldering, and glazing your work. If you can have separate tables for these operations, as each requires slight alterations to the original plywood surface.

Glass cutting is best done on a slightly padded surface. The ideal is a tabletop covered with one layer of felt that is stretched smooth and taut and tacked under all edges. Indoor/outdoor carpeting can also be used as a cushioning material. Buy the kind with the lowest, tightest pile you can find. If the padding is too springy, the glass will break with what is less than normal pressure; the same is true of cutting on a very hard surface.

If you have only one table, use it for constructing your work and improvise a cutting surface by covering a separate piece of heavy plywood with felt. The board should be 21 inches by 21 inches (1 m by 1 m), or slightly less if it would prove easier for you to handle. This board alternative conserves space, is portable, and eliminates the need for a separate table. When you need to cut glass, you can simply move your cutting board to your work table.

In a pinch, three or four layers of newspaper spread out on your construction table will do. This is commonly called the "kitchen-table" method of glass cutting.

Always keep your cutting surface clean of glass particles with a *bench brush* or a *whisk broom*.

For pattern layout work, you will need a smoother surface than plywood can offer. A hard floor, a kitchen table, or even a wall will serve this purpose best.

For assembly work, you will need two *guide strips* made from lengths of 2.5-by-5-cm lath stripping. Cut these to the length and width of your construction table and nail them at a right angle onto the lower lefthand corner of your table (Fig. 5-1). These serve as a brace against which to build. Make sure they are at a right angle and make sure that the angle is *square*. Check it with your T-square to make sure—the eye plays deceiving tricks. I stress this point

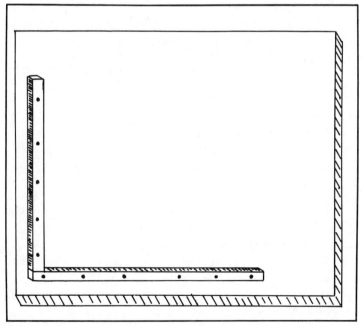

Fig. 5-1. Construction table top showing guide strips nailed in place.

because, if the first corner in your stained glass work is not square, neither will your last corner be.

Tool storage is an important factor to consider. You will want your tools where they are easily accessible, yet not where they are going to be in the way of hands and soldering iron cords. A *pegboard* hung on the wall next to your work table will provide you with handy storage. If you are careful to return tools to their proper places when you are finished with them, you will be able to reach for them easily the next time you need them, and they will be out of your way.

Another alternative is the old-fashioned toolbox, but you will need a fairly large one to accommodate all of your tools. This creates somewhat of a jumble sometimes, but it's better than nothing. Small metal strongboxes are deep and narrow and make good toolboxes. They lock, too. There are also tool stands and revolving tool holders that set on your work table to keep things organized and within reach.

Whatever you use, make sure that tools are properly stored and returned to their original place when you are through. It will save you much time, especially if you are working in confined quarters where things seem to almost misplace themselves.

You will want to be sure that there is adequate *light* wherever you end up working. It's hard on the eyes to work in dim or poorly lit space—and it can be fatiguing and depressing too. Cutting glass, like reading and sewing, causes eyestrain, so have a good light over your table. You might also be certain that there is an outlet nearby, or at least within reach of an extension cord.

Carpeted workrooms are impractical. No matter how thorough, vacuuming and sweeping cannot possibly remove all those small glass slivers from any kind of carpet.

Even on hard floors, such as cement, linoleum, or tile, sweep up after you have finished your glass cutting. This applies particularly if you have set up shop in a part of your own home, where the unsuspecting tread.

Good *ventilation* is necessary wherever soldering is done. It's nice to have windows that can be opened, both for circulating air and for cheerful, natural sun light. If you solder on cold days, set up a small fan so that it moves the air and the fumes do not become so concentrated. Don't aim it directly at yourself, as this is usually bothersome and can cool off the iron just enough to keep it from its maximum performance.

Making stained glass windows entails the use of some chemicals. Few are lethal in small amounts, but most are potentially dangerous. Keep all bottles containing chemicals, such as fluxes, patina, and etching cream, plainly marked so that you can tell what they are at a glance. If there are small children or roaming pets around, it is wise to keep these materials on a high shelf or in a cabinet that can be locked. You can leave them out while you are working, but when you are through be sure to replace them where they are out of reach.

If you keep large quantities of chemicals on hand, pour out only as much as you will need for your work or for the day into a smaller container and put the rest away. This is suggested for the safety of others as well as for the fact that if you spill a small jar, it won't matter as much as if you knocked over a quart.

Sooner or later you will have to store glass. As you go along, you will begin to accumulate glass—scraps that are too large to throw away, special pieces that you just had to buy, or even larger sheets of glass purchased for large projects. Because glass cannot be folded up, hung on a peg, or stacked in a corner, storage can present a problem, especially if your space is quite limited.

Glass racks or bins of the type commercial dealers use for glass storage are ideal. These can be built with 2-by-4s and plywood. Make them about 15 cm taller than the normal size of glass that you buy (see Fig. 5-2). If you buy 30 cm (foot-square) pieces almost exclusively, make your bins about 46 cm tall and

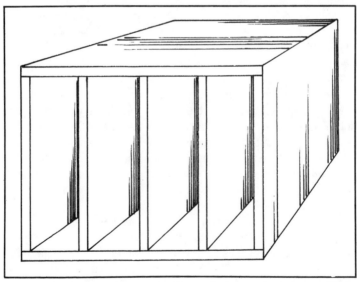

Fig. 5-2. A bin for glass storage can be built to hold any size sheets of glass.

about 30 cm wide. These will look like small cubbyholes. If you make them of heavy plywood and of a uniform size (say 30 cm wide, 30 cm deep, and 46 cm tall), you can stack them to suit the limitations of your work space. For larger sheets, make your bins taller and reduce their width so that the glass doesn't sit at too much of a slant.

Glass bins can usually be made to fit under your work table. This is possible a fine idea but only if you still will have easy access to the glass. If, however, in the interest of saving space, you find yourself having to weave in and out of the table legs on your hands and knees to get a particular piece of glass, then try some other more workable arrangement. This is not only frustrating but dangerous.

Glass is best stored vertically, and for anything over 30 cm square, it is almost essential. Do not stack large and irregularly sized pieces of glass on top of each other: they will slip and slide and eventually break. It is also too much weight and uneven pressure for the pieces on the bottom, and they will break from the sheer stress.

You will also need several *small boxes* about 30 cm square and 15 to 20 cm deep, preferably made of wood. These will be scrap boxes for those leftover pieces of glass or new scraps that you buy to use some time in the future (almost all stained glass stores sell scrap glass by the kilogram or pound). These can be stacked to conserve space if you wish. You can sort the glass to go in them by general size or type of glass or by the color. Or you can just fill them indiscriminately, although you may regret this when you go looking for that little piece of emerald green glass you need for a special touch.

A table made especially for glazing would be most convenient if you can spare the room—the farther from your work area the better. Glazing is a messy procedure, and the use of the whiting, or any other such substance, proves to be a real nuisance. A thick layer of this powder builds up on surrounding areas, no matter how hard you try to keep the dust down. If you can't manage a separate table, you should cover your tools and liquids when you glaze.

The basic points on storing lead are covered in Chapter 2. The "where" is more or less your business, but here are a couple of suggestions. If you are working at a table 2 meters in length or longer, a lead box such as described in Chapter 2 can be built to fit under the table. This will enable you to store your lead uncut, to waste less of it, and to protect it from oxidation. If your table is shorter than a meter, build a box that will fit to whatever length the table is. This will make it necessary for you to cut your lead came in half or to the length of the box. Don't double lead over in order to make it fit into such a box; you will end up with a tangled mess. One full meter is really the smallest you should make your lead box if at all possible.

If you've already planned to put your glass racks under your table and there is no space for a lead box, you will have to resort to another method, such as taping the came to a small board, wrapping it in newspaper and standing it in the corner, or hanging the lead on a large hook.

If you can, bolt your lead vise onto your work table. It will only take up a few inches but will make its use handy and simple. Mount it to the corner farthest from your right-angled guide strips; the teeth of the vise should be parallel to the long edge of the table (see Fig. 5-3).

By now it may seem to you that you will need a warehouse in which to work and adequately store your tools and supplies. What I've described is, of course, the ideal—and the ideal too often falls

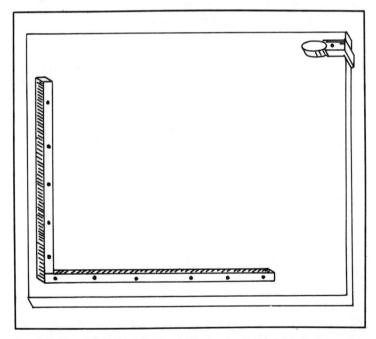

Fig. 5-3. If possible, bolt the lead vise to your work table in the corner diagonally opposite the right-angle guide strips.

quite short of reality. Even with all of the tables and storage equipment described, a garage or basement would most likely fit the bill. But what if you are an apartment dweller, or don't intend to make glassmaking a career, or just don't have this sort of space in which to design, cut, and build? A part-time workshop is difficult buy by no means impossible.

The studio in which I work full-time is a large building—indeed almost a small warehouse—that is well organized and equipped. There are six large tables, and tool shelves and glass racks line almost every wall. It is truly a pleasure to work in this kind of atmosphere, to know that tools can be found easily and glass identified by a simple tag above each rack.

At home, however, it is a different story. My kitchen often turns into a workshop at night, and I have built some large stained glass pieces on the very same table on which I eat meals. Here's how I've done it: I have a large table (although it is in a small kitchen), which serves well for making initial layouts and patterns. For glass cutting, I use a small piece of felt-covered plywood about 5 cm by 5 cm, as, described in Chapter 4. I keep this standing up in the closet. When I'm ready to cut glass, I move it to the table. When I work with large pieces of glass I use a few layers of newspaper laid out on the table.

For constructing the piece, I use two different plywood sheets, which are stored vertically against a wall. I don't put them outside because the elements, especially rain, would quickly make them useless. (Don't use warped boards.) One sheet is about 135 by 76 cm; the other is about 1 meter square. Both have square corner strips already nailed onto them. I use whichever one will best suit my purpose for my particular job, and it, too, is set on top of the kitchen table. If I am working on a small project, the entire board (project and all, can be lifted off and placed somewhere level and sturdy to free the kitchen table when it is needed, such as meal times. Usually, however, the family eats in the living room (with the TV as an added bonus) so that my work can be left undisturbed. You will need a tolerant family to get away with this for more than a couple of days at a time. If the job is small, I try to do my glazing outdoors, transporting the entire board and project to the backyard where the breeze can blow the whiting away.

You must have a strong back for carrying sheets of plywood and stained glass windows—especially since the board must be carried flat, at least until your work is completely soldered front and back. Stained glass, soldered and leaded, will weigh approximately 1.5 to 2 kg per 30-cm-square area. The plywood itself isn't exactly light as a feather. So if you're not sure whether you can manage the weight and the awkwardness, get a friend to help. Better safe than sorry, as they say.

For storage, again, the word is *improvise.* One of my kitchen cabinets holds, on its five shelves, four boxes of glass scraps, sorted for size and color; a revolving tool caddy, which holds most of the tools I use; a shelf for extra tools; lamp forms; glass glues; books; and assorted sundry other tools and materials. Flux, patina, kerosene, and all other dangerous chemicals are kept on a high shelf, out of the reach of my young son. Large pieces of glass and half sheets are stored, vertically, in a closet.

Lead came is hung on a hook in an unnoticed cranny, although I really would like to have the room to store it properly. Over the table there is a window, which opens, and an electrical outlet within arm's reach on the wall. The floors are linoleum, and I'm close to the coffee pot. What more could you ask for?

Working in such limited space does not require as much contortionism as it sounds like. It is more difficult than working in the proper space, but as you can see, it can be done. I have built 150-by-120-cm windows there in much the same manner, although I used a sheet of plywood that occupied nearly my entire kitchen on top of the table, and we watched TV with our dinner for several weeks. As long as your work board does not overhang your table by more than about 15 cm, you're okay. Beyond this, because of lack of support from beneath, the plywood can not withstand the pounding of nailing into it, and the constant bouncing may well put one or more cracks in your glass work.

You will doubtless come to find the best arrangements suited to your available space and your own working habits. Cramped accommodations do not necessarily mean cramped creativity.

Light tables are handy devices to have in your home workshop. They allow you to compare the colors of your glass to see if they go together before any glass is cut. By laying out your samples on the table and arranging them in the approximate order they are to be in, you will be able to tell if they will match well or clash. Keep in mind, however, that the best light is always natural light—regular old sunshine— and that the fluorescent light used in light tables tend to flatten the glass colors somewhat.

A light box is simply an open-topped box over which a sheet of sandblasted plate glass (0.6 cm thick) is placed. It is lit from within by fluorescent fixtures. The box itself can be almost any size, as long as you can fit a fluorescent tube into it. If it is small, one light will probably do. A large table may require several bulbs wired together and attached to a single switch. The switch should be on the outside.

You can buy plate glass from your regular glass dealer, and he can sometimes arrange to have it sandblasted. Or you may have to take it somewhere that does only sandblasting work. Sandblasting the plate glass makes it look frosted and acts to diffuse the light from the bulbs below. For safety, have the edges ground smooth.

Chapter 6
Cartoon Layout and Pattern Making

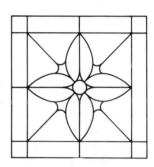

The term *cartoon* refers to the finished drawing of the design to the exact dimensions of the finished piece. It includes all lead lines. From this cartoon, a *pattern* or *cutline* as it is sometimes called, is made to serve as a guide for the actual glasscutting. Another copy of the cartoon, called the *working copy*, must also be made.

For your cartoon use kraft paper or other strong paper.

Copying the cartoon on pattern paper may be done with carbon paper, a lightbox, or a window large enough to which to tape the drawing. If your cartoon is small, you can use carbon paper in the same manner you would for typing. Simply sandwich the carbon between your cartoon and the piece of pattern paper and draw carefully over all the lines. You can tape several sheets of carbon together for larger projects, although carbon, being so thin and flimsy, is hard to work with this way. You will need to do this twice.

If you have a lightbox, this makes the job considerably easier. Lay out your cartoon first, then position the pattern paper over it and tape it securely to the table to keep them both from shifting. When you turn the light on, the lines will show through the pattern paper, making it easy to trace them.

This same principle can be used with a large window, such as a picture window. First tape the cartoon flat to the window. Over this lay the pattern paper, again taped securely. The sunlight will make a vertical lightbox and allow the lines of the pattern to come through sharp and clear.

Now make a second copy of the cartoon for your working copy. You should now have three papers, all exact copies: the original design, the cartoon; the working copy, and, on heavier paper, the pattern. The cartoon will be your guide: it will lay flat on your work table and the leaded glass will be constructed right on top of it.

The working copy is used as a layout. Each piece of glass as it is cut is laid on top of it. When you have finished cutting all of your glass and laying it out on the working copy, you will be able to see the project as it looks without the lead. Naturally, you won't be able to see the true colors of your glass until it is leaded and soldered and can be lifted, but you will be able to tell if there are any pieces that fit poorly and need to be recut. Remember that there will be a 2-mm or so gap between all of the pieces to allow for the lead. If you find there are large gaps between the glass at this point, check each piece against the pattern to which it was cut. Often you will need to groze the edges or perhaps cut the piece over again. On very, very simple projects with few pieces, it may not be necessary to have this working copy, but in general it's a good idea for the beginner. It is easier to spot and correct mistakes made in cutting here.

Cut out each piece of your pattern with pattern shears. As noted in Chapter 4 the pattern shears cut out a 2 mm paper strip. This is the measurement of the lead heart. When the pattern is cut out, lay each piece on top of your glass sheet and cut around it so that the glass will be cut in the same shape and size as the pattern piece. It is important that the paper on which the pattern is made is not too thick; it must be sturdy enough to hold its shape, but thin enough to allow the cutter to run exactly along the edge. The wheel of a glass cutter protrudes slightly beyond its axle; the pattern paper must be able to fit under this small "shoulder" (Fig. 6-1).

Number each piece as it is cut. The numbers for each piece should be the same on each drawing. These numbers will help you to know where each piece goes, on the working copy and in the actual project itself. For instance, if the first piece to be set into a window is number one, you would be able to quickly locate the piece and be able to tell that that indeed is the correct piece (Fig. 6-2). The process of making leaded glass is somewhat like a jigsaw puzzle. If you had the entire puzzle numbered to correspond with numbers on each piece, it would go much more smoothly, right? Of course, in puzzle working, finding out where the pieces fit is the fun part; in leaded glass work; it is simply frustrating.

If you should discover that you missed a piece in your number-ing sequence, either fill it in with the number that comes after your

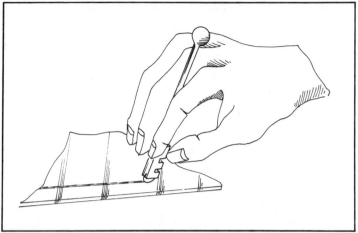

Fig. 6-1. The shoulder of the glass cutter rides on top of the pattern; the wheel moves against the pattern's edge.

last number, or make it a subscript of a nearby number or assign an alphabetic designator. For example, if you missed a piece and it is flanked by number 51, make the blank one 51A. Be sure to mark it on your other copies as well.

You may start numbering at the bottom, the top, or in the middle if you want; it makes no real difference. I find it easiest to begin in the lower lefthand corner and to number across to the right edge, then start back, working back and forth until I reach the top. It doesn't matter in which order you number a pattern, as long as the number is the same on all three copies. This has no bearing on the order in which the glass will be cut or leaded. It is simply a code to let you know where each piece fits in the window.

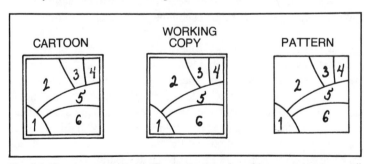

Fig. 6-2. The three drawings. The cartoon and working copy have a small margin to compensate for the width of the border lead. The pattern is the same size as the cartoon and working copy less the area to be taken up by the border lead.

You will also find it helpful to mark each pattern with the color of glass from which it is to be cut. By doing this, you will be able to put all the greens in one pile, all the blues in another and so forth, so that all the pieces to be cut from one color can be cut at one time. This is easier than cutting one piece of green, putting the glass away, then a piece of blue, and then having to get the green back out because you have another piece to cut from it. This can be done either by writing the name of the color on each piece or by drawing a line of color on it (with crayon, colored ink, felt-tip pen, or whatever) that will represent the glass color. Do the same on the cartoon to enable you to cross-check colors as you cut, if need be.

CUTTING THE PATTERN

When you cut your pattern with pattern shears cut down the very center of each line. The thin strip of paper that the scissors removes should have the drawn line on it. Any veering to the right or left of the line will show up in your glass.

The actual cutting should be done with the back portion of the shears, using small bites. If you attempt to use the entire length of the blade, your pattern will fray badly along the edges and the paper strip will clog up the blades, making it necessary to stop and pull the paper out. Pattern cutting should be done in a continuous forward motion.

As you will discover, turning corners or changing angles as you cut can be a little tricky, and if you're not careful, you could tear the pattern. These cuts are easily made by cutting slightly into the adjoining piece (Fig. 6-3). The shears can then be drawn back enough to cut true on the center of the adjoining line.

What you want are smooth edges, free of fraying and mashed paper. Should either of these problems occur, trim the edge carefully.

If you have taped paper together to get the correct size for your pattern, you may find that when you cut through the tape with pattern shears the cutting becomes more difficult or the paper gets jammed easily between the blades. Cutting through any amount of tape will sometimes gum up the inner edges of the blades and cause the blades to mash or fray the paper edges as it cuts. If this occurs, dip a rag into acetone and poke it through the blades far enough so that you can get a grip on it. Pull it up and down and slide it along all of the inside cutting edges. This should remove the sticky residue and improve cutting. Do this periodically in any case to keep the blades clean and free of dust, oils, and grime.

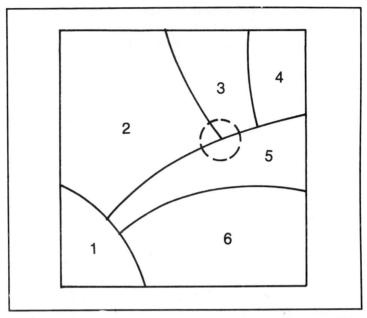

Fig. 6-3. When cutting patterns, cut slightly into the adjoining piece. This will enable you to turn corners and to cut odd angles.

Never force any tool or hard object between the bottom blades as this could spring them and ruin them.

I find it easier to cut with the single blade on top. This allows me to see the line on which I am to make my cuts. Some people, however, find the reverse suits them best. Use whichever way feels most comfortable to you and allows you to follow accurately the lines and cut in their center.

SCALING THE DESIGN

Oftentimes you will want to use a small drawing or design from a book and will need to enlarge it to the size you want your finished stained glass to be. You may be able to accomplish this by freehand drawing to the desired size. For those without such talents, however, there is a way to do this that will produce excellent and accurate results.

Suppose you have taken a design from a pattern book and wish to make it into a full-scale cartoon for a leaded-glass window, and the design as it appears in the pattern book measures 16 cm by 24 cm. First you must determine the final size of your window, and (for this method of enlargement to work) it must be in the same proportions as the smaller drawing. That is, if your drawing is 16 cm wide and you want your window to be 64 cm wide—four times wider—the height of your work must be four times taller, or 96 cm. If the dimensions of your drawing are not the same proportions you want your finished lead window to be, you will have to modify one or the other.

Next you must transfer the pattern-look drawing into graph paper or a sheet of quadrille pad paper, which has 5-mm squares. To do this first draw in on the graph paper the outline of the rectangle you are transferring; then place the graph paper over the drawing and trace the design. You will have something that looks like the drawing in Fig. 6-4A. On the graph paper you can make each square represent any unit of measure you like—1 centimeter, 10 centimeters, ½ inch, or even 1 inch. The important point is that the pattern will be properly proportioned.

Now you must reduce the number of squares in the tracing. Do this by drawing a heavy line, horizontally and vertically, every four squares. These larger squares will be reference squares for creating your full-sized cartoon. The appearance of your drawing will look something like the one in Fig. 6-4B.

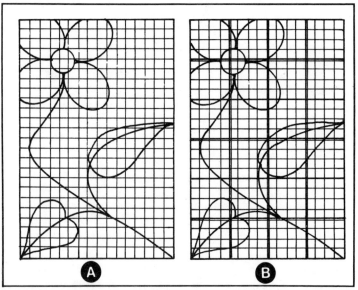

Fig. 6-4. (A) Design traced onto graph paper. Each square on the paper can be used to represent a centimeter, several centimeters, an inch, or whatever unit you designate. (B) The graphed design with reference (heavier-lines drawn in).

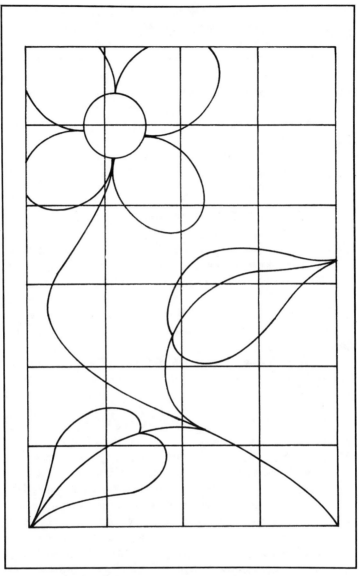

Fig. 6-5. Full-size cartoon drawn "two up" or two times larger than the original shown in Fig. 6-4.

To transfer this design to its full size, you will need a piece of cartoon paper a little larger than you want your leaded glass work to be. Measure off your perimeter lines (in this case they will be 64 cm wide by 96 cm and draw them in on the cartoon paper. Square the corners. Be sure the corners on your graph paper are also square; if they are not, redraw them so that they are square.

On the cartoon rectangle, mark off points on all perimeter edges at intervals four times greater than the width of your reference squares. (If you are making your cartoon drawing five or six or seven times larger than the graphed drawing, you would mark off intervals proportionally, that is, five, six, or seven times greater than the reference squares on the graph paper.) Connect the intervals horizontally and vertically with a pencil (the pencil lines can be erased later if you wish) so that you have a grid of squares covering the space. (In this example your squares would be 16 cm wide and 16 cm high.) These squares represent the 4-cm reference squares on the graph paper.

From this point it is a simple matter to enlarge your design. On the cartoon paper, sketch your design freehand using the reference squares as guides. Where a design line crosses in the middle of a reference line on the graph paper, your design line should cross the middle of the same reference square on the cartoon paper, for example. Following the graphed design square by square, you will be able to transfer the design onto the cartoon paper in the right proportions and to the desired size you want your leaded glass to be.

This method of "scaling up" is, of course, easiest when you are working with even measurements. On uneven measurements or smaller-scale drawings simply use the same graph principle and figure out the divisions so that the squares will be evenly spaced.

Before you start, remember that whatever the width of your border lead, it must be compensated for in the full-scale drawing. This is most important if you will be installing your leaded glass into a premade sash, jamb, or window frame. The outer edge of the lead must not extend beyond the drawing's perimeter lines. Different border leads are different sizes so plan accordingly. For illustration purposes, let's say that your border lead is 10-mm H lead. This lead, as you know by now, has a channel on both sides, but since it will be used as a border, only one side will hold glass. The lead heart is just shy of 2 mm (about 1/16 inch), and it is to this measurement that the glass will be cut—*not* to the outer edge.

A full-scale drawing is illustrated in Fig. 6-6. The perimeter of the drawing represents the outer edge of the lead border. The broken line marks where the lead heart will fall, and also where the glass will be cut to. This is marked at 4 mm in from the perimeter line. Draw this line in around all edges. The glass must be cut to the

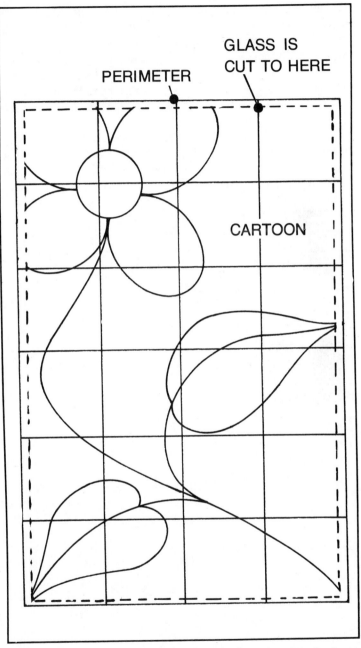

Fig. 6-6. The outside border represents lead. Glass is cut to the inner broken line.

broken line, *not* to the perimeter line, which means that your pattern itself must be drawn only to the broken line. In simpler words, the pattern when drawn will be smaller than the cartoon drawing by 4 mm on all edges. This may seem to be a confusing concept, but it is most important. Read this over and look at the drawings until you are sure that you understand it. Otherwise, you will end up with a window that is too big for its intended opening, a most frustrating prospect.

To adjust this measurement to any size border lead, measure the lead across the face to get its correct width. Measure the distance from the edge of the lead, whether U or H, to the heart and add 2 mm to this measurement. Draw this line in around each edge (*inside* the perimeter line). This is the line to which your pattern for glass cutting is to be made.

Chapter 7
Glass Cutting

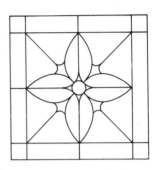

Learning to cut glass is probably the hardest part of stained glass work. Learning to cut accurately to a pattern makes it that much more difficult, but don't give up already! Like most of the technical aspects of the craft, practice does make perfect (or just about perfect, anyway).

Glass cutting is not an innate skill; it is an acquired one. And we all must begin with knowing nothing and going from there. Everyone does.

During first projects, I am deluged with students asking two questions: "Is this close enough?" (it usually is not), and "Will it show?" (it usually does). But I always remind them that practice is the key. With practice you will become better, then good, and finally excellent at glass cutting.

While I do not either rigidly insist that you cut one piece over and over again until it fits right (and in this context "right is a very loose term), I also do not encourage you to "make do" or be satisfied with mediocre craftsmanship. There is a fine line between the two criteria. By appealing to the integrity of any craftsman, whether beginning beginners or seasoned oldies, one quickly weeds out those who are serious from those who are not. Even if you are working merely for your own pleasure, you have an idea of your own standards and how you can best serve them.

Don't expect a masterpiece from your first window, but do the very best that you can. It helps to keep your first design simple, using a small pattern and inexpensive glass until you become competent in the basic procedure. Practice, practice, practice!

You will need the proper cutter for whatever glass you have selected and the necessary lubrication for it. Various cutters and their purposes are covered in Chapter 4, but briefly, here is what you need to know.

If you are cutting window glass (single- or double-strength), cathedral glass, mirror, or most of the antique glasses, you will want to buy a No. 2 glass cutter, either a Fletcher (metal with a ball on the end) or Diamantor (green wooden handle). For all opalescent glass and a few of the antiques, you will need a Fletcher No. 7 for straight cuts and gentle curves and a Fletcher No. 9, a smaller wheel, for pattern cutting. Be sure to buy oil or make the oil (a mix of light oil and kerosene) as explained in Chapter 4. Use the oil religiously.

Holding a glass cutter is an awkward affair for the first time. There is a recommended "proper" way, to hold it, but the proper method does not work for many people, no matter how hard they try. There are also alternative ways. I suggest you grasp it in whichever way feels most comfortable to *you*. As long as your grip is secure and the cutter does not wobble or slide around in your hand, you will be able to cut glass. Three ways to hold a glass cutter are shown in Fig. 7-1.

Always stand when you are cutting glass. While it may be tiring to stand for a great length of time if you are cutting a lot of glass, it is close to impossible to cut glass sitting down. The score line will be irregular because you simply cannot get the correct amount of steady pressure in a sitting position.

Stand close to the edge of the table with your right hip slightly angled away from the table. Your left foot should be forward so that your body weight falls on your right. This makes the pressure from the shoulder a natural thing. This is for right-handed people. If you are left-handed angle your left hip slightly and stand with your right foot forward.

MAKING THE SCORE

Two actions occur when a piece of glass is cut. First, it is scored with a glass cutter. This leaves a visible (usually) fine line inscribed in the surface of the glass. You can also hear the cutter scoring the line. Then the glass is broken. If the score was a good one, the glass will break along it. If it was not a good score line, the glass will usually break raggedly wherever the score was faulty.

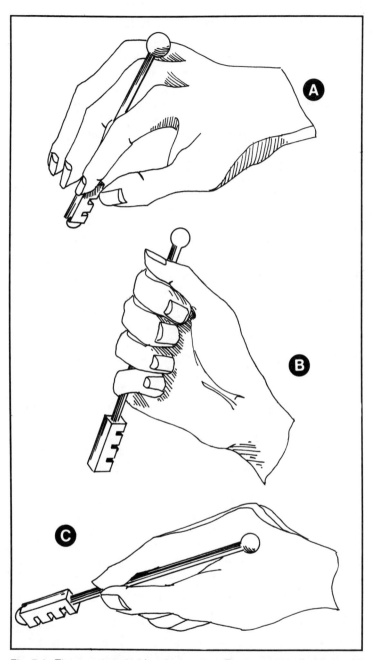

Fig. 7-1. Three ways to hold a glass cutter. The recommended "proper" grip is shown in *A*, but use one of the others if it is more comfortable.

Beginners often ask which side of the glass to consider as the cutting surface. Glass is always cut on the *smooth* side; and in cases where both sides are smooth, you will usually find that one side is somewhat smoother than the other. If you cannot tell after careful inspection, make a test cut on a corner of the glass. Whichever side scores and breaks most easily is the side on which to cut.

Hammered and ripple-back glasses are cut on the smooth side, which is obvious at a glance. Mirror is cut on the shiny mirrored side, never on the backing.

Antique glasses are difficult to judge because sometimes both sides seem equally smooth. By holding antique glass up to a light, you will see small striations or very fine lines running through the glass. These are more predominant on one side, and that is the side to cut on.

Flashed glass is cut on the white or clear side. This can be discerned by holding the glass to the light and looking at the edge. You will be able to see the side the color is layered on and know to cut on the other side.

The surface you will be cutting on should be slightly padded, as was mentioned in Chapter 5. The padding allows for the irregularities in the glass surface. Bare wood, metal, and Formica allow no "give." The pressure applied to the bottom of the glass from the hard surface when combined with the pressure above from the glass cutter will probably shatter the glass.

When glass is cut in straight lines, either freehand or along a straightedge of some sort, you draw the cutter toward your body. When you cut to a pattern, you push the cutter away from you.

Always be sure that your glass is clean before you begin any cutting. Use a glass cleaner to remove dust, lint, or other particles that may hinder your cutting.

To make a score line along a straightedge, first dip your cutter in the oil. Start at the top of the glass, as close to the edge as possible, and draw the cutter (toward you) steadily across the glass. Allow the cutter to run off the bottom edge of the glass. This is hard on the cutter, so don't let it hit the table with a great deal of force. The padded surface also helps absorb some of this shock on the cutter. (Later, you will learn to stop it at the edge of the glass). Trying to concentrate on scoring the line any stopping the cutter at the edge, however, usually means you will be thinking of stopping the cutter, and so ease up your pressure as you near the edge of the glass. If you do this, the score line will be weak, and you will probably lose the cut. If you can manage it without losing pressure, stop the cutter at the edge of the glass. This is healthier for the cutter and the glass.

One thing often misunderstood about glass cutting is how little pressure need be applied to the cutter. A score line that will break correctly really takes very little effort—certainly not the grunting and groaning that is often heard from those who are learning. The secret of this pressure lies not in the wrist but in the shoulder. Any weight applied to the glass cutter should be coming from this point of your body. Using the wrist to apply pressure will end up giving you a stiff joint. You will find that you do not really need such severe pressure to make a good score.

Use enough pressure to make a score, but not so much that you are *gouging* the line out. You can actually hear the cutter scoring, a difficult sound to describe, but it sounds something like a sharp object being drawn across a piece of fine-grain sandpaper or like paper being torn. If you do not hear this or any sound, or if it stops and starts intermittently, it is a faulty score and may be difficult to break.

If, on the other hand, small chips and slivers of glass fly off from your cut, you are pressing too hard. One of my more energetic students bore down so hard on the glass that I could not bring myself to watch him cut; it's surprising that the glass didn't shatter into bits. This kind of brute force is tiring and unnecessary.

Different types of glass require different pressures. The same amount of applied pressure that would score a piece of the harder opalescent glass will probably destroy a softer, sometimes very thin sheet of German antique. As you cut more glass, you will learn to gauge the amount of pressure needed.

Never go over a score line twice with your cutter, because this will ruin the wheel immediately. If the score is bad, break it out and start over.

In pattern cutting, the pattern piece is laid on top of the glass, not under it, and the cutter is then run around the edge of the pattern. Usually, more than one complete score line is needed to cut each piece (Fig. 7-2). Each score is broken as it is cut not after the entire piece has been cut. This is done because some glass has a regenerating quality; if it is not broken immediately, the score tends to "heal," making it difficult or impossible to break the piece out.

It takes a bit of practice to be able to hold the pattern piece in place and keep it there while you cut around it. Some individuals adhere their pattern pieces to the glass with a small bit of tape

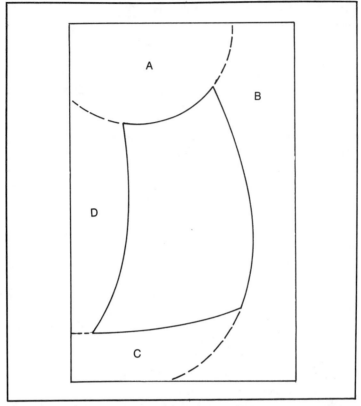

Fig. 7-2. One piece often requires several cuts to break it out. A single cut will release piece *A* in the upper left corner. The next cut will free *B*. A third cut trims away *C*, and *D* is removed with the final cut.

folded in a little tube and stuck to the back of the pattern. Use this method if you must, but discontinue it as soon as possible. For some reason, pieces cut in this manner are usually slightly larger than the pattern, and the slight increase in each piece adds up to an appreciable difference by the time all the pieces are cut.

As you cut each piece of glass, check it against the pattern. Looking at the piece from the top, with the pattern next to it, you should not see any glass protruding from under the edge of the paper. Small bits and nubs can be grozed away, but if there is an overall difference, the piece should be recut. Likewise, when you turn the pattern and the glass over, you should not see pattern paper sticking over the edge of the glass. Pattern and glass should both match exactly. Lay each piece on the working copy before you go on to the next.

BREAKING THE SCORE

There are many ways to break the score line, some better than others. This is the part that frightens some people because it means actually handling glass, breaking it, and controlling the break. As long as the basic procedures given here are followed and their precautions observed, there is no reason for discomfort. Really, this is one of the fun parts, because it is the first fruit of your labors: the transference of a paper pattern to a glass shape.

Hand Breaks

It is always best, whenever and wherever possible, to break the piece by hand. This gives you the greatest amount of control over the break and is in itself a pleasing sensation. To break a score by hand requires the proper grip and positioning of the hands. Both thumbs are placed on either side of the score, close to the line but not on it. The hands support the glass from beneath (Fig. 7-3). Your fingers should be closed into fists as shown. When this is done, snap the glass in a down-and-away motion (Fig. 7-4). It feels almost like *pulling* the glass apart; and if you are fortunate and have made a good score, it will be that easy.

It is essential that your hands are closed beneath the glass, and that your thumbs are next to the score line. To open the hands up below will give the wrong pressure in the wrong place and simply invites a serious cut. Break from the edge closest to your body. Don't try to break from the top of the score line, farthest from

Fig. 7-3. Proper position for hand breaking: thumbs are placed on either side of the score; the remaining fingers support the glass from beneath.

Fig. 7-4. The break is made by snapping the glass at the score line with a down-and-away motion.

your body. Your hands should be right in front of you where you can see them and what's happening with the glass.

The score line should always be facing up when breaking glass unless specifically mentioned. Do not break glass with the score on the bottom.

For breaking larger pieces of glass that are scored with straight lines, there is an alternate method. For this, turn the glass so that the score line is parallel to the table edge. Hold the glass firmly with both hands (spaced as shown in Fig. 7-5) and pull the entire sheet toward you until the score line is about 1.5 cm past the edge of the table. The glass will be half on the table and half off of it. Now simply raise the glass very slightly, no more than 1 to 1.5 cm, and snap it down on the table. The glass will break along the score. You should be prepared to hold the weight of the glass as it swings down. This sounds like an elaborate process, but it is actually a smooth and rapid motion.

If the piece is not so large but you wish to break it in this manner, use only one hand to hold the glass (in the middle, as shown in Fig. 7-6). Place your other hand flat on the glass to hold it in place on the table. If this is not done, the glass could fly up and hit you. On larger sheets, the weight of the glass itself is enough to hold it on the table; you must supply that weight for smaller pieces. Remember, though, this method can only be used for straight-line cuts.

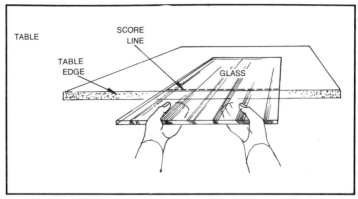

Fig. 7-5. Straight cuts on large sheets can be broken over the table's edge.

Tapping

Although I try to discourage the separation of glass by tapping, it seems there is always someone who has seen it done or heard about it wants to know how to do it. Few people who do tap glass to break do it correctly, and the sound of it alone is nerve-wracking, but here is the proper way.

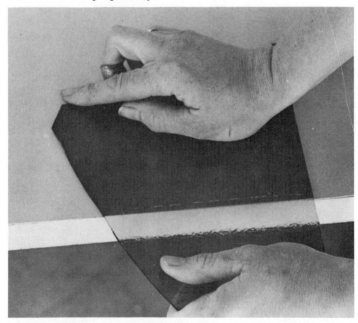

Fig. 7-6. Straight cuts in small pieces can also be broken over the table's edge, but one hand must hold the glass in place on the table.

The ball on the end of Fletcher cutters is the instrument most often used, although the grozing teeth on the front end of the cutter are also sometimes used. I shudder to see some people tapping with their glass pliers.

The glass must be supported on both sides of the score line, so that in the event that the pieces separate by themselves, which they often do, neither piece will fall on hands or feet or the floor. To do this, hold the glass in your fist so that your thumb is on top of the glass on one side of the score line or slightly over it and your index finger is underneath the glass on the other side of the score line.

When you have gotten the glass firmly in hand and properly supported, tap the end of the score line gently with the ball end of your cutter (Fig. 7-7). It is not necessary to use force; simply tap in one place at the beginning until you see the score begin to run. The principle involved is not to bang away at the glass until it falls apart, as many do. When the score fractures and begins to run, what you will be doing is "leading" the run across the glass by tapping it gently. Tap again wherever the run stops, and the run will shoot forward a little more. Each time the run moves, move your tapping up to where it stops. By doing this, you will be able to run the line across the glass and simply pull it apart by hand with the greatest of ease.

Tapping glass has many drawbacks in comparison to its few dubious advantages. When you do separate the pieces, you are quite apt to find a very splintered edge, with small slivers of glass all along it. This occurs each time you tap not directly in the center of the score line. Any variance to the left or right, even if it is imperceptible to your eye, will cause splintering on that edge when the glass is finally broken. More than anything else, this is a nuisance because you must then go back and clean up the edges with your grozing pliers.

If you get carried away with your tapping, you are also liable to end up with a chunk of glass in your eye. As I said before, force is not the issue here. Don't hammer away at the glass or keep time with a song playing on the radio. Slow and steady all the way.

And, as if this were not enough, tapping glass does make a noise that has about the same effect as Chinese water torture. I suppose it might not be so bad in the privacy of your own home, but until you have heard an entire class of people tapping away at their glass, you do not know what noise is. About the only use I have found for tapping is for trick cuts in glass, or those that require a great deal of caution in breaking, again because of the difficulty of

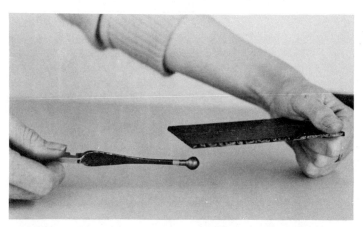

Fig. 7-7. The proper way to tap score lines. Note that both sides of the score line are held.

the particular cut or the type of glass. Learn to use your pliers well and, between them and your hands, you should not need to use this method much.

Using a Fulcrum

This is yet another way of breaking glass, used primarily for breaking larger pieces. It will work only if the glass is scored in a straight line or a very gentle curve. A small object, such as the head of a leading nail or the cutting end of your glass cutter, is inserted under the glass, directly below the score line. You need only about 1 to 1.5 cm of whatever item you use, just enough to provide a fulcrum at the edge of the glass. Once you have positioned your fulcrum, simply place your hands on either side of the score line, palms down, and press (Fig. 7-8). The glass should run the entire length of the score. A flat, narrow piece of lath stripping also works well for this.

When you use this method, be careful not to press too hard or too abruptly with your hands. Also make sure that there is only a small portion of the fulcrum under the glass. The use of either too much pressure from above to too much leverage from below has an almost certain effect—a shattered piece of glass.

Glass Pliers

Glass pliers are perhaps one of the best investments you will make, and I urge you to get a pair. They are invaluable for going

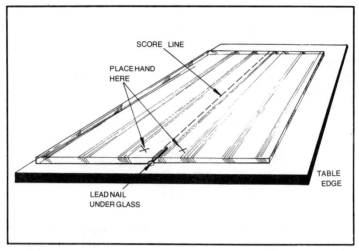

Fig. 7-8. Another method of breaking is with a fulcrum. Use it primarily for straight cuts or gentle curves in large glass sheets.

where fingers cannot to break out a piece of glass, such a small pieces and very narrow ones, and they make the successful cutting of difficult curves and other shapes much easier.

To use glass pliers effectively is an art in itself. First score the glass in the desired shape. Then pick it up and hold it in your left hand. Your hand should be positioned as if you were going to break the piece manually; this is, a fist gripping the edge of the glass, close to the score line. Place the thumb on top of the glass, again close to the score (Fig. 7-9). This gives the necessary support to the glass and will keep you from getting cut.

With the pliers in your right hand, place the jaw nose parallel to the score line, but *not* on top of it. As shown in Fig. 7-9, the pliers are kept fairly close to the edge of the glass. This gives better control to the break by utilizing the correct pressure point. By grabbing indiscriminately along the glass with the pliers, you risk having the score run off the line, as it will almost certainly do.

When you have the pliers in place, simply repeat the down-and-out motion used in breaking glass by hand. This is done with a steady motion rather than a frantic jerk. The latter will cause you to lose the piece.

For added support and stability, you may place the glass on the table, pull it out so that the scored part of the glass is suspended, and break with the pliers while holding your other hand firmly on top of the glass set on the table.

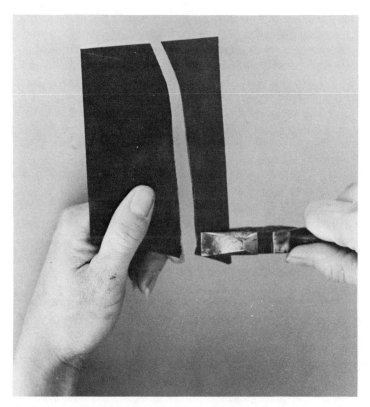

Fig. 7-9. To break glass with glass pliers, position the glass pliers so that their nose faces the score.

GROZING

Grozing pliers will supplement your glass pliers. As I said in the chapter on tools, both serve specific individual functions.

Grozing pliers are used after the glass has been cut in the desired shape. You might find that the glass overhangs the pattern in a small area or that there are small slivers or "nubs" along the edge that result from a poor break. There are a few glasses that do not break clean but rather on a slight angle, so that the bottom edge of the cut will jut out slightly while the top edge is true. This is where grozing pliers prove their worth.

Hold the glass in your left hand and, with the pliers in your right, move the jaws along the edge of the glass in a gentle chewing motion. For little bumps of glass or small overhangs, you might need to apply a bit more pressure, but generally, grozing is not a forceful action. The handles of the pliers should be held in a loose

85

grip; if the axle is well lubricated, you should be able to use the pliers with a minimum of strength.

Grozing pliers are also useful for removing glass bit by bit in difficult cuts, such as in deep, narrow, concave curves. These cuts are not so much scored and broken as they are chewed away with grozing pliers.

Neither of these methods involves taking large bites out of the glass. A hard pressure over a larger area will only crush the glass to bits. Likewise, using grozing pliers to break glass instead of the proper glass pliers will result in the same problem. The teeth along the jaw are there to provide the irregular pressure needed to clean up and smooth the edges of the glass; the flat jaws of glass pliers provide an even, steady pressure.

Do not mistake grozing pliers as a substitute for accurate cutting. Their use in this way is tiring and unprofitable. To groze every piece of glass down to its proper size increases the chances of leaving unsightly chips in the glass, gives ragged edges, and only paves the way for other bad habits.

If you accidentally take out a bigger bite than you had intended when you are grozing, or if the glass should for some reason chip along the edge, it would probably be best to recut the piece. These chips may not look like much, but after they are leaded and light shines through your finished work; they show up as black spots, regardless of the color of the glass. Even clear glass does this.

If the chip is very small or you are sure that the lead will cover it, go ahead and use the piece. Hold a piece of the lead along the edge of the glass to make sure. If you can still see the chip, try again.

DIFFICULT AND SPECIALTY CUTS

There are some cuts that are impossible to make in glass (in one piece, anyway), and there are those that are classed as impossible simply because they are generally impractical in terms of both time and wasted glass. These are usually trick cuts and are made mostly to see if one can do them and in how many tries (always more than one).

Concave Curves

Deep concave curves (Fig. 7-10) are among the most difficult cuts to make and the ones that seem to show up most often in design. Once you have a little practice with glass cutting, there is not need to redesign such curves in order to break them up.

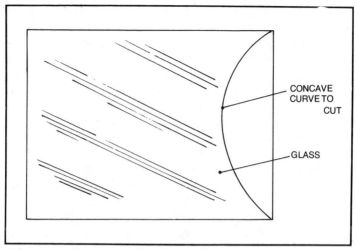

Fig. 7-10. A deep concave curve is difficult to cut.

To make a cut like the one shown in Fig. 7-10 first score the line. Trying to break this piece out by any single method will result in the score line running off the score and right across the piece you want. So, to ease the tension set up the glass by scoring it, make a series of graduating curves from the original score line to the edge of the glass (Fig. 7-11). Break these out gently with glass pliers, one at a time. Do not position the pliers in the middle of the curve; you will lose the corners of the piece. Place them so that the jaw is close to the edge of the glass and close to the score, as shown in

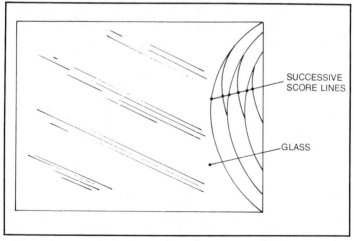

Fig. 7-11. To cut a deep concave curve, succeeding scores are made.

Fig. 7-12. In this manner you should be able to successfully cut and break a concave curve.

For very severe or narrow cuts that are concave, more caution must be exercised. Again, the original score is made as are succeeding smaller scores to the edge of the glass. With your glass pliers break out all but the last one or two scores. The remaining pieces may be gently grozed away with grozing pliers. If you are careful and take your time with this, you will find that nine times out of ten you will be able to get the piece you were trying for. Hastiness has no place here.

For gentle inner curves you may either use this same method of several scores broken out one by one, or you may simply break the piece out in its entirety either by hand or with your pliers.

The success of making concave cuts is also somewhat dependent on the type of glass with which you're working. Again, this is something you will have to gauge for yourself after you have been cutting glass for a while, because there are no hard and fast rules, just a few generalities. Antique glass usually requires slightly less pressure when cutting than do opalescents, some of which are very hard to cut. Antique glass also seems easier to break in tight curves and odd shapes. Cathedral glasses range from dependable to dubious in their ability to be scored and broken out, especially in curves.

Inside Right Angles

The inside-right-angle cut (shown in Fig. 7-13) sneaks most unobtrusively into many beginning glass designs, and the best thing to do about it is to change it. Because glass will break in a

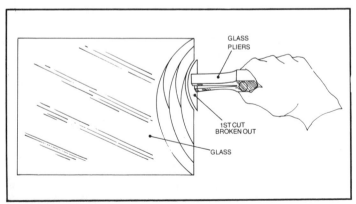

Fig. 7-12. Each piece is broken away with glass pliers.

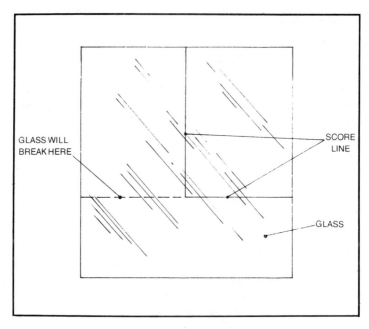

Fig. 7-13. Avoid having to make an inside right-angle cut. L-shaped pieces such as this are not worth the effort needed and the glass wasted in making them.

fairly straight line by its own preference, you are asking for trouble in trying to make this type of cut. All pieces of glass must be scored from one edge to the other; you cannot simply stop in the middle or radically change directions.

The only way to make this cut successfully (and it may take many tries) is to round the extremity of the sharp corner, and score successive lines out to the edge of the glass (Fig. 7-14). Break these out with glass pliers. Now go back and groze away at the corner, very gently, until it is almost, but not quite, square. During leading, it can be leaded so that it will look as if it *is* a square corner.

Chances are that even if you make this cut, you will lose it somewhere along the way. During leading, the tapping done to seat the pieces of glass will probably cause this shaped piece to crack whatever way it wants to. During the glazing process, even the small amount of pressure used will have the same effect.

If you want to see if you can do it (and that is a valid reason in itself), go ahead and try it on a piece of cheap glass, but don't plan to use such a piece in your work for the reasons given above.

Doughnuts Shapes

Cutting doughnuts out of glass, or for the matter cutting a circle out of the middle of any shape, can be done, although its use is limited in design work and is used mostly for novel touches. It is simply too time- and glass-consuming an operation to include regularly in your designing. Again, this is something you might want to try in a dull moment to see if you are able to cut it.

A soft glass is best for this—window glass, cathedrals, and some of the antique glass such as German antique.

The inner circle to be cut cannot be very small, nor can the distance between the inner circle's edge and the edge of the entire piece be any narrower than 12 cm to 15 cm.

First, score the circle in the center. Make a series of small crosshatched scores all over the circle. With the ball end of your cutter, gently begin to tap along the circle's edge. When you have gotten a run started, continue tapping at the end of the run to lead it very carefully around the entire score. Tap very gently; force will only shatter the whole piece. When you can see that the run is complete and has met its starting point, you are ready for the next step.

Begin to tap—again, gently—along the crosshatched score lines. You should be prepared to spend a bit of time doing this; there is no way to speed the process without losing the entire piece. Eventually and hopefully, all of the crosshatched score lines will run within the center of the circle.

To separate them continue tapping with the metal ball. Keep moving your taps around the inside of the circle. Stay away from the outer, original score. The pieces will eventually loosen and fall out of their own accord. Be sure you are holding the piece over your work table or board so that the pieces don't drop on the floor or your feet—or whatever else is below. You can clean up the splintered edges with your grozing pliers.

This cut is more easily made on larger pieces than on smaller ones, and it will most likely require several attempts. If you want to try it anyway, use cheap glass.

Points

Another cut to avoid in designing, if possible, is the long, narrow point. While fat, trianglelike peaks are a snap to cut, the longer and thinner the shape gets the more the difficulty the cut becomes. This goes for both the regular single point and the piece that requires a curve which tapers into a long point (Fig. 7-15).

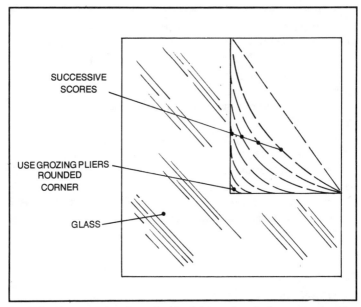

Fig. 7-14. If you must make an inside right-angle cut, do so one step at a time by scoring and breaking out successive areas. Also modify the corner so that it is rounded.

When planning long, narrow pieces in your design, keep in mind that when it is made in glass, lead will overlap both sides of such pieces. Thus, the last few centimeters or so of your carefully cut point may end up obliterated by lead and solder.

There is no real trick to cutting long, pointed pieces; they are just difficult to make successfully. You must get a good score and use a minimum of pressure to break the glass. Sometimes it helps to break from the thin end of the point rather than to start at the broader base. This allows the tension in the glass to be absorbed over a larger area.

Straight, Narrow Pieces

Cutting long strips of glass for borders or other uses is not as easy as it sounds. As with points, the difficulty increases in proportion to the narrowness of the piece. In additions, the longer the strip, the more tendency the break has to run off of the score line. If you plan to cut long pieces that will eventually be cut into smaller lengths, having the break run off the score in one place may not be too critical. When the entire length is needed, it can be nothing short of aggravating. After all, it's just a straight line, right?

To break long narrow pieces get a good, singing score and hope for the best. If you will be cutting lots and lots of these for some reason, you may want to get a pair of running pliers, like those discussed in Chapter 4. Otherwise, break the thicker, wider strips out by hand (this should not be much of a problem) and use your glass pliers or a pair of breaking pliers for thinner strips.

Once the score is made start at the bottom edge of the glass (always with the nose of the pliers facing the score) and apply a steady pressure until you see the glass fracture and begin to run. Then simply move the pliers along the run, applying the same pressure wherever the run stops until you can easily separate the strip from the rest of the glass.

For short strips, up to 50 cm or so in length, you can break them in any manner you desire. They usually respond with equal ease to hand breaking or glass pliers.

Circles

Circle cutting is not difficult at all; it just requires a certain technique that is easy to master. Circles may be scored with a lens cutter or beam compass, as described in Chapter 4. These are most useful if you plan to be cutting a lot of circles, but the investment (about $20 to $30) may not be warranted if you only need a few.

You can score the circle freehand, either to a pattern or by marking it on the glass with a felt-tipped pen. From this point, then, there are two ways in which to break the piece out.

One way to cut circles is to turn the glass over so that the score line is face down on the table. With your thumb, press on any point around the circle, on top of the score line. You will immediately see a run begin in the glass where pressure has been applied. Continue pressing along the score line until the run has followed the circle completely around and met its beginning. Now turn the glass over again and score tangent lines, or small lines running from the edge of the glass to the score line. These should not be made at a right angle to the score, but should look like those in Fig. 7-16. The circle can easily be broken out with glass pliers by breaking the tangent lines.

When you have gotten the circle out, you will probably have a few rough edges that will need to be smoothed out with grozing pliers.

The second way to cut and break a circle in glass is to score it as before—freehand—either to a pattern or to a predrawn mark.

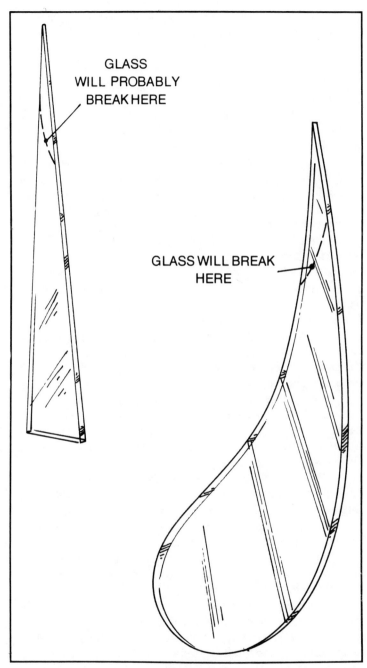

GLASS
WILL PROBABLY
BREAK HERE

GLASS WILL BREAK
HERE

Fig. 7-15. Avoid having to cut long, narrow points.

Instead of turning it over and pressing on it, however, simply score the tangent lines and break with glass pliers.

Diamonds and Squares

Geometric designs, in particular diamonds and squares that cover a large area or even an entire window, appear to be one of the simplest designs possible. In a way, this is true, and they can be quite pleasing if they are done carefully.

The problem here is that the pieces must be cut with great accuracy and an observant eye when they are being assembled into the window. Any small deviation in the size of even one glass piece from the pattern will throw the entire design off. In the case of diamonds and squares, looks are truly deceiving.

A straight line that suddenly wavers and then begins to fan outward or contract is very noticeable in geometric designs. It disrupts the continuity of line and space. Use care not only in your glass cutting, but especially in pattern cutting. Be sure all lines that are meant to be straight are as straight as they can possibly be and that all sizes are uniform if they are supposed to be.

If you are making a large project made up of pieces all of the same size, such as squares, the best way to ensure accuracy is to measure the width of the square and cut strips of glass to that width. Be sure to allow for the lead heart if you are measuring from the cartoon. (A better idea is to cut the pattern and measure the width of a pattern piece that represents the average size.) When you have cut the glass strips, it will be a simple matter to cut squares from them with a straightedge. Only one additional cut will be necessary for each square.

When you have cut all of your pieces, hold them together and set them vertically on a flat, even surface. The edges should be matched on all sides if you have cut each to an uniform size. Discard those pieces that are too small and recut them. Groze or recut those that are too large.

This principle can be used for cutting almost any geometric shape, with some modifications. For cutting large numbers of such shapes, you may want to make up a small jig.

Remember, too, that when cutting along a straightedge, such as a ruler, you must make allowances for the space that the axle of the cutter takes up. The wheel will not ride exactly along the edge; the axle of the glass cutter pushes it away about 2 to 2.5 cm—a small amount indeed, you may say, but unless you allow for this,

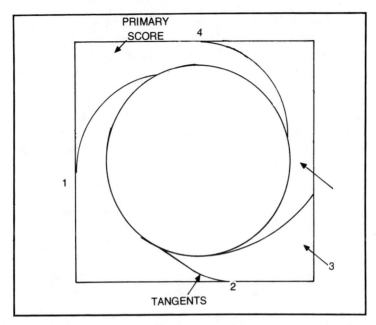

Fig. 7-16. To cut a circle, first make the score, then score tangent lines from it to the edge of the glass. Free the circle by breaking out each piece around it.

your piece will be all that much larger. You know what will happen next, right?

GLASS CONSERVATION

Undoubtedly, you will accumulate a healthy scrap pile in the early stages of glass cutting. Most people do. Save the larger scraps for future use and discard the rest, unless you are interested in doing some mosaic work or other projects that can utilize small, sometimes tiny, pieces.

Glass, however, is not cheap by any standard, so learning to conserve it will stand you in good stead now, in the beginning, and more so as you advance to bigger and better (and more expensive) projects.

My first word of advice is this: begin with inexpensive glass, at least for your first project, and the second or third if you still are fairly shaky. Cathedral glass or window glass is best; rummaging in scrap bins at your supplier for usable bargins helps, too. Don't start off by buying a lot of antique glass, which starts at about $6 per square foot and averages about $8 to $10. A woman in one of my classes spent $30 on her first project, a five-piece panel that measured about 13 cm by 18 cm. She insisted on using antique glass and went through quite a bit of it to cut just five pieces.

Second, learn accurately to calculate just how much glass you need so that you can get the maximum number of pieces out of the minimum amount of glass. This does not mean that you line up your pattern pieces edge to edge and fill every little area, but do try to conserve your glass. I've seen many individuals place their pattern smack dab in the middle of a piece that extends 15 cm out on all sides. They are then left with one cut piece and a pile of scrap.

For regular pattern cutting, 1.5 cm all around suffices. As you become more accurate with your cuts, you may be able to lessen this to about a centimeter, although it's wise not to go much below this amount. Line up straight pattern pieces along straight edges of the glass to cut down on waste; just be sure that the edge *is* straight.

If you have to cut one piece from a large sheet, figure approximately how much glass you will need, allow about 1.5 cm on all sides, and cut a piece this size from the sheet. *Then* cut your pattern piece from the smaller amount.

Before cutting up a sheet of glass, lay your pattern pieces out with a reasonable amount of space between them, 1.5 to 2.5 cm. See how you can get the most out of the sheet by turning the pieces in different directions or switching them around until you are satisfied that waste will be kept to a minimum.

If there is a strip or area of glass that will not be needed, cut that off before you begin cutting your patterns.

If you place your pieces too close together, you won't be able to get a clean break along the edge, and much grozing will have to be done as a follow-up. Too much glass around the edge is wasteful. If you take the time to lay it out first, you won't be left with a pile of scraps that are all a bit too small to use.

On some glasses, such as the opalescents, you will need to take into consideration the *grain* of the glass when you figure the amount of glass you will need. You will want the grain to be running in the same direction throughout your design. To do this you will need more glass than you would if you were to use glass that shows no grain.

Some people incorrectly consider glass grain as similar to that of wood and anticipate problems that do not exist. The grain on opalescent glass refers to the general direction of the color as it is swirled and mixed throughout the sheet. Glass grain does not affect the cutting qualities of glass; it is only a surface appearance and unlike wood grain that runs throughout wood's thickness, glass grain does not go any deeper than its surface.

While grains are most obvious on opalescent glass, there are similar surface treatments you should watch for in other glasses as well. In some seedy glass — glass with a great many small air bubbles, called seeds, that trap and refract light — the seeds run predominantly in one direction. If they are jumbled around in a window, the effect can be quite noticeable, often unpleasantly so.

Rippleback glass often has the ripple running in one direction, also.

There, is no rule, of course, that says you cannot have the grain or ripple running in different directions if you so wish. If you plan it that way, that's another story. Too many, however, don't take this fact into consideration and don't discover it until it's too late and the window is finished.

THE ENGLISH METHOD

The English method of glass cutting actually involves much more than differences in cutting techniques. It *is* different in this respect, since no pattern is used for cuttings, but it also entails a completely different manner of construction. In the English method, instead of laying cut glass out on a working copy before it is leaded, the cut pieces of glass are placed on a large plate glass easel. This lets the craftsman see the true colors of the glass as light passes through it. The glass design is "constructed" on the easel, but without lead. In this respect, the easel acts as a working copy of the design.

To hold the glass pieces together and to the easel, the most common material used is wax, melted and dribbled down around the edges of each piece or applied with a soft brush.

The artist can then view the window much as it will look after leading. The colors will all be true, undistorted by false lighting or bland or "flat" as they lie on a table. If a color needs to be changed, it can be seen immediately and remedied before the window is leaded.

The English method evolved when staining glass was the rule rather than the exception. Although staining is still done today, it is a closely guarded art. Leaded glass has replaced true stained glass in popularity.

When the glass pieces were all placed on the easel, the artist could then apply the glass stains without worrying about how the lines would meet up. He could continue a line from one piece of glass to another without interrupting the flow of the line and could make shadings gradual and uniform from adjacent piece to adjacent piece.

When the staining is completed and ready to fire and any necessary color changes have been made, the glass pieces are removed and the stained pieces are fired in a kiln to fuse the paint to the glass. They are then cleaned and leaded up in the traditional manner.

Many people who practice the English method actually only use the different cutting technique and do not construct it on a glass easel. Variations of the cutting technique allow the beginner more flexibility as he is learning and simply increase his knowledge of what can be done in the craft. For this reason, I am including the standard usage of this method and its widely practiced diversities, although I feel that pattern cutting is still the most accurate and dependable.

The primary difference between the English method of glass cutting, as noted earlier, is that the English method uses no pattern. Two drawings are made, as with the traditional method. They are exact copies of each other. One becomes the cartoon; the other is the working copy. No pattern is made. The design is scaled up to the correct size. The glass is then placed directly on top of the cartoon and the cut is made freehand to conform to the lines given on the cartoon.

As the pieces are cut, they are laid aside on the working copy of the design. When all the pieces are cut and laid out, the table is then readied for building the window. And leading begins.

I have known some individuals to cut a piece of glass and immediately lead it up. Their window is already set up for construction on another table and each piece is fitted as it's cut. This seems to me to be an exhausting process, prolonging both the cutting and leading processes beyond what they should normally be.

The English method of glass cutting was devised when most of the glass being made and used was antique glass or clear glass. An obvious problem arises when you work with a denser, colored glass, and especially opalescent glass. The lines of the cartoon are not so visible through such glasses; or they are badly distorted.

Most artists who use the English method today confine themselves to using transparent glasses, mostly antique. When denser glass is used, a light table or lightbox, such as described in Chapter

5, is used. This delineates the lines of the cartoon clearly, making it possible for them to be seen through the glass. Even with the aid of a light table, however, very dark glass or very thick glass is usually avoided.

Another problem that arises with this method is accuracy, a must when working in glass. You remember that when a pattern is cut with pattern shears, the shears automatically cut out the area for the lead heart (just under 2 mm). When cutting the English way, you must also take into consideration the area take up by lead, but it is a little harder to do.

The way it is usually done is like this: after the cartoon is drawn up to full size, the lead lines are blacked in to represent the lead heart. A felt-tipped pen with a tip that makes a line measuring a scant 2 mm (about 1/16 inch) is usually used for this purpose. When the glass is cut, it is cut to the inside of this line on all sides, and adjoining pieces are likewise cut to the inside.

Theoretically, this takes care of the proper lead allowance. Eventually, however, the pen wears down, and if it is not caught at the right moment, it could conceivably affect the size of your entire design. Simple human error also makes this a somewhat hit-or-miss way of glass cutting, in my opinion. Doubtless, the studios that practice this method exclusively and over long periods of time have it down to an art, or they would probably be out of business.

An offshoot of this method is to use the pattern as a guide, not for cutting around, but from which to draw the shape of the piece onto the glass. To do this run a felt-tip marker around the pattern. Then lay the pattern aside and cut the piece freehand to the lines drawn directly on the glass. This is sometimes helpful for beginners, who have trouble holding the pattern still and in one position while trying to cut along its edges. This is an acceptable alternative to try if you find yourself having such a problem. Because the pattern is made and cut with pattern shears, the allowance for the lead heart is automatic. There is no problem cutting the opaque glasses because the lines are drawn on top of the glass.

If you wish to try this method of cutting keep in mind that, as the pen goes around the edge of the pattern, it adds a slight bit, perhaps 1 mm or so and sometimes even 2 mm, depending on the marker. If you do not take this into consideration when scoring the outline, you will be defeating your original purpose for making the pattern in the first place. These small additions, minute as they may seem, will add up and add up and add up until you find that you have a considerable problem.

To avoid this, when you cut the glass, cut to the inside of the line you have drawn, not right on it or along the outside. In this way you allow for the difference between the cutting wheel, which would cut right to the pattern, and the marker, which moves slightly away from the pattern edge.

Match each piece to its pattern piece to check its size. It should be exact, with neither the pattern nor the glass hanging over. Groze of any small differences and lay the piece on your working copy.

Chapter 8
Leading

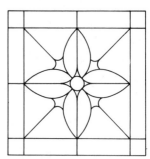

In leading, the design begins to be less of a two-dimensional object of paper and moves toward three-dimensional reality, toward being a leaded glass design. It is an exciting process, a rewarding process; and as is true of all aspects of leaded glass work, it is an exacting process. If you have painstakingly cut your pattern and carefully cut your glass, you should be prepared to apply the same care here, or else all your efforts will be wasted.

SETTING UP

When you set up for construction, you are readying the tools and work area for leading, or "leading up" as it is sometimes called. At this stage you should be working on a table, where you do not have to move things around too much and put them away at the end of each day. Especially when you are a beginner, leading up may be a process that requires several days (working a few hours each day until you tire). It is best to leave your work undisturbed when you are done for the day. If the project is small and can be accommodated on a small working board, this won't be so much of a problem, but it is nice to be able to spread out a little.

The first thing, then, you will need to consider is your work space. Whether it is a workbench or a work board, you will need two lengths of lath stripping or similar board measuring approximately 2.5 × 5 cm, and about 15 cm longer than your cartoon's height and width. For example, if your cartoon 30 cm by 46 cm, the lath strips will be 2.5 cm by 5 cm by 46 cm and 2.5 cm by 5 cm by 60 cm. Nail these strips at a right angle in the lower left-hand corner of your work board. If it seems more natural to you, nail them in the lower right-hand corner; it really is only personal preference. You will be building from this corner, so use whichever one feels right to you. Again, be sure the corner is square. To do this, nail your bottom board down along the lower edge. Place the lengthwise board so that it meets at the corner. Lay a square along the bottom edge and move the lengthwise board so that it lies flush along the square while still meeting the lower board. When you are sure the corner is square, nail the lengthwise board securely in place.

If you want to be extra ordinarily neat, you can miter the corners of your board so that they meet in a 45 degree angle, but it is easier and faster to nail them in a butt joint. It does not matter which board is butted against which, as long as they meet snugly and there are no gaps in the joint.

Make sure that the lath strips are not warped. Sight down them like you would with a rifle barrel. They should not bow or bend in either direction, but should be straight and true.

By taking this care at each step, you are ensuring a better final result, so do not take shortcuts and do not make assumptions. There are no shortcuts, and assumptions often cause disasters.

Next, lay your cartoon down on the board. You should have about an inch of margin on all sides of the cartoon. Depending on what size border lead you will be using, you will need to cut away some of this extra margin. For a 6 mm U-lead border, trim the pattern margin to about 3 mm on all sides; for a ¼-inch U-lead border, trim the pattern margin down to about ⅛-inch. Thus, when you fit the cartoon in along the corner, you will have allowed enough space on the cartoon to accommodate the border lead. If you do not do this, your succeeding pieces of glass will not match up to the lead lines drawn on the cartoon. While this is not a matter of life and death, you will discover that it is much easier to have these as guidelines in the beginning. Leave the cartoon loosely in place or tape it down. As long as it can not move around, either way is fine. Alternatively you can leave a large margin on your cartoon and place this part of the paper under your guide strips so that when the boards are nailed down, the pattern is secured to the work board.

Your cartoon can go on the board anyway you wish, but do bear a couple of considerations in mind. One is that, usually, the beginning corner of the design correlates to the numbering sequence; that is, piece number 1 would generally be the first piece to be placed. So whatever corner number 1 falls in is the corner placed against the corner strips. This is not a hard-and-fast rule, however. You might study the design and start in whatever corner has the largest pieces, or the least number of small ones. There are a couple of reasons for this. First, by starting with the largest pieces, it makes it seem as if your progress is moving rapidly, because so few pieces occupy so much space. This is primarily a psychological consideration, but there is another practical purpose served by it.

When leading small pieces of glass, particularly a lot of them, progress is often slow and frustrating because the pieces tend to shift and move around while you try to keep them secured, or they twist and roll just when you thought you'd gotten them in place. By leading large pieces first, you set up more of a stable base or framework against which to set small pieces. Also, because small pieces tend to shift, you will find that all pieces generally fit together better in the long run if you can avoid starting right off with many small pieces to be leaded. This will not always be possible, but it is a useful suggestion where it applies.

You're ready now to stretch your leads and begin leading. As I've said before, all lead must be stretched, and this is best done immediately prior to its use. Try to buy all the lead you will use for one project at the same time; buy slightly more if you're not sure. You can always use extra lead on another project if you have leftovers. Don't forget to buy border lead if you will be using lead made specifically for that purpose, although in beginning projects it's perfectly all right to use an H lead for the border.

Stretch your leads. Cut them in half if you do not have enough room for them to lie straight in one piece. Cutting them is preferable to folding them. After you have stretched your lead, run a lathekin along the channels to open them up. This will make seating the glass easier later on.

Cutting lead is an art that is often overlooked by the beginner. Lead, being a soft and pliable substance, will crush beyond repair if you approach lead cutting as you might approach carving a roast.

CUTTING LEAD

Cutting lead is not simply a matter of whacking a piece off here and chopping a corner there. Approaching it in this way you will give the lead many little kinks and bends that is shouldn't have. Trying to repair these defects will give you nothing but headaches.

Cut leads through the face, not through the channel. An exception to this is some of the flat-faced leads, which tend to crush rather easily.

Set most lead up then so that you look down on the face of the lead. Hold it with your fingers close to where you will be cutting, but not so close that you lose a fingertip. Place the blade of the lead knife on the lead and rock the knife gently, using only a slight pressure. Increase the pressure slowly as you feel the blade begin to cut through the heart of the lead. If you are using a curved leading knife, as recommended, this will go much more smoothly. When you have cut through to the heart, simply rock the blade forward once more and then back, using enough pressure to cut through the rest of the lead. Figure 8-1 illustrates how to do this.

Avoid cutting straight through the lead in one hard motion; the lead will most likely twist away from the blade and become crimped. The entire process takes no more than a few seconds; it just sounds as if it takes longer. Once lead has been bent or twisted as a result of either incorrect handling or improper cutting, it is very difficult to remove the disfiguration. By cutting lead correctly, you will also avoid mashing it down or crushing it. Crushed lead, again, is a pain to correct and can affect not only its appearance, but how the glass seats in the channel.

The angled blade of the lead knife sometimes cuts the lead at an angle (Fig. 8-2) through no fault of your own. If this happens, just trim away the lower overhang, so that the end is even. Leaving an angled cut such as this without repairing it will make a weaker joint when it is soldered.

For cutting wide, flat H or U leads or any U leads larger than standard 6 mm or ¼ inch, I find it better to cut through the channel. This is, no doubt, frowned upon by some craftsmen, but if done with care, I feel it gives better results. The lead should be opened with a lathekin first, on both channels if it's an H lead. With H and U lead, begin the cut slowly, with gentle pressure and somewhat less of a rocking motion (Fig. 8-3). When you reach the heart of the lead, continue the cut with one steady motion. Again, you may have to go back and trim the edges a bit to even them out. Do *not* use this method of cutting on any of the rounded-face leads; it will not work properly.

When cutting in either manner, you may have to reopen the ends of the lead after cutting. Sometimes they become slightly mashed or flared out and will have to be opened or straightened. Use a lathekin for this, or the tip of your lead knife blade.

LEADING UP

Once you have stretched your lead, you are ready to start leading up. Have your working copy of the design close by, with the

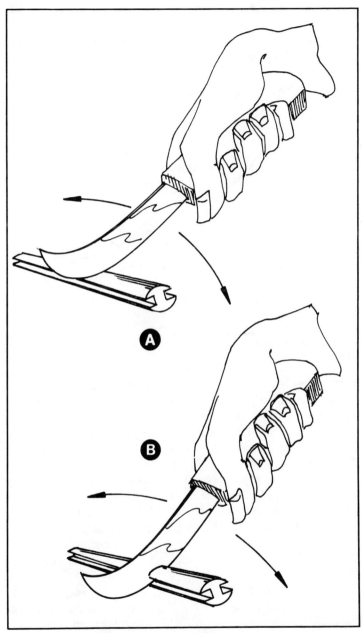

Fig. 8-1. Cutting the came. Begin the cut (A) by rocking the knife gently back and forth. After you have cut through to the heart, rock the knife down (B) in one cut.

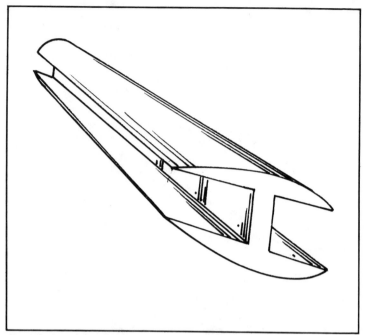

Fig. 8-2. If the lead was cut at a slant, trim the lower edge of the sloped cut so that it is flat.

glass pieces laid out on it. Having it on another table or across the room means walking back and forth for each piece, so it's better if you can place it within arm's reach.

You will need your lead knife, leading nails, lathekin, cutting wax, hammer, and, of course, your lead. Have these tools at your fingertips.

For illustration purposes, we will use a 6 mm U border lead and 6 mm H lead for the interior. The nonmetric equivalent standard sizes are given in parentheses. (Please note that the "equivalents" are not direct metric to U.S. conversions; they are the nearest size standard to the metric values given.) The nearest "inch-equivalent" to 6 mm is ¼ inch, and the nearest to 3 mm is ⅛ inch.

Place two border leads first, one cut to the length of your finished design and one cut to its width. They will fit right up along the guide boards in a right angle. If you are going to join these two leads in a butt joint, cut either one the full size and the other 1.25 cm (½ inch) shorter than the final measurement of your piece. For a butt joint, it is often easiest to allow the leads to run long, or about

106

2.5 cm (an inch) more than the ends of the cartoon. This will allow adjustments to be made should the window "grow" in the process of building.

The neatest way to join the corners with this or any border lead is to meter them at a 45-degree angle. A mitered joint is stronger and is a must when you are constructing a large design or window. H lead, when used as a border, is the only lead that really does not need to be mitered.

When you've set your first leads in, nail them at about 7.5 cm (3 inch) intervals to hold the leads still, and set a nail at the end of each piece to keep it from sliding in or out. You should be using your leading nails for this.

Cut a few small pieces of lead to be used as buffers. Buffers are small bits of lead that go between the glass edge and the leading nail. They hold the glass tightly in position while you prepare the next piece to be placed. Their use removes the risk of chipping the glass by driving the nail in right next to it, so always use them. Buffers need only be about 1.25 cm (½ inch) long. The ends of the lead that bear the teeth marks from the lead vise and pliers are fine to use for this. Certainly you would not use them in your window.

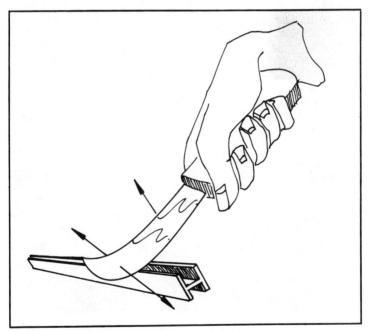

Fig. 8-3. Flat-faced lead is cut across its face.

To begin leading, take the first piece of glass to be placed from the working drawing and set in into the corner leads. (Fig. 8-4). Make sure that it is well "seated" in the channels and will not move. When a piece of glass is *seated,* it means that it is tight in the lead channel and does not wiggle around.

When the glass is secure in the channel, take a buffer and place it next to the glass, then hammer in your lead nail next to the buffer. When you let go of the whole thing, nothing should move; that is, the glass should not fall out of the lead channel and the nail should not fall out of the wood.

A word about nailing: because you will be pounding in and removing the lead nails continuously during leading, it is not necessary really to *pound* them in. Give them a couple of firm taps with the hammer or the end of your lead knife (it's made for that), and let it go at that. The nail should be nailed in firmly enough to

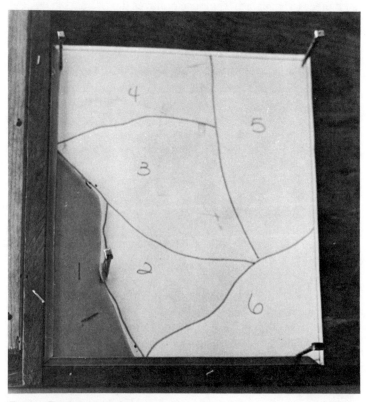

Fig. 8-4. The border leads are nailed in place; the first piece of glass is set in and held in place with a buffer and a nail.

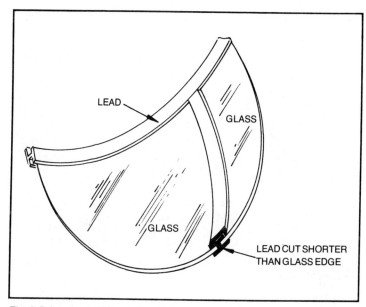

Fig. 8-5. Lead must be cut slightly shorter than the glass edge to allow for other lead to run by.

hold the piece in, but you should be able to pull it out with your fingers.

With your first piece of glass in place, the next step is to measure off the next piece of lead and to cut it. You may remove the nail and lay the lead next to the glass itself to determine where to cut. Or you may do as I do and lay the lead along the edge of the glass—but on top of it, not next to it. Mark it with your fingernail or lead knife and put the lead back on the board to cut it. Do not try to cut your lead on top of the glass or in your hand—put it on a solid surface.

You must remember to allow room for any adjoining lead to run by. This means that you must cut the lead slightly shorter than necessary, anywhere from 1.5 mm (1/16 inch) to a larger amount, depending on what size lead you are using. Figure 8-5 shows how this works. If you were to cut the lead exactly to the needed size, the other leads running by at this joint would be pushed away from the glass slightly, making an odd little bulge there.

You have cut the lead for your first piece. Remove the lead nail and place the lead against piece number 1 as shown in Fig. 8-6. Make sure that it is tight against the glass. Seat the next piece of glass in the channel. Now put your buffer against piece number 2

Fig. 8-6. Pieces 1 and 2 in place. Piece 1 is leaded in place; piece 2 is held in place with buffers and nails.

and hold it in place with a lead nail. You are now ready to cut the lead for piece number 2 and then set in the next piece of glass.

Very few of the cuts you make on your lead will be straight ones. There is usually something of an angle involved for the lead to meet flush with the other leads. You will have to cut whatever angle is required to get the piece to match evenly. Use the same cutting technique as that given for straight cuts.

You want your lead joints to be as even as possible, without gaps. Several tries may be necessary to get the lead to fit right in there flush, but it is much easier to correct this now. Remember that any gaps in the joints will have to be filled in with solder, and too many filled joints look just plain sloppy. After you have finished one or two projects, you will have a better feel for how long or how short to cut your leads, so don't give up. If you find that you have a large gap in a joint, recut the lead for that piece. You can use your too-short piece somewhere else.

Pieces 1 and 2 are now set in and leaded. To set in the next pieces, the same procedure is followed. Each time a piece of glass is set in, hold it in tightly with buffers and nails. Sometimes more than one buffer and nail will be needed to hold one piece of glass.

When the remaining pieces of glass are set in, you should have something that looks like Fig. 8-7. Notice how each piece is held in place around the edge with buffers and nails. You are now ready to measure off and cut the last two border leads. When you have done this, remove the nails along one edge of the window. Lay the border lead along the edge and nail it. When you have gotten it in, you can go back and tighten it up. To do this, remove the nails, this time one at a time. Take out the first nail, lay your lathekin sideways against the lead, and tap it a few times gently all along its length. Holding the lathekin in place, slip the nail in between it and the border lead and then tap the nail into the board. Repeat this along the width of the border and then do the same thing on the lengthwise border. This will "pull it all together," so to speak, and tighten up the window.

This is the basic leading process, although unfortunately it does not always run as smoothly as this, especially for beginners. You now have the general procedure; let's get down to specifics, and pitfalls.

Each piece of glass, as it is inserted into the lead channel, must be seated well. First, make sure that it really *is* in the channel. Sometimes it will catch on an underside of the lead. When this occurs, what happens is that it mashes the lead into the channel itself and the glass edge protrudes. This usually happens on the bottom side so that you do not know it has happened until you have

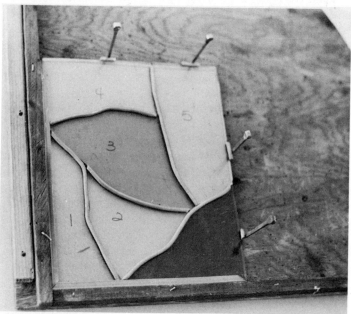

Fig. 8-7. All glass pieces are in place and ready for the border leads to be put on.

aded the entire piece and turned it over. To avoid the problem, lift each piece of glass slightly as you slide it.

Once the glass is in the channel, place your lathekin next to it and give it a few taps to push the glass in tight. Don't tap, however gently, directly on the edge of the glass. If you are lucky, you will just get a few chunks out of it; and if you aren't, you could split the piece in two. Always use something between the glass and tool when you're doing any hammering or tapping.

If the pieces are not seated in the channel (and I mean *every* piece), the window is not only prone to a frightening rattle, but it is inclined to "grow," a term use for when a window seems to be expanding for no apparent reason. So take care to seat each piece of glass carefully; it is apparent *and* important. All glass pieces should be tight against the lead.

The cartoon is placed beneath the glass pieces for a reason. As you place each piece of glass on the cartoon, it should fall slightly short of the line on your cartoon (Fig. 8-8). The lead, when it is cut and placed, should cover that line.

If this does not happen, it could be because of a slight error in the cutting of the pattern or an error in cutting the glass. If the mistake was in the pattern, you need not worry about it too much unless you want to start all over. Chances are that if you accidentally cut the pattern piece a little small (and thus cut the glass a little small too, since it was cut to the pattern piece), the adjoining pattern piece will have the extra from the undercut piece. If these two (or three, as the case may be) pieces fit together well and there is no more growing, all will be well.

If the mistake was in the glass cutting itself, you may have more of a problem, however. If, for instance, there is an additional few millimeters on the glass that was not on the pattern, this means that your leaded design will continue to grow as it is built. You can remove the piece, match it up against the pattern, and either trim or recut it, or you can plunge blindly ahead and hope for the best. You will probably end up with considerably less than best, I might add.

There are other reasons, of course, why the lead may not line up exactly with the cartoon, and they are not all as traumatic as they appear at first. Depending on how you plan to use your first project, you may decide to not lose any sleep over the fact that all the lines and glass aren't matching precisely.

In the event that each piece seems to fall farther and farther away from the lines as the pieces are set in, you know then that you

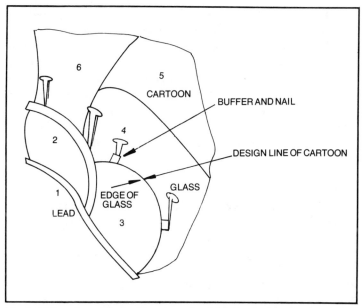

Fig. 8-8. The edge of each glass piece should fit just inside the design line on the cartoon drawing so that there is space to accommodate the thickness of the lead came's heart.

are in for trouble somewhere along the way. The difference usually begins with a very slight discrepancy and becomes greater with each piece cut. Again, you are faced with choices. You can let the discrepancy go, and maybe end up trimming the glass along the border when you get that far. You can trim the offending piece itself. This does not always work out too well because, once you trim one piece in a window, you can bet that you will be doing quite a bit more of it before you're done; and heaven only knows what the thing will look like when it's finished. Or you can try to figure out where the problem began and see if it can be solved there.

It is also necessary to plot and plan how you will set your pieces. It is quite possible to "box in" the glass in such a manner that you can not place a central piece without removing one or more of the other ones which you have carefully set in.

In planning your leading sequences, if you need to, you can let some of the leads run long. After you have set several pieces, you can cut lead to its proper length. This is usually done when you wish to follow the flow of the line without cutting it. No matter how smoothly lead joints are made, once they are cut it is difficult to make them look as if they weren't

You want to keep the lead line as smooth and unmarred as possible. A long straight run, such as might be found in a glass border, is best done with one long piece of lead rather than several shorter ones. In this way, the width of the border is kept uniform and the lead does not undulate in what obviously should have been a straight line. Lead lines that are supposed to be straight but are *not* are quite noticeable in leaded glass, and they are a sign of poor workmanship.

Lead that has been crushed and fixed (but still looks bad), lead with dents and nicks and teeth marks in it, should not be used at all. It looks bad.

I have heard tales of one craftsman who sat on top of his work-in-progress in order to work on the middle or the far reaches or whatever. This is unthinkable, and I hope you don't ever consider it. This was apparently a very large work, but still, just the thought of it is horrifying. Don't sit, lean, or rest on top of your glass, and don't set anything heavy or hot on it, either. This also goes for sharp blows. Replacing broken pieces is not really much fun.

For some pieces of glass, such as circles and severe inner or outer curves, it is often easiest to wrap the lead or form it to the glass before the glass is set in. It is difficult to get the came to conform tightly to such pieces, and doing it beforehand ensures that the glass is well set in the channel and that your next piece will fit correctly, too.

PIECING LEAD

As much as I've stressed the importance of even lead joints that closely and neatly meet without gaps, there are times when the difference is so slight that it is simpler to piece the joint.

You can fill in small gaps, thereby avoiding the necessity of recutting a piece of lead that fell short of its mark. To do this, a small piece of lead came, just large enough to fill in the gap, is cut. Lay the piece on its side (Fig. 8-9) and cut off one face so that you have a piece shaped something like a T. Insert the T-shaped piece in the gap, without removing the surrounding leads (Fig. 8-10).

The edges of the piece should evenly match both edges of the leads that it meets. If it does not, the discrepancy will show when it is soldered. Don't cut off the "tail" of the lead (the heart) or the piece will not fit properly.

Do not try to use this method for large gaps. Recut the lead to the correct size. You should not try piecing gapped joints greater

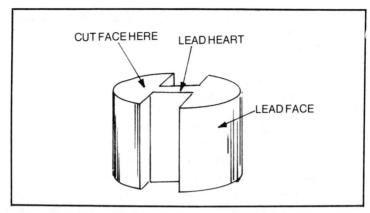

CUT FACE HERE   LEAD HEART

LEAD FACE

Fig. 8-9. To piece a lead joint, cut a small piece of lead to fill the gap. Then cut away one face of the lead.

than 6.35 mm (¼ inch) at the most. If you try to piece larger gaps, you will also have to cover that area with solder, and the result will look messy.

Piecing lead joints is not a desirable working habit to acquire. It is to be used *occasionally,* with discretion. Pieced leaded joints only weaken the solder joint, they also reflect poor workmanship, as do most shortcuts. This technique is only presented here be-

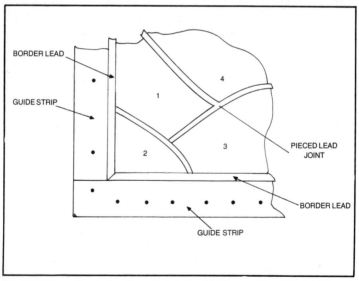

BORDER LEAD

GUIDE STRIP

PIECED LEAD JOINT

BORDER LEAD

GUIDE STRIP

Fig. 8-10. The edges of a pieced joint should align neatly with all adjacent lead.

115

cause there are times when it is more practical, and it is always preferred to filling in gaps with solder alone.

In your beginning leading attempts, it is wisest to do your best. Recut any leads that are too short and make sure you angle the leads so that they match well. Good leading can often do much to enhance an otherwise poorly cut work.

I am *not* suggesting that you can work wonders with your leading techniques if your cutting was abominable. What I am saying is that your beginning projects will do much to form your future working habits and attitudes. If you start with the idea that you can fix it up later, you will be letting yourself in for a lot of frustration. If, on the other hand, you do your honest best and follow the proper procedures right from the start, your beginning works will reflect that effort, too, and you will advance with much more ease and confidence.

LEADING CIRCLES AND OTHER ODD SHAPES

One of the questions I am most frequently asked by students is how to lead up a design that is flat but not square, such as a circular shape. It is really not as mysterious or complicated a technique as it seems.

To lead a circle, start by laying your cartoon on the work board. Beginning at an arbitrary point somewhere in the lower right quarter of the circle, drive your leading nails in, just outside of

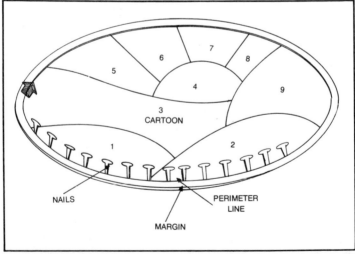

Fig. 8-11. To lead a circle, hammer nails around the shape up to the point indicated by an X.

116

the border line on the cartoon itself. The nails should be evenly spaced and about 2.5 to 4 cm (1—1½ inch) apart—but no more. Pound the nails in securely; they will be your guide boards and they must not move or shift.

Continue nailing around the circumference of the cartoon. Set the last nail at the very top of the circle or a little ways beyond, so that your board looks like that shown in Fig. 8-11.

The border lead (usually a U lead) is then laid inside this circle of nails. Press it gently to conform with the shape, but not so that it bulges out between the nails. Nail leading nails on the inside of the lead about every 7.5 to 10 cm (3-4 inches). What you now have should look like Fig. 8-12. There is the very outer border of nails, which will represent the outermost border of the finished piece. The lead lies tight along these nails and is held in place securely with more nails on its other side.

Let your border lead run long so that when the glass is all in, you will be able to cut it exactly right. You must be sure that the gap between where the nails stop and where they start again is sufficient to allow you to place any larger pieces of glass.

To begin leading, set your first piece in and nail it in with a buffer. Start close to the bottom and work upward and then outward. The interior leading procedure is the same as for any other

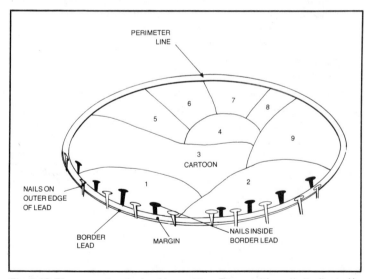

Fig. 8-12. Place your border lead in position. The outside nails (indicated in black) serve as guides. Hammer the nails inside the border lead to hold it in place.

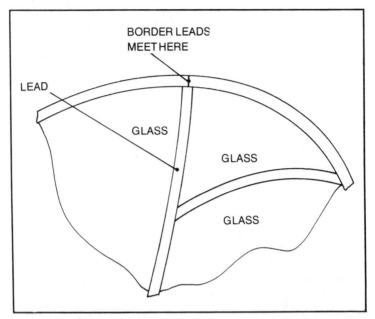

Fig. 8-13. Neatly join the two ends of the border lead at a point connecting with an interior lead.

project. Check the border periodically to make certain that it is still smooth and does not bulge or bump as the glass is set in.

When you have leaded all the pieces, you are ready to close the circle. To do this, simply fit the border lead along the glass, nailing as you go. Cut the lead and make sure the edges meet tightly. Try to cut your border lead so that its solder joint will be met by a lead running from the inside of the window, as in Fig. 8-13. This avoids having a solder joint hanging out in the middle of nowhere along the border—a very noticeable and unpleasant look.

For leading other somewhat unconventional shapes—hexagons, octagons, and the like—use guide strips, as you would for a square project, but nail them to an angle that conforms with the irregular shape.

Chapter 9
Soldering

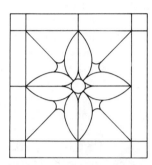

When a window is entirely leaded up, it is ready to be soldered. Heat (from the soldering iron) is applied simultaneously to both the lead joint and the solder, causing the solder to become liquid and fuse the leads together. Solder, once applied, requires no "drying" time; it hardens as soon as the source of heat is removed.

For stained glass work, only 50/50 solder or 60/40 solder should be used. Make sure that it is solid-core (rather than resin-cored) wire solder. This is usually sold in one-pound rolls. A few shops sell it off of large spools, which allows you to buy the exact amount you need. Solder is not cheap (about $6 to $7 per pound). It used to be cheaper, but the price of tin has risen considerably lately, and, likewise, the price of solder keeps going up.

For soldering you will also need flux for lead (this is properly called oleic acid), a flux brush, a large sponge, a small wire brush (handy, but not essential), and, of course, your soldering iron.

TINNING

Nearly all soldering irons are pretinned when you buy them, but ask the salesman to be sure. This means that a thin layer of solder has been applied to the tip, and it is ready to be used for soldering. Tinning allows solder to adhere to the tip and to flow easily onto the lead to be joined. An improperly tinned tip (or one that has not been tinned at all) will not pick up or hold solder; it will not distribute heat evenly, and if it does the job at all, it will not solder the lead easily or properly. A tinned tip on a new iron will appear a bright, shiny silver color; as I have said previously, most tips are already tinned when you purchase them. If you are using a soldering iron that has been lieing around the house, it is best to clean and tin the tip before you begin working with it.

To do this, plug the iron in and allow it to heat up slightly. When the iron is hot, wipe the tip quickly with a clean cloth. Then slightly form a small cup out of a piece of tinfoil. Into this cup, pour a small amount—a few drops—of oleic acid. Now melt a small bit—a couple of centimeters depth—of solder in with the oleic acid flux and swirl the tip of the iron around in this mixture until the tip is coated with solder. There will be a good deal of smoke (from the burning flux) and nasty fumes, so have a window open nearby. If the solder does not adhere to the tip, the iron is probably too hot. Unplug it and let it cool a bit, then try again.

If there are any pits or ridges in the tip, file them down before tinning. Do this with a flat file, and be sure to retain the original shape of the tip. File down to the bare metal—in this case, copper. Then, when all the deformities are removed and the surfaces are flat, tin the tip as directed above.

It is important to know how to file and tin soldering-iron tips. As you do more and more soldering, the tip of your iron will eventually wear down and become pitted or uneven, and you will have to file and retin it. Of course, you could alternatively replace the tip with a new one. I knew one woman who simply discarded the iron when the tip got bad, an extravagant and needless waste, in my opinion. You can file and retin an iron countless times before you will have to buy a new tip for it. You need not replace the entire iron for such an easily remedied problem.

FLUXING

Flux—in leaded glass work, oleic acid—prepares and cleans the lead surfaces to be soldered. Without flux, the solder will not adhere to the joint but will glob up or roll off. Therefore, it is important that the correct flux be used, and used correctly. Oleic acid is a liquid flux with a somewhat oily consistency. It is not corrosive in the sense that it burns holes through wood, but you would not want to drink it either. It will be more of a nuisance than a real danger should you get it on your hands (which you undoubtedly will). This is because it is oily and has a slightly unpleasant odor. There are paste fluxes available, but they are more difficult to control during application. They are also much more difficult to remove from the glass during the cleaning process.

Flux is applied to each lead joint with a small flux brush, which is a metal-handled brush with bristles that are stiffer than found on regular brushes. You can try a regular small paintbrush if you like; for the price, however, a flux brush works better, lasts longer, and is easier to handle. It is not worn down or eaten up over a long period of use.

It is never necessary to use much flux, although a little excess here or there will not harm anything. A brush dipped in flux once should be able to handle about three to five joints. Do not use so little, however, that the solder won't flow properly.

As you are soldering use a sponge to clean and slightly cool down the iron. Use a large sponge like those used for washing cars, not the kind made from natural sponge or nylon. Thoroughly wet it and then wring it out before each soldering attempt so that it is slightly damp. It may be easier to use if you make several parallel slashes about an inch deep on one side. The iron tip can sink into the slashed sections without flipping the sponge off the table and you won't need another hand just to hold the sponge still.

As you solder, periodically wipe the iron's tip off on the damp sponge. This will remove the dirt that accumulates on the tip and will also cool the iron slightly.

As we said in Chapter 5, ventilation of some sort is an absolute necessity, so work where there is adequate air circulation either through windows or from a small, portable fan.

A small wire brush comes in handy when the solder does not seem to want to take and you are sure that the joint is fluxed because you've fluxed it three times. What has probably happened is that either the lead has oxidized through incorrect storage or insufficient or frequent cleaning, or it has simply accumulated grime and skin oils from handling. It's no earthshaking matter in either case, and you can correct it by scraping the surface of the joint a little bit with the wire brush. This will roughen up the lead and remove the layer of oxidation. Flux the joint again and it should take solder with no problem.

Care should be exercised when scraping joints; don't go wild with the brush. Unless the area that is scraped will be completely covered by solder, the little scratches will definitely show; there is nothing you can do to hide them. Confine the use of this method to the lead joint only and leave the surrounding areas alone.

SOLDERING

Because soldering requires good timing and nimble hands, it is a skill that must be "felt" rather than taught. Indeed, first attempts (my own included) often range from a frantic, pecking motion with the iron to the heavy-handed, count-to-one-hundred method. Neither of these produce long-lasting satisfaction *or* good solder joints. Finding the middle ground (there is one, believe it or not) is not as difficult as it may seem at first.

To begin make a final measurement of the project to be soldered to make sure that it is the correct size. This is most important if it is to fit into a preexisting space, such as a window frame. Also be sure that all measurements are true and square. If it is a rectangular piece and the top measures 25 cm in width, it also should measure 25 cm in width at the bottom and in between. If it deviates from the correct measurement at any place along the way, remedy this by either pulling the lead out slightly (but not so much that you can see the edge of the glass) or tapping it in, using the lathekin and a hammer or the end of your lead knife (*gently*, please!).

Be sure that all lead joints are tight and meet smoothly. If you have pieced any of them (not *too* many, I hope), make certain that the pieces fit snugly.

Flux all joints. After you have done this, especially with larger windows, check for those you missed (I'll wager you find at least one, and probably more on a larger piece). Have the flux and brush nearby so that if you run across any others when you are soldering, you won't have to stop everything to find them.

A small amount of solder is used for each joint. Remember that you want a small, even joint. Many students in their beginning efforts treat the solder as if it were paint, and it ends up being smeared not only on the joint but three inches out in all directions as well. Solder is not easy to remove once it has been laid on, and sometimes it is just impossible. Joints that radiate solder in every direction look messy, even if they are smooth.

To solder, then, hold the iron in your right hand (if you are righthanded). Hold the coil of solder in your left hand and pull out about 15 to 20 cm (6 to 8 inches). If your project is small, this should carry you well throughout it. If you need more solder, you can pull out more as you need it, but it's easiest to begin with a good length in order to avoid having to unwrap it a few centimeters at a time while holding a hot soldering iron in your other hand.

Touch the end of the solder to the tip of the iron—holding both right at the point where the iron touches the work. If the iron is the right temperature, the solder will melt immediately. If the solder remains hard or begins to melt slowly, wait a few more moments before you begin. An 80-watt iron takes about 3 to 5 minutes to heat up. The closer to the work you apply the solder onto the iron, the better your chance of making a good joint. The farther up the tip you touch the solder, the greater your chance of ruining the joint. At the same time, bear in mind that the iron may be too hot a few centimeters up the tip from the joint, because the lead cannot effectively carry the heat away. If you consistently apply solder too far up the tip, you will be replacing tips quite often. This is because the directly applied solder causes very hot tips to pit prematurely.

To make sure the iron is not too hot, lay it on a piece of scrap lead. If nothing happens begin soldering. If the lead melts, unplug the iron and allow it to cool for a few minutes.

To solder, lay 3 to 6 mm (up to about ¼ inch) of solder across the joint, as shown in Fig. 9-1. Lay the flat surface of the iron on top of the solder and, as the solder melts, pull the roll of solder away. This does not require much pressure other than the weight of the iron itself. If you lean on it, you are liable to find yourself repairing the lead or, worse yet, the glass. Pick the iron up as soon as the solder has melted under it, which will take only a second or two.

Go right on to the next joint and repeat the steps above. Do not stop between operations to admire your work, at least not for more than a quick look. Keep soldering. If you mess up a joint, leave it and go on to the next. You can come back to it later and decide what to do about it. For now, you want to maintain the momentum that keeps you in control of the situation.

Fig. 9-1. Lay about ¼ inch of solder on the joint.

Once soldering is begun, it should be smooth and almost rhythmic process. Because the iron is constantly heating up, it must be kept in motion in order to keep it at a manageable temperature. Each lead joint that is soldered reduces the temperature of the iron slightly, so you can keep the iron from getting too hot by moving it from one joint to the next without hesitating in between.

Sometimes one of my students will stop for a full minute between joints or will fiddle and smear around one joint for what seems to be hours. It is agonizing to me because I know he or she is only trying to get the solder to look just right, while the iron is heating up more and more each wasted moment. I gently remind him of this fact and urge him to come back to it later, but for now to keep soldering. At this point the student usually gets flustered at the thought of burning cames or cracked glass and becomes positively frantic, dabbing solder helter-skelter all over the place.

Obviously, this approach is as bad as is the ponderous one. You may find yourself the victim of one or the other during your first project anyway; but don't let it discourage you. In only a short time you will have more confidence and your soldered joints will show marked improvement.

After all joints on one side of your project have been soldered, turn the work over and flux and solder the joints on that side too.

Any gaps that have been left between the lead joints while the window was being leaded will also have to be filled with solder if you haven't pieced them. This requires more solder—as much as it takes to fill up the hole and form a rounded top (it is supposed to look like lead is under it). This is not a good practice to get into, because solder is more pliable than lead, it represents a weakened joint, it doesn't look very good in most cases, and it takes too much solder. In soldering work, you will always want to use as little solder as possible because a little goes a long way, and a neat joint that is relatively small looks best.

If you should find that you have used too much solder on a joint and it looks awkward and bulky, restrain yourself from trying to spread it out on the adjoining leads. This will not remove or "thin" the solder; it will only make it look messier. In some circumstances it is possible to remove excess solder by scraping it off the joint with the iron and then flip it off of the iron, either onto the floor or the work table. This takes a practiced hand and caution to make sure that in flicking the solder off of the iron, it doesn't land on you or on an innocent bystander.

It is wise to avoid getting solder on the glass or on yourself. It is very hot and will burn badly. If some should accidently drop on the glass, remove it right away if possible with your lead knife or a similar object but do not attempt to pick it up with your fingers. If it is a very small drop, you can just leave it until you are through soldering and then scrape it off. Solder will not stick to any flat nonmetallic surface that does not have flux on it, but it *is* difficult to remove from clothing and carpets.

Most windows are "built," or leaded up, entirely before soldering is begun. Occasionally, though, you may have to solder the window in sections. This is done when a particular part of the window contains many small pieces of glass that must be leaded together. You will find in this kind of situation that, after you have painstakingly gotten such an area leaded, the whole thing will rise up from the center like a volcano and the pieces will be scrambled. This results from work going on in an adjacent part of the window because of tapping the glass, pressure, and fitting pieces. When this takes place, it is most frustrating, especially when you go back and relead the whole area only to have it happen again. In this instance, then, the area is leaded and then soldered to hold it in place and keep the pieces from rolling.

Solder only the particular area that is causing the trouble, not the entire window. This allows you to make adjustments when the window is finally completely leaded up without taking the whole thing apart.

Soldering Temperature

Getting the solder to flow smoothly is important to producing attractive finished joints. A good solder joint is smooth, fairly flat, and does not extend too far in any direction from the joint itself (Fig. 9-2) To get this kind of a joint, the solder, then, must flow evenly from the iron to the joint and permeate the spaces between the two leads. This is largely dependent on using the iron at the correct temperature. An iron that is too cold will leave lumpy little patches of solder that more or less sit on top of the joint; an iron that is too hot is likely to take care of the matter by burning up the lead entirely.

Between when the iron is hot enough to melt solder easily and yet not so hot that it leaves gaping holes in the lead, there is a place called ideal. At the ideal temperature, the ideal solder joint is achieved.

On a project with many joints to be soldered, the iron almost certainly will become too hot to use without burning the lead. When this is felt (and it *is* felt; you will come to know that point,

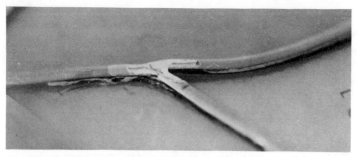

Fig. 9-2. A good solder joint is flat, smooth, and even.

too, as you solder more), you must unplug the iron. Continue soldering with the unplugged iron until it begins to cool too much. When this point is reached (it is noticeable by the appearance of the solder joint, discussed below), plug in the iron and resume work. Unless your iron has a heat control and thermostat, you'll have to create your own heat control plugging and unplugging the iron. Primitive as it may seem, with all of our modern technology, it still seems to me to be the best method. You can purchase a soldering iron with a rheostat to control the heat, but I do not endorse their use. On/off switches are a more convenient method of controlling applied power because they are installed about 15 cm below the handle of the iron, on the cord. They allow you to turn the iron off when it becomes too hot without reaching for the outlet, and the same for turning it back on. If it's easier for you, use an on/off switch, but remember that the principle is the same. The iron's power switch does not regulate heat.

I said before that soldering is not so much a thing to be taught as a thing to be felt, and this is true. There are the technical aspects, of course: how long to stay on the joint, how much solder to use, how to correct this or eliminate that—but one develops a feel for the work along with this knowledge, and these two combined are what makes for proper timing and good solder joints.

The iron that is too cold performs sluggishly. The solder will not melt readily against either the iron itself or the lead. When it warms up a little more (but still not to the correct temperature), the solder joints begin to resemble the Swiss Alps, with sharp little points. The solder at this point still does not flow to any degree, but forms ridges and bumps and all kinds of other strange formations, all of which look bad. If you try to smooth out the joint until the iron is hotter, the joint will look worse yet. Figure 9-3 illustrates how such a joint might look.

The iron that is too hot is frightening to behold. No sooner do you set it down on the lead joint than, presto-chango, no more lead joint. It will burn instantly through the lead came before you know it, so watch what you are doing at all times. If you don't, you may well be left with a hole in the lead.

If you do not pull the iron away fast enough, you also run the risk of cracking the glass below the lead. This would be unfortunate indeed. Under normal soldering circumstances, chances are slight that you would allow the iron to come into contact with bare glass long enough for it to crack, but with an excessively hot iron these chances are greatly increased.

For this reason, be aware at all times of what you are doing and how long your iron has been plugged in. Don't plug it in and then go away to do something else, or start talking to a friend and forget about the time. You should not leave an iron unattended at any time, so unplug the iron first if you must answer the phone or the door.

To determine the correct temperature before you begin soldering, test the iron against a piece of scrap lead. If it does not melt, you can proceed.

Okay, you may be saying, but what do I *do* about those little mountain ranges in my solder, or the Grand Canyon holes in my lead, after they're already there?

For the joints produced by the too-cold iron, the answer is almost obvious. When the iron has heated to the correct temperature for soldering, you can go back and flatten out the joints. You will usually not need to apply any more solder for this. Just lay the tip flat on the joint for a few seconds and then remove it. The solder should flatten out quite nicely with this simple remedy.

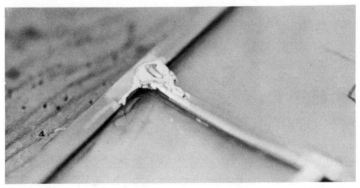

Fig. 9-3. This is a poor, bumpy joint, made by an iron that was too cool.

For gaping holes, you may need to do a bit of lead patchwork, unless it is a very small hole. For a small hole you may be able to smear enough solder over it to cover the gap. This is best done with a slightly cool iron; an iron at soldering temperature may not cover it well. You can always come back later with a hotter iron and smooth it out a little. This must be a fast operation. If you linger over it, fiddling and smearing it around, you will only become frustrated as the solder refuses to span the gap and builds up all around the edges. For this, use as little solder as you possibly can.

For larger holes or where your patience wears thin on the smaller ones, you may have to patch the joint. To do this, carefully trim the edges of the burned leads so that they are even, as in Fig. 9-4. Since this is done with a lead knife, and usually right on top of the glass, caution must be used not to exert too much pressure. From your scrap lead, cut a small piece to fit the gap and then cut away the face of the lead, as shown in Fig. 9-5. This operation is similar to piecing lead, except here only the face of the lead that you have cut off is used. Lay it over the hole and make sure that it meets the other leads flush. Now you can flux it and solder it together.

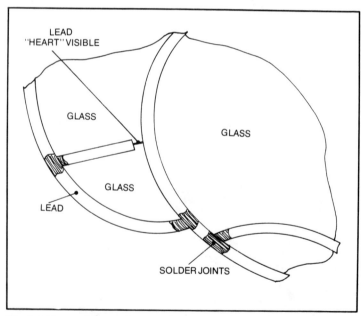

Fig. 9-4. To repair burned cames, first trim ragged edges so that they are even.

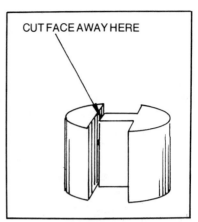

Fig. 9-5. To fill gaps created by burning lead, use only the face of the lead came.

CUT FACE AWAY HERE

Turning the Work Over

Leaded glass must be soldered on both sides before it can be glazed. This naturally requires turning it over once the first side has been done. On small projects of 30 cm (about a foot) square or less, the window can be picked up and turned rather easily.

For anything larger, however, there is a proper method that must be observed. A larger project will sag or actually bend in its weakest areas or in places where there is a lot of stress as soon as it is removed from the table that has given it support. To turn a large piece that has been soldered on one side only, then, here is the correct procedure.

Pull the project out so that the border is lined up with the edge of the table. Grip it with one hand in the middle of that edge and place the other hand in the middle of the opposite edge. Now bring the project straight out, toward you, supporting it with the one hand as seen in Fig. 9-6. Pull it far enough out so that one half of the project rests on the table and the other half is supported by your hand.

When you have gotten this far, slowly drop the outer edge downward, pivoting it on the table. Your other hand should bring the far edge of the project up as the lower edge goes down (Fig. 9-7). From this position, it is then possible to lift the project and set it back on the table, holding it upright and supporting it by a hand placed in the middle on both sides.

Carefully turn the project around so that the unsoldered side is facing you. At this stage you are likely to be handling a very flimsy project so be sure that it is always supported and does not lean in either direction. Keep it upright.

After you have turned the project around, lift it off the table and place it against the table's edge. This will be the reverse of what you have just done. Hold it against the table—the pivot point again is its center. Slowly let your far edge down to the table from this position, moving the edge of the project closest to you up along with it. When it meets the table, you will again have half of the project on the table on and half of it off. From here, simply push it so that it slides back onto the table.

When you are turning a leaded-glass piece, it is especially important to be sure that you do not pull up or push abruptly on either edge. Keep the movements smooth and support the window as evenly as possible with your hands. A leaded piece weighs about 30 grams per square centimeter, which is about 2 kg for each 30 cm square (3½ to 4 lb per square foot). As I mentioned earlier, leaded glass of any appreciable size will seem frighteningly flimsy, and you will almost certainly break some of the glass panels if you do not handle the work with utmost care.

For very large or long and narrow projects, it is necessary to have someone help you turn them. One person should be on either end and the steps are the same as above. When two people are involved, the movements of both should be well synchronized so that one is not pulling when the other is pushing or whatever. This, too, will result in breakage.

After both sides are soldered your leaded glass must still be handled in the above manner to get it off the table or to lay it down. Never, never pick it up just as it lies, like you would a mattress or anything else. It will be supported only where your hands are, and the rest of it will sag or bend and suddenly break.

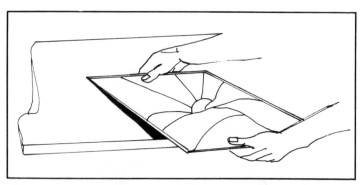

Fig. 9-6. To turn a project so that the other side can be soldered, pull *straight* out from table edge, while supporting the leaded glass with your hands on opposite edges.

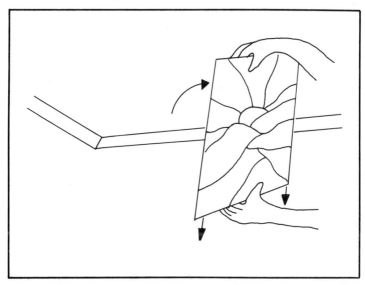

Fig. 9-7. Tilt the leaded glass using the table's edge as a pivot point.

When carrying leaded glass, whether it is soldered and glazed or just soldered, carry it vertically by the edges.

Don't lean leaded glass at an angle against anything; this will almost certainly result in sagging. If you must lean it on edge, make sure that it is flat against the wall or whatever you have, and that it will not fall or be accidentally kicked.

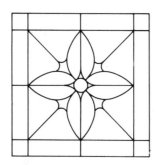

Chapter 10
Glazing

Glazing is also called grouting, cementing, and sealing. In this step, a glazing compound is applied to the window to make it weatherproof, waterproof, and fairly solid. Glass that may rattle alarmingly in the lead channels will be silenced forever.

There are probably hundreds of recipes for glazing compound, but I will give only two here. The first is for those who prefer to mix their own. You will need casting plaster, which can be bought at paint stores; turpentine; boiled linseed oil; and lamp black (powdered or in a tube), which is usually available at art stores. If you cannot find lamp black, a tube of slate gray or flat black oil paint will do.

Use a large container for mixing; a big coffee can is good because it also has a tight lid. To mix, add 2 parts linseed oil to 3 parts turpentine. Add to this 7 parts plaster. Mix this all up so that it has an even consistency. When the paste is free of lumps, add enough lamp black to color the compound a dark gray or black (gray is preferred). Make sure that the lamp black is distributed evenly and mixed in well.

The mixture should be the consistency of a thick pudding or mud. If it is too thick, add a little more turpentine. If it is too thin, add more plaster, a handful at a time, until you get the right mixture.

At the studio we use a recipe that is a little easier to make up. To make this mixture you will need turpentine; whiting, also called

Chinese whiting, and DAP glazing compound. DAP is also called metal sash putty. The most common DAP, sold in almost all hardware stores, is white; if you can; purchase the gray colored DAP; which is scarce in some areas. If you can't find gray, you will have to color mixture with lamp black.

To mix, thin out the DAP with turpentine until it is the consistency of pudding or mud. When it is thinned, add about two handsful of whiting and mix well. If this thickens the mixture too much, add a bit more turpentine. If you are using white DAP, now is the time to color it.

The differences in glazing compounds seem to rest on a few subtle nuances. The most important one is the length of time a particular mixture takes to set up, but other considerations are how long it lasts and how well it keeps.

I find the recipe we use in the studio suitable in all areas. It sets up relatively quickly (about a week in good weather), lasts, keeps well, and makes a good bond. As a beginner I used the first method of mixing the compound, but our studio's recipe is much easier and less messy to mix.

For glazing, you will need a couple of stiff-bristled brushes. A pair of rubber gloves and a coverall-type apron are also good investments, since this is a messy process.

Be sure to work in a ventilated area. It is best if it is also contained so that putty and whiting (especially whiting) won't be spread from one corner of the room to the other.

Don your work clothes and you are ready to begin. First, take a healthy scoop of the putty on one of your brushes and plop it down on your leaded glass. Begin by scrubbing it over the project and forcing it under the lead. It is important to get the compound under all of the leads, including the borders. Be careful along the border leads that you don't push them away from the glass—they are hard to get back into position once this happens.

Your leaded glass will look like quite a real mess at this point, with putty all over it. The first time, I witnessed this procedure I was most certain that the piece was ruined and the compound would never be completely removed. Little did I know!

Use enough pressure to get the putty in along all of the channels, but not so much that you break the glass. When you have done this, take a small, flat object and run it over all of the leads, particularly the border leads. An old, smooth lathekin works very well for this, but you can also use the blade of a putty knife, the back wooden handle of the glazing brush, or any similar object. Remember not to press too hard. This will crimp the leads down so that they are holding the glass tightly while at the same time forcing out any excess putty.

Once you are sure that the glazing compound is under all of the leads, it's time to begin removing it. Much of it can be removed with the stiff-bristled brush, by brushing along the lead in the same direction. Do not angle the bristles of the brush; you want only to remove the excess, not the putty under the lead.Periodically, when the brush is full, scrape it off on the side of the can. Continue this until you have gotten as much compound as you can off of the glass.

To remove the remaining putty, sprinkle a fine layer of whiting over the entire window. A flour sifter works well for this; you really don't need more than a handful or so for a medium-sized project. When you have applied the whiting, begin to scrub it off, using a different brush than the one you used for the putty. The whiting acts to absorb the oils in the glazing compound and makes it easier to remove. It also cleans and polishes the glass.

Continue brushing the putty and whiting away and off of leaded glass. When you have finished, there should be very little of either remaining on the glass. As with the putty, don't angle the brush as you scrub. You don't want to remove the putty under the leads.

Sawdust is sometimes recommended as a substitute for whiting. It usually proves unsatisfactory, however, as it becomes embedded in the putty and makes it difficult for the final cleanup of your leaded work.

Both sides must be glazed. It is preferable to let the window set until the first side is dry. This normally takes at least a week. However, small projects may be turned and glazed on the other side as soon as you have finished the first, if you are impatient. For larger projects it is best to let them dry some. If you can't bear the thought of a whole week, at least give them one to three days (the longer the better, of course).

When the glazing compound has had a chance to set up, turn the window over and glaze the other side, following the same procedure as above. After this is done, the window *must* be allowed to lie flat and undisturbed for at least a week—and preferably a week and a half to two weeks—before any further cleaning or installation is done. To attempt to install or hang a window that has not dried or set up properly involves the risk of breaking the seal of the putty. A window is also much easier to handle when it has been properly glazed. The putty, when it dries, makes the leaded glass more rigid and solid; it will not be as flimsy as it was before it was grouted.

When you have finished the first side of the window you will notice that the lead has taken on a dull sheen and the solder joints have darkened naturally, blending well with the lead and having almost an antiqued look. This, to me, is a pleasing transformation from the shiny solder joints and bare leads.

When both sides have been glazed and allowed to set up well, it is time to finish the last stages of cleanup. If you did a good job removing the glazing compound, the cleanup job will be that much easier.

While the leaded glass was drying, any excess putty will have oozed out from the leads and hardened on the glass. You will first need to remove this. There are no sophisticated tools involved in this process. In fact, the best tool is a manicure stick, sometimes called an orange stick. You can easily run the pointed end around the edges of each lead and scrape off the putty. Popsicle sticks that have been sharpened with a knife also work well and are less expensive. You will need to sharpen both fairly often. Any other similar object that you can think of will do the job. Leading nails are useful for getting into tight corners, and they do not wear down.

Be careful not to dig the putty out from under the leads. Remove only that which protrudes from them or any that is on the glass itself.

A stiff brush is useful for brushing the putty off once it has been loosened.

If you can perform this task in a place where there is light coming through your leaded glass, it will be much easier for you to see where you need to clean. I use a large plate glass easel lit from behind. It works on much the same principle as a lightbox except that it is vertical. The light shining through the glass makes the dirty areas much more visible. For small projects, such as a setup is not really necessary; you can use a regular window in your home in much the same way.

On leaded-glass works that have many pieces in them, it is sometimes easiest to do most of this cleaning while the project is still flat on the glazing table and in a matter of a day or two after it has been glazed. Because the putty sets up quite hard, it can be difficult to remove. To make the rest of the cleanup simpler, you can do the majority of the putty picking a few days after it has been applied, while the compound is still somewhat soft. It will probably continue to ooze a little afterward, but you will at least have gotten the big stuff off. Allow the work to set a few more days before the final cleanup.

On ripple-back glass or any glass that has a definite texture to it, it is most important to remove all of the putty before the window is allowed to set up. The reason for this is almost obvious. The putty hardens and becomes embedded in the finish of the glass, and will at least double your cleaning time trying to get it out. So make sure that the glass is as free of putty as you can get it before leaving the project to set.

Should you find that you have missed some putty, a small wire brush is useful for covering larger areas, although a good deal of it will probably have to be picked away with a stick or nail—a tedious job.

When all of this has been done, clean the glass with glass cleaner. Use one that does not contain ammonia, as this will work to slowly erode the putty. Some books recommend that no glass cleaner of any kind be used on leaded glass windows, advocating instead the use of soap and water or some other method. This seems to me to be an extreme effort. Just use the cleaner and several clean, soft rags to shine the glass.

It is after this has been completed that you may finally get to have your first sustained look at your masterpiece. A glimpse here and there as you turned the work over for soldering or glazing does not compare with unadulterated gazing, so enjoy!

A word to the wise here about the entire process of glazing and cleaning. All arts have their share of dull work, and leaded glass is no exception. There are days when I think that if I must glaze another work; I will surely go mad, just as there are some days when it is a genuine pleasure to play in the putty and not have to really think about anything in particular. Either way, this final step in construction is one that should be taken just as seriously as cutting glass or soldering.

Regular dirty windows are bad enough, but dirty leaded stained glass windows can be an eyesore and embarrassing, so don't invest heavily of yourself in the first stages of making something and then not follow through. Leaded stained glass should be shown off to its best advantage.

If you feel the glazing blahs coming on as you solder your last joint, the best thing to do is glaze as soon as you are done soldering, even if it seems difficult. If you let it go, thinking you will get to it later or tomorrow, you will usually find that tomorrow never comes, and the project sits somewhere to become a glass skeleton in your closet.

Chapter 11
Bracing and
Reinforcement

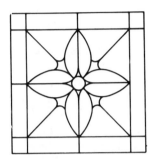

Adding brace bars could almost be called a finishing technique in that it is the last construction step necessary before you actually install or hang your finished work, but it is really more than that. While brace bars add nothing to the beauty of a stained glass piece (indeed, if done improperly it can greatly detract), they do add considerably to the strength of the piece and its ability to endure stress and age.

As discussed in Chapter 2, a brace bar is a flat steel bar, usually about 10 mm (⅜ inch) wide, although there are other widths available. It must be galvanized steel, however, or the solder will not adhere to it. There are also round brace rods, but these cannot be bent to blend with the design in a manner that does not detract from its overall effect.

Old stained glass windows were braced almost exclusively with round bar. Usually the bar extended straight across the window's width beyond the window's edge and was sunk or drilled into the wooden window sash itself. Copper wires were soldered to the window at lead joints and the wire was then pulled tight, twisted around the bar, and cut short. Although this method is still being used today by some, the disadvantage is that the shadow of the bar must fall where it will and is most visible when the window is viewed. It appears as a dark line running straight across. Since a window must usually be braced in two or three places, there are that many lines to interfere with the design of the window. I have seen many instances where this type of reinforcing completely ruined the appearance of stained glass, and as a result I am a firm believer in what I feel is the proper and most aesthetically pleasing method.

Perhaps one of the questions I am most frequently asked regarding the use of brace bars is this: How do you tell if you have to brace your work? While there are no hard and fast rules, there are a couple of considerations you must take into account. In general, it never hurts to brace a window; so if you are not sure, you cannot lose anything by doing it.

The very first thing you should consider is the size of your work. I feel, generally, that anything over 60 cm by 60 cm should carry at least one brace bar, and a meter-square project should have two. There are exceptions to this, naturally, but in the beginning it is better to be safe than sorry. When you have a feel for the kinds of pressures that are combined in a stained glass window and can easily determine the areas of stress, you will be much more capable to decide the question for yourself. For now, the dimensions given above seem to be a good guideline to follow.

Another element to consider is where the leaded glass will be used. In a frame to be hung? In a window sash or a door perhaps? A window that is installed in a door will take much more of a beating than one that is hung in a place where it will remain serenely untouched. For this reason, almost any window to be installed in a frequently used door must have bracing. If it does not, I can assure you that you will be sorry when the whole thing crashes to the floor after that once-too-often door slam.

As leaded glass ages, even the strongest lead will begin to sag and pull away from the glass. This is partially due to age and the elements, but also to sheer gravity. Brace bars in strategic places help combat this effect because they are soldered directly to the lead and sort of hold it up. Sagging from age usually takes many years, of course, for the window to come to such disrepair that it must be removed and releaded, but you will add to its life considerably by reinforcement of this kind.

A leaded glass window installed in a door or one that is opened and closed frequently, such as a slider-type window, must hold up against not only the natural effects of gravity and age but the stresses that come with frequent, sometimes less-than-gentle use. So think about where your work is to be placed.

A brace bar normally runs horizontally from side to side rather than up and down. It is soldered all the way across at each lead joint and to each of the two border leads. The bars, if there are to be more than one, should be somewhat evenly spaced, although you cannot always work this out because of the design.

The best solution to the bracing dilemma is to plan ahead. Consider the size and the place the leaded glass will go and make allowances for the brace bar or bars while you are still in the design stage. In this way, you can perhaps modify the design in such a manner as to lend itself to the incorporation of a bar. While you are doing this, keep in mind that the bar will have to be bent (steel, remember) to follow a lead line, and the fewer angles and wild curves in your lead line where the bar will go, the more smoothly the job of bending the bar will be.

To cut the bar you will need a hacksaw. It is best to angle the cut as much as you can. This leaves less of a protuding angle along the sides of your work. If you have a grinding wheel, it is also a good idea to smooth the edges of the cut a bit. A large file will work as well for this.

The ends of the bar, as I said, are soldered to the border leads of the window. It is important to affix them approximately in the middle of that lead. This will allow room for ir tallation and, if necessary, some trimming of the leads.

To measure a length of bar, particularly if it is to make a few bends in the span of the window, cut a piece about 15 cm or so longer than you will need and, beginning at one end, bend it to conform to the design. When you get to the other side of the window, mark where the bar falls (in the middle of the lead, not at the outer edge) and cut at an angle as described. By cutting it longer, you will assure yourself enough lead to be able to bend the bar to the specifications.

Bending a brace bar can be wonderfully simple or a real headache. I'm not quite sure what the variable is, but some brace bars seem to bend easily, almost like wire, while others take great effort. At any rate, what you will need for this job is mostly muscle and a hammer. A vise is most helpful, also, to hold the brace bar steady if you need to pound it. You alone know what kind of curves you must make your bar accommodate, but here are a few tips to help you along.

For straight runs, the job is a snap; no bending is necessary, but do not shy away from this task by incorporating lots of straight lines into your design. It's not really as difficult as it sounds. For very gradual curves, you may be able to bend the bar with your hands or by using a solid tabletop as support.

To make more difficult curves and angles, hold the bar along the lead so that you can see where you need to start bending it. Mark this point with a marker. Place the bar in the vise and tighten down the vise, slightly *before* the mark you have made. The bar will not bend exactly on the mark, but slightly ahead of it, so you must compensate for this. Then begin bending, either by hand or with a hammer. You will have to remove the bar from the vise after each slight bend and match it up against the lead line to see where you go from there. Try to keep it so that it lies right along the middle of the lead.

For corners and sharp angles, you will have to use a hammer. Bend as much as you can by hand and then use the hammer to tighten it up.

Bending brace bars may go a little slow the first time, but I can guarantee you that your work will look much better than it would if you ran the bars straight across. It's worth the extra time and trouble.

Soldering is not begun until the bar is entirely bent, cut, and the ends filed. For soldering you will need a small jar of muriatic acid or liquid copper-foil flux. Copper-foil flux is carried by some suppliers. Either one of the two will work.

Dip both ends of the bar into the acid flux and then lay it aside. Check over the lead where you are planning to solder the bar and be sure that it is free from dirt and flux. Expecially clean away any of the glazing putty that may still be along the solder joints. The putty will resist both flux and solder, and you will get either a poor bond or none at all.

After the areas are cleaned, lay the bar on top of the lead and make a final check to be sure that it does not hang over anywhere. Apply the flux to both ends of the bar and to the lead border it touches. Again, be sure that the bar does not reach all the way to the edge of the lead, but falls in the middle of it, about where the lead heart is.

Plug in your soldering iron and allow it to heat. When it has reached normal soldering temperature (you can still burn the leads), apply the solder to one end of the bar and form a good bond to the lead. When this is done, do the same for the other end. You will now have the bar soldered to both edges, although no soldering has been done in between. By doing this you ensure that the bar will not move around as you solder along its length.

Now you are ready to flux each of the solder joints along the lead. At each joint the bar will be attached to the window. Flux each

140

joint and apply a liberal amount of flux to the bar at these spots also. All you should have to do then is lay the tip of the iron on each joint until the solder becomes liquid again and bonds to the bar. Use a little more new solder to make sure that the solder bond is strong and solid. Solder on both sides of the bar.

The brace bar must be flat along the lead for a proper soldering bond to occur. Sometimes the bar may tend to bow up a little, and this should be corrected before the bar is soldered. You may have to hold the bar down while you solder it in place; but beware, because the brace rod will get very hot close to the soldering area.

When you have attached all brace bars, go back and clean off any flux that may have gotten on the glass during the process. Since it is acid-based, and flux that is left on can pit the glass.

As with any other soldering, you should strive to make these joints as smooth as possible. It is a little more difficult because you are soldering the lead, which is running horizontally, to the bar, which is set up on its edge vertically. By placing only the chisel tip of the iron along the bar and on top of the lead, you should be able to get good, clean joints.

These newly soldered spots will be a shiny silver in sharp contrast to the now darkened solder joints on the rest of the leaded glass. This is where that great stuff, patina, comes in handy.

Patina is a chemical substance used to darken solder. It gives it anywhere from a very dark, almost black color to a nice gunmetal gray. To apply patina, dip a small rag into the solution and rub it across each of the solder joints. It will instantly turn them dark. All you have to do then is buff them up a little.

A better applicator for this is a sponge cut into bite-size pieces. These get into small, tight spots where the patina is needed and don't get much of the patina on the glass or surrounding leads. It is difficult to clean patina from glass, so a little caution here will save you time later.

If the joint does not darken enough, apply the patina again and repeat the procedure. If it becomes too dark, about all you can do is to try to rub it out and hope for the best.

After all this is done, you will need to do a final cleanup with glass cleaner. The project will now (finally) be ready for installation.

For leaded glass measuring more than 20 cm on a side that are to be hung without a wooden frame, you might consider using zinc came instead of lead around the border of the piece. You'll be amazed at how much extra strength this simple addition will add to your work. Free-hanging pieces, especially, are in need of all the support they can get, although zinc can also be used on almost any other project.

The main limitation of zinc is that it does not bend. Some thinner zinc came, such as 3 cm or 6 cm (⅛ or ¼ inch), can be made to take a gentle curve (in round designs for instance), but bending must be done by hand, a little at a time to avoid crimping. For this reason, zinc is employed mainly as border pieces where it requires no bending and serves its purpose admirably.

Zinc cames are available in the same shapes as lead (U, Y, and H) and in just about as many sizes. It can be obtained through your stained glass supplier, most likely; if he does not have it in stock, he can probably order it for you.

It is somewhat more expensive than lead, but all in all the extra cost is usually worth it. It also must be cut with a saw. Zinc is not very hard to cut, and a small jeweler's saw or similar type will do well.

Zinc came requires no special preparation and can be soldered easily using the same flux you'd use for lead (oleic acid).

Chapter 12
Installation, Hanging, and Display

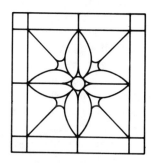

Once you have finished your stained glass work, you will doubtless want to display it where it can be admired. Perhaps you have even made it to replace a plain window pane in your home.

Smaller panels may be hung directly from the border lead. When I say smaller, I mean about 30 cm or so square (about a square foot) to about 30 cm by 40 cm. Anything bigger really should have a frame around it to give additional support. To hang a larger panel by its border lead alone is asking for trouble. In time the weight of the glass and lead and sheer gravitational force will pull the lead away from the glass.

CHAINS

To hang a small stained glass panel, the best method is to attach small loops or rings to the border lead to which you can attach small chains that can be hooked to the ceiling or wherever you want the panel to hang. Use copper or brass rings because they can be easily solderable to lead with a minimum of preparation.

To make rings, you will need a heavy-gauge copper wire, usually sold on small spools at the hardward store. To obtain a number of rings that are uniform in size, wrap the wire as it comes off the spool around a pencil or other cylindrical object. The circumference of the object you use will determine the size of the loops, so use a thicker form (such as the handle of a wooden spoon) if you want a larger ring. Wrap the wire tightly so that if forms a coil along the length of your form. Then snip the wire with wire cutters down one length (Fig. 12-1) so that you have individual rings. Slide each off. You will then have what will probably be a lifetime supply of copper rings. You do not need to solder the two ends together as this will be done when you solder the rings to the border lead.

Copper will not solder directly to the lead, so you will have to coat each ring with solder before it will adhere. Because copper easily builds up a surface before it will adhere. Because copper easily builds up a surface residue of dirt and oxidation, you must also clean each ring. Muriatic acid will both clean the copper and make it solderable.

Some stained-glass supply stores also sell a flux made specifically for copper-foil work. This flux works equally well for soldering other metals such as brass, copper, and galvanized steel to lead. If you can get hold of some of this, it will do the job just as well and probably easier than muriatic acid.

Both muriatic acid and copper-foil flux are highly corrosive inorganic chemicals. Extreme caution should be observed when using them. It is of particular importance to keep them out of the reach of children.

To prepare copper for soldering, first dip the ring in the acid. Use a pair of needle-nose pliers for this and wipe them off when you are done, as this acid erodes metal. Lay the rings on the table. When the iron is hot, drop a small bit of molten solder on the ring. Move the iron around on the ring until the copper is completely covered with solder. Turn the ring over to make sure that the other side is also coated. Either flip it over with the iron or use pliers; it will be very hot.

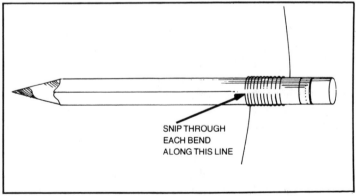

SNIP THROUGH
EACH BEND
ALONG THIS LINE

Fig. 12-1. Rings can be made by wrapping wire around a cylindrical object.

Do as many rings in this manner as you will need. Usually only two will be per panel, but doing this operation all at once will save time if you have other projects to hang.

Because copper is a highly conductive metal (meaning it heats up very hot, very quickly), it's just not possible to hold the ring in your fingers and solder it onto the panel at the same time. A number of ways have been devised to position and solder rings to panels with the least amount of contortions, but it still remains a slightly frustrating experience at times.

One way to do this is to hold the ring to the lead with a small metal clip sold at stationery stores for about $.30. A medium-sized clip one works best. Position the rings at the two top corners of the panel. Then simply set the iron on the inner edge of the ring. The solder should melt enough to allow some kind of bond, however weak, to take place. From this point you can then carefully add a little solder at a time until you have a strong joint there. Building up a small hill of solder around the bottom of the ring will give more strength to the bond. Do not remove the clip until you have a strong enough joint formed. If you do, you will find that the ring will fall over each time heat is applied from the iron, an aggravating experience.

Repeat the same procedure for the other ring, making sure they are lined up.

There is an alternative method for positioning each ring, and it may work a bit more smoothly. Lay the panel flat on the table. Place a small piece of scrap window glass along the upper edge, where you will be soldering the ring. Lay the ring on the glass, just touching the border lead. You will find that it is lined up in just about the middle of the border lead. It is then easy to solder the ring onto the lead. Again position both rings so that they are soldered in the same place on opposite sides of the border-lead edge. The best place is at each corner.

Position the rings so that the two unjoined ends of the copper (where the coil was cut) are at the bottom, next to the border came, or where they will be soldered. Do not leave them at the top of the ring, where the chain will be attached. They will not look good and will weaken the ring.

Try not to build up so much solder that you get a ridiculously large bulge at the joint. As in any other soldering job, the joint should be as smooth and tidy as you can make it.

If for some reason you plan to set the rings in from the corners, and not right where the two border leads meet, make sure that they are soldered close to or aligned with another lead joint as illustrated in Fig. 12-2. The rings should be soldered at the outside corners or at a place where an interior lead meets the outer border lead. By doing this, you cut down the chance of having the lead pull away from the glass.

Chain can usually be bought at a hardware store or from a jewelry findings supplier. Some stained-glass suppliers also carry it. Buy chain that is thick and strong enough to support the panel, but don't use one that is so heavy it is out of proportion with the size and appearance of your panel.

Fig. 12-2. Rings are best placed at outside corners, but if you wish to move them in, place them where interior leads meet the border.

Heavy, clear plastic fishing line can also be used; this has the added advantage of being almost invisible. Again, use a heavy enough line or "test."

SUCTION-CUP HANGERS

When they first appeared on the market, these little inventions seemed to be an ingenious device for displaying small stained glass works. They are small, clear plastic suction cups that have a little hook embedded in the plastic. They can be stuck anywhere and are wonderful for displaying small hangings in a window. They eliminate the need for hooks in the ceiling, nails in the window sash, and other visible means of support.

Unfortunately they are meant for hanging very small trinkets, not panels measuring as small as 30 cm square. It is amazing the number of people who do not realize this and attempt to hang such a weighty panel from these small cups, only to be up in arms when they let go under the stain and the panel drops to the floor with a crunch. So if you want to use these for some of your stained glass, fine, but use them only for very small, lightweight objects such as trinkets meant to catch the sun or little free-form pieces.

FRAMES

A wooden frame is perhaps one of the most handsome ways to show off your stained glass. The wood and the colored glass seem to complement each other. Frames can be very rough (almost crude) or refined, sanded, polished, and stained, and they almost always look good regardless of their finish.

You can make a very simple frame from redwood, which is a beautiful wood in itself. Ask the man at the lumberyard for a redwood strip of 5 cm by 5 cm (about 2 by 2 inches). Measure the length and width of your panel and double each to get the length of piece you need. Either have it cut to size at the lumberyard or cut it yourself. A very simple frame can be made by joining the strips together in a butt joints, instead of the neater mitered corner. You might call this frame a beginner's beginning frame.

The edges of the panel are inset into a groove or channel that is cut into the frame's inside edge. Before you can cut the framing pieces you must determine how deep you want the panel's edge to inset into the frame. The width of the border came's face is often the amount used (Fig. 12-3).

Now measure the height of that portion of the panel that will be visible in the frame (the panel height less the width of the top

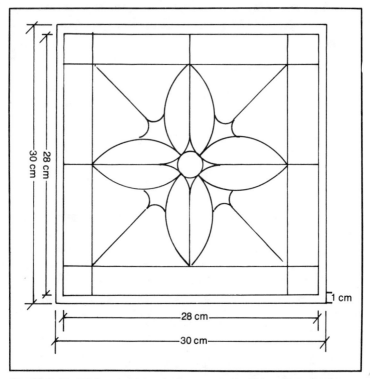

Fig. 12-3. First determine how deep your panel will inset into the frame. The width of the border came (1 cm in this example) is a good measurement to use. To determine how long to cut the side framing pieces, first measure the height of the panel minus that portion that will be inset (28 cm in this example).

and bottom border cames). To this number add the height of the top framing piece and the height of the bottom framing piece. Cut two framing strips to this measurement. Cut the top and bottom framing strips to the width of the panel less the width of the two side border cames that will be inset (Fig. 12-4).

Once the strips are cut, you must cut the groove or channel (in which to inset your panel) in the inner edge of all four pieces. The channel is cut to the depth your panel will inset and to the width the border came's thickness (Fig. 12-5). The channel can be cut easily with a table saw or with a router. If you have neither of these woodworking tools, you will have to find someone who does. A cabinet shop (they are difficult to find in some areas these days) is usually well equipped to handle such a request and will generally charge you no more than a few dollars for this service.

148

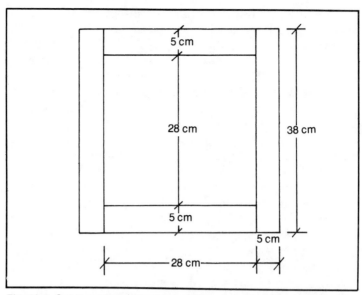

Fig. 12-4. Cut the side framing pieces to the height of the panel less the portion that will be inset, plus the height of the top and bottom frame pieces (28 cm + 5 cm + 5 cm = 38 cm). The top and bottom pieces are cut to the width of the panel less the portion that will be inset (28 cm).

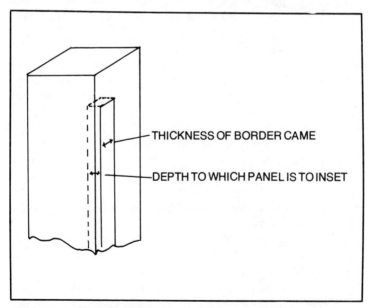

THICKNESS OF BORDER CAME

DEPTH TO WHICH PANEL IS TO INSET

Fig. 12-5. The channel or groove that holds the panel is cut as deep as you want the panel to inset and as wide as the border came.

Now you are ready to fit the frame together. To do this, assemble three sides and join them together. Slip the window into this part of the frame and then attach the fourth side to the others. Naturally, you will need to use a great deal of care in this procedure so that you won't have to replace any broken glass.

There are several methods that can be used to join the frame pieces together. They can be nailed together, but hammering must be slow and gentle once the panel is in place in order to avoid breaking the glass. Long wood screws can be used in place of nails. Right-angle corner braces screwed on provide another method. Apply them to the back of the frame where they are out of sight. Braces provide extra support to the frame if you want to outdo yourself, you can drill holes in the frame and attach the pieces with doweling.

Join three edges of the frame and secure them by whatever means you have chosen. If the joints do not meet flush, you may have to trim, plane, or sand the edges to get them to fit snugly, depending on how radical the discrepancy is.

Once you have these put together, set the frame on edge and slide the panel into it, making sure that it is well seated in the grooves. Now gently pull the wood tight to the border of the panel.

Lay the window flat on the table. Since it is in the frame, the wood will raise the glass off the work surface. You must be able to support the glass as you work, and this is best done with styrofoam sheets placed under the glass. When you have done this, fit the last piece of the frame along the open end and secure it tightly to the two edges of the side pieces. Make sure that the glass is seated within the channel on this piece as well. Be extra careful that you do not apply too much force in whatever method you are using to join the framing pieces.

Now you are ready to attach the hooks for hanging the frame. Buy a couple of heavy-duty screw eyes at the hardware store. These can be screwed into the top of the frame near each corner. Either chain or nylon rope can be used to hang the panel. Just make sure that it is secured well in the ceiling, the inside of the sash, or wherever you are placing it.

This frame is not the most finished looking one you could construct, although with the bare cut edges of the wood sanded and a coat of varnish applied, it will look quite satisfactory. The best thing about it is that it can be put together rather cheaply, and for the most part it does not require that you possess any special tools. What specialty work does have to be done can be done inexpen-

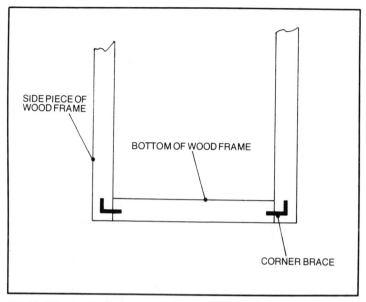

SIDE PIECE OF
WOOD FRAME

BOTTOM OF WOOD FRAME

CORNER BRACE

Fig. 12-6. Top and bottom pieces of frame will fit inside the two side pieces. Here they are shown joined with right-angle brackets and screws.

sively by someone else. If you have a workshop with all kinds of saws and tools at your disposal, you can naturally make much more elegant frames.

The more customary frames for leaded glass look like picture frames, or regular window sashes. They have mitered corners joined by pegs, doweling, or finishing nails. The wood is usually hardwood as it is more aesthetically pleasing, but pine frames are fine and can always be stained if you wish. Like the redwood frame described above, they are grooved down the inner edge of each side to accept the lead border of the window. They can also be cut out with molding added to hold the panel in the frame.

To make this kind of frame you need a table saw, miter box, and a few other tools that may not be included in your home workshop.

A number of woodworking shops specialize in making custom frames for stained glass windows, and some stained-glass supply stores also offer this service. If you want to have your panel framed at one of these places, you can expect to pay a bit for it. There is usually a minimum charge and it goes up from there. However, you can also count on getting your money's worth with a professional job.

WINDOW-SASH MOUNTS

Installing a panel into an existing window sash has its advantages and disadvantages. When a panel is made a permanent part of a room, such as in a window frame, it can greatly enhance its surroundings, being decorative as well as functional. The disadvantages occur in the dirty work: removing old putty from the sash and dealing with a leaded glass panel that may be slightly too large or too small for its new setting. Taking accurate measurements can be crucial.

Stained glass can be installed into both wood sash and metal sash windows frames. They can be put in slider-type windows and hung sash frames that can be opened and closed. About the only places they cannot go are in tub enclosures, sliding glass doors, and cars. The limiting factor here is not the glass panel itself, but health and building and safety codes.

Wood Sash Installation

To install a window in a wood sash, the first job that has to be done is to remove the old putty holding the present glass pane. If it is held by wooden stops or molding, so much the better. Putty can be a real pain in the neck to remove, especially if it is many years old, baked in, and hard as a brick.

You will need to use a putty knife at least, and more likely a chisel and a small hammer. Just begin somewhere and start chipping away. Progress will probably be pretty slow at first, until you get a good 20 cm to 25 cm (about 10 inches) out. After that it may be a little easier to get extra leverage. If you are trying to save the glass, this task will necessarily be even more time-consuming than it would normally be, so your best bet is not to worry about the window glass.

An L-shaped device (although there are other shapes, too) is available to simplify this job. It has an asbestos base and a coil heating element. This is laid along the old putty and plugged in. The heat softens the putty and makes it a cinch to scrape away with a stiff putty knife. The fumes from this process are enough to gag you, though, so avoid breathing them directly.

After the putty is removed, look closely along the edges of the existing glass and remove the small glazing points that are holding the pane in. These are usually small pieces of metal with a point on one end. This point is pushed in under the glass to provide extra support. When you have found and removed these (there are usually two or three on each side of the pane), remove the old glass and clean away any excess putty or debris with a putty knife and a brush. Now you are ready for the moment of truth—will your panel fit or won't it?

Hold the panel and insert it into the opening. It should fit snugly, but you shouldn't have to force it in. There should ideally be 1.5 mm to 2 mm (1/16 inch) space around the edges of the panel. If it fits correctly, remove the panel to prepare for puttying it in. Never leave a panel sitting in the sash while you get your tools together, no matter how tight it seems to be. Too many times it has happened that somehow the panel falls out as soon as your back is turned. So remove it, place it out of harm's way, and then go about your business.

You will now need a can of wood sash putty, a hammer, glazing points (also called push points) or 2.5 cm brads, and a putty knife with a stiff blade.

First take a good handful of putty and knead it for a few minutes to soften it. Take half the putty and run a bead of putty along the bare edge of the sash, where you removed the putty from. Press it in well with the heel of your hand. Have a rag dampened with turpentine handy to wipe your hands after handling the putty.

Place the stained glass panel into the opening and make sure it is firmed up against the "bed" of putty you have laid. Place two glazing points for each of the four sides of the window, spacing them 10 to 15 cm (4 to 6 inches) from the corners. In larger window frames, of course, you will need more, spaced at regular intervals. You may also use the brads for this purpose, driving them in (carefully) with the hammer. The points or brads will hold the panel well enough while you get ready to putty the outside.

Soften the putty as before by kneading it in your hands. Start laying a small bead of putty along the outside border of the panel. Press the putty in well so that it fills any air pockets. After you have gotten this putty in, you can go back and add enough putty to make a good solid bead along all four edges. With the putty knife, smooth and bevel the putty to about the same angle that the old putty was. Figure 12-7 shows a cutaway view of how an installed panel will be positioned.

Another way to handle the last step of this operation (and preferred by some) is to set the panel in and apply a small amount of putty all the way around. After this, wood molding is set in and nailed to the sash. Miter the corners of the molding so that they meet smoothly.

Determining on which side of the window frame to work from in installing the window is somewhat a matter of choice. Inspect the panel in the frame from both sides before it is puttied. See which side the glass is set *against* and which side it is set *into*. In some cases it is more feasible to remove the molding (from the inside) and work inside than to work from the outside, especially if the window is, say, on the second story.

If you are removing the molding from the inside, be sure that the panel will be set against wood on the outside, not putty.

These instructions suffice if your initial measurements of the window frame and the panel were accurate and the stained glass fits in as if it were made for the opening (it was, of course). But what happens when you go to install the panel and it seems to be too big or too small for the hole? You might start by screaming. Then you are ready to rectify the problem

If the window is too big for the window frame, hopefully, it will be only slightly too big. This means no more than a couple of centimeters. This problem can usually be solved by trimming the border lead. You should figure out the total difference in size and trim a little from all four sides rather than trimming from only one of two sides. Of course, if the length fits but the width does not, the trimming will have to be divided equally for each of the two side widths.

This method will work only if you have used H or a Y lead came for your border. With a U lead there is nothing to trim away except the very heart of the lead, and you don't want to do that. If you have used a U lead and find that your window is too large, there is not much you can do except remove one side of the border and trim the glass itself.

Since window sashes are seldom truly square, you may find that the panel fits fine in all but a certain area. If the panel itself measures the correct size at this point, you can assume that the sash is what is not quite right. In this case, if the difference is very slight (and it usually is), you may be able to work the window in by using the blade of your putty knife for leverage. Do not apply any real muscle here, or you will probably end up with a cracked panel.

Another solution to this problem is to trim the lead at the point of difficulty. It should then slip in easily. Sometimes this can be achieved without any trimming at all. Simply tap along the lead with a hammer (very gently) or with the heavy end of your lead knife. Lead, being a soft and malleable metal, often flattens just enough to allow the panel to fit in.

If the window is too small and the difference in size is really great, there is not too much, unfortunately, that can be done about

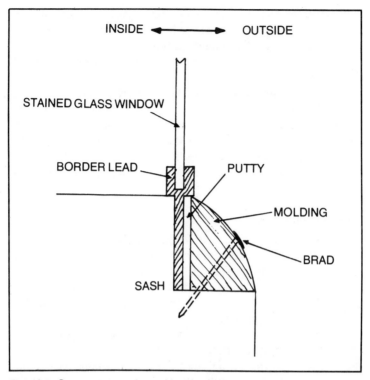

INSIDE ⟷ OUTSIDE

STAINED GLASS WINDOW

BORDER LEAD

PUTTY

MOLDING

BRAD

SASH

Fig. 12-7. Cutaway view of panel in wood sash.

it. If the difference is slight—a relative term, I know, but slight here means 6 to 12 cm (up to ½ inch), seldom more—you may be able to shim the window so that it fits the opening well enough. Shims are small pieces of wood or shaved wood that are used to lift the panel up a little from the bottom of the sash and to square it off. They are placed after the first small bead of putty is laid and the window set it.

Don't try to install an impossibly small panel in this manner. It will end up looking bad. The border lead of the window should still extend at least halfway, and hopefully farther, beyond the actual window opening, into the sash itself. If the panel is just too small, you will need to either recut the border pieces to enlarge the panel or, if the design will allow it, add a small border to the panel.

Before you remove the old glass in the window, it is a good idea to remeasure everything: the window that you will be installing and the existing sash. If your window is too small or too large, you will, in this manner, be able to anticipate the problems that may arise. If there is a drastic difference, you will not have removed putty and glass only to have to put it back in again while you make adjustments in the stained glass piece. If in doubt, measure!

After you have installed the panel, you will have to clean it once again to remove putty prints. The putty itself has a tendency to ooze along the edges of the window inside, especially if it is installed in very warm weather. Note this fact and check the panel periodically. Scrape off the putty when it appears. This should stop after four or five days if you have a problem with it at all. The outside putty usually sets up hard in a few days to a week—check the instructions on the putty can. After this, it can be painted if so desired.

Metal-Sash Installation

Metal is more rigid than wood and allows for very little leeway. To install a window in a metal sash, first remove the metal stops by unscrewing them. If you cannot see any screws, the stops are most likely of the spring or snap-on variety, and these can be removed as you remove the old putty. Use a screwdriver or similar tool to take these types of stops out.

As with installing a panel in a wood window frame, first size it against the opening by setting it in. Adjust the fit if necessary with shims to fit a too-small panel, for too-large by trimming the lead.

Run a bead of putty around the frame. Silicon sealer may also be used for this. Now set the panel in and if the frames uses snap-on clips, put the clips back in their holes.

Another bead of putty is applied around the leaded panel after it is set in place. Use the putty knife to smooth the putty firmly and to even it out. If metal stops were used to hold the window in place, these should now be replaced in the frame. Whether the sash uses clip springs or screws, clean away the excess putty after installation, wash your hands, and then clean the window with glass cleaner.

Semipermanent Installations

It is also possible to install a panel over an existing window pane without removing the old window or putty. This is a handy technique, especially if you rent your house and would like to take your work with you whenever you move.

The panel is installed from the inside; therefore, no putty or sealant is needed. The glass that is already in the window will provide the necessary weatherproofing.

To install the window in this manner, make two wooden frames from square molding to fit inside the sash. Miter the corners of each frame and be sure that they meet snugly. Nail one frame into the window frame with 2.5 cm brads. Insert your leaded glass panel into the opening and fit it so that it is firm against the wooden frame you have just put in. Fit the second wooden frame over the leaded panel. Nail this frame in with brads, so that you have wooden frame, the glass panel, and then another wooden frame.

Installing leaded glass over an existing window pane, or alternatively installing clear glass against the leaded glass after it is in place, is always good idea. Many stained glass shops recommend this method of installation. The clear glass keeps out dirt so the stained glass work does not need to be cleaned so often, and, of course, the clear glass can be cleaned easily. It also serves to deflect small twigs and stones that could damage or crack your work. It is much simpler and cheaper to replace a broken window pane than to repair a stained glass window that has been damaged. If you choose to install your panel in this way, consider using heavy plate glass instead of window glass. It will cost a little more, initially, but will be worth it in terms of protection and easy care for your stained glass. Plate glass can be bought and cut to size at any regular glass supplier.

OTHER INSTALLATIONS

The methods described above are the most traditional and widely used ways of showing off stained glass. There are countless other methods, however, and using your ingenuity, you may be able to devise even more.

A lightbox or shadow box has gained popularity with those who wish to display their glass in a totally different way. This works on much the same idea as the light table, discussed in Chapter 5, except that it is smaller, designed to be hung on a wall, and the stained glass panel is attached to it.

The simplest form is a box that is the same size as or slightly larger than your panel. It is lit with fluorescent tube lights that are recessed into the frame. The lights must be fitted with some kind of reflective material, such as tinfoil. The backing of the light box is attached by screws instead of nails so that you can change the bulbs without tearing the box apart.

Lightboxes for this purpose are not too expensive, either to make or to have made for you. They provide an interesting alternative to the usual methods of display and have the added advantage of being able to be hung anywhere there is an electrical outlet, as they provide their own light source.

A very small one, perhaps 10 cm by 10 cm would be a delightful change from the traditional nightlight, and both the glass piece and the box could be constructed from scraps. For something of this size, you could even use a small incandescent lamp such as a refrigerator bulb. Normally, incandescent light creates "hot spots," or areas of very high and disturbing glare. In this case, all you can see is the bare lightbulb glowing through, especially if the glass is antique or transparent.

Because light bulbs show through antique and transparent glass opalescent glass is usually used. This type of glass will also show color when not lit, something not possible with the antique glasses, which usually appear black or very dark without light to give them life.

Room dividers of stained glass are also a new way to display your work. These can be installed as a permanent part of the room (the best way), or smaller folding screens can serve as frames for stained glass. Placed where they will allow some light to pass through, this method can be a breathtaking sight.

Fire screens are sometimes made from stained glass, although it is probably wisest to place a specially treated glass fire screen. They will not obstruct the stained glass, and will protect it from the heat of the fire.

Small free-form pieces and little glass objects known as suncatchers can be hung in a sunny window. French windows with a suncatcher hung in each pane are especially pretty. These small pieces can be fashioned from any scrap glass that is lying around and hung by means of a copper ring.

Stained glass can be incorporated into so many forms of display that there is literally no end to the list. Stained glass lampshades are popular and most loved, but how about a stained glass votive holder or patio lantern? Use your imagination to show off your work. No doubt you will come up with some original ideas of your own.

Chapter 13
Safety

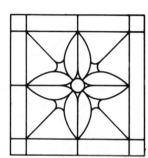

Although potential hazards involved in glass crafting have been noted throughout, I feel it best to include a summary of what has already been stated and to add some others. So many people fear working with glass and lead and often ask many questions about the correct handling of these materials. Following are some of the most frequently asked questions (with answers to provide you with an easy reference on safety.

GLASS

I have seen many students who devoutly wished to learn how to make stained glass windows, yet harbored almost paranoid fears about glass. We were all brought up to respect its razor-sharp edges and jagged points, not to mention its fragility, but those ideas must be somewhat set aside for glassworking. Correct handling and storage will remove most of the dangers. There is always the fluke occurrence, but *you* should at least be out of harm's way if the measures given below are followed.

1. Store glass upright, on its edge, and out of the way of feet or household pedestrians. Glass bins for this purpose are described in Chapter 4. They should never be positioned so that you have to climb or reach over your head to get to the glass. If the edges of the glass protrude beyond the bin, cover them with some sort of padding.

2. When carrying glass, always hold it by its edges and to the side of your body. Do not carry it in front of you, or tucked under your arm, and under no circumstances should you carry it above your head.

3. Don't stack odd-sized pieces of glass on top of each other on your work table, or anywhere else for that matter. It's not a very stable arrangement.

4. Don't run your hands or fingers along the edges of glass. This is a sure way to get cut.

5. Scrounging around in scrap bins can be fun. If you're trying to get to a piece you've spotted down below, however, remove the glass on top of it instead of trying to reach in and pull it out.

6. It is best not to work with glass, either cutting it or storing it, in carpeted areas. Small slivers do occur (lots of them), no matter how contained you think you are, and they are next to impossible to get out of rugs. If you have no other area in which to work, cover the entire carpeted floor surface with a tarp or drop cloth, and be careful. When you pick it up be careful to shake out any glass slivers that have accumulated.

7. Needless to say (I hope), you should always wear shoes around glass.

8. Keep your work table free of slivers and chips while cutting glass by frequently sweeping it off with a bench brush or small wiskbroom. This will not only keep those chips out of your hands, but will keep them away from your glass and eliminate the possibility of your good glass getting scratched or broken by them. Never brush off the work surface with your hands, for obvious (but apparently not obvious enough) reasons. It's also a good idea not to lean on the table where you are cutting your glass.

9. If you do happen to get a sliver (and you will know it right away), remove it by hand if it is big enough, or use tweezers if it isn't. Often these small punctures and tiny cuts seem to bleed more than a fair-size cut, so have a box of bandages at hand as part of your regular tool supply.

10. Glass in the eye is one of the most common scares, and it does happen. Don't panic. Hold the lid it is under away from your eye until you can get to a mirror. By that time the piece should have washed down to the lower lid where it can be removed with a pointed twist of toilet tissue or a cotton swab stick. Colored glass, at least, can be seen more easily than clear glass. Usually, the glass is easy to remove. If you remove it and are bothered by pain or strange sensations, see a doctor. I've had many bits of glass in my eyes and never has it developed into anything. It takes a few seconds to remove the piece, and I'm back to work. Safety glasses, or even regular eyeglasses, provide adequate protection from this hazard under normal working conditions.

11. Gloves are not really necessary, but you will find a few people who insist on wearing them (very few, I suspect). Amateurs and professionals alike for the most part find them bulky and awkward. They do not allow much manual dexterity and thus are likely to cause at least as many accidents as they prevent, and very likely more. If they are worn at all, it is usually for handling large sheets of glass, which the beginning student will probably not be involved with for a while.

12. For the last work of warning concerning glass, I must say that, all else aside, you should *expect* a few cuts and scrapes. Rare is the scratchproof glass worker. In spite of the warnings I give to my students, most of them inevitably show up with an occasional bandage wrapped around their fingers, waving as both a battle scar and a flesh-colored flag of victory.

This does not mean that you are to become one of the walking wounded. It simply means that some days are better than others, and small accidents do occur from time to time. Have your first-aid supplies handy, follow the correct procedures for handling glass, and may your glass always break where (and when) it's supposed to.

LEADING AND SOLDERING

The prospects of lead poisoning appeal to no one, and occasionally a flurry of concern arises in connection with leaded glass work and this possibility. While it is not beyond the stretch of the imagination, such voluminous amounts of lead fumes would have to be inhaled that even professional studios doing a great deal of soldering pay the matter scant attention. Detailed tests and surveys have been done in very large professional studios. These tests proved the dangers to be practically nonexistent as long as the following simple and proper procedures were followed.

1. Work in a well ventilated area.

2. Avoid "hanging" over the iron while soldering as much as possible. If you do not, the fumes have nowhere else to go but into your face.

3. Wash your hands after you have handled lead, and particularly before you eat, drink, or smoke. You probably have a better chance of contracting lead poisoning by ignoring this step by than breathing fumes.

4. Always use a stand for your hot soldering iron.

5. Keep electrical cords and extensions out of your way as much as possible to alleviate the chance of your tripping over them.

When you are finished soldering, place the cord on the table rather than leaving it dangling. Put all extension cords away.

6. Always look before you reach for a hot iron. Grabbing it by the shaft instead of the handle will be an experience you will never forget.

7. Leading knives are very sharp—treat them with the same deference you would any other knife.

CHEMICALS AND FLUXES

There is not too much to say about these except that all fluxes and chemicals used in stained glass work should be stored on a high shelf where children cannot reach them. Clearly label the contents of all chemicals and fluxes.

Don't store them near heat. Oleic acid is the one exception here. While it should not be *stored* near heat, it tends to separate if it gets too cold. This does not usually happen; but if it should, warm the bottle slightly and mix or shake it until it combines properly again. It can then be used as effectively as ever.

FATIGUE

One safety precaution often overlooked is guarding against fatigue by breaks during your work. Aha, you're probably saying, sheer laziness masquerading as a safety precaution. Not so. Few aspects of glassworking can be done "automatically"; glass cutting, especially, requires a great deal of concentration on relatively small areas. You will find it immensely helpful to take a short break every so often as you are cutting or leading. It gives you a chance to set down for a few minutes (since most of the work must be performed standing up) and will give you a fresher perspective when you return.

If you are having a real problem cutting a particular piece, this is especially advisable. To keep trying after four or five unsuccessful attempts can be very frustrating, especially to the beginner. You will end up ruining more glass and getting more frustrated and upset. Either take a short break or go on to another piece and save the "toughie" for later.

Everyone has bad days. You know them right away, as soon as you begin glass cutting and go through a couple of hundred square centimeters of glass without getting one usable piece. Do not work when you are very tired and very crabby, unless this sort of thing does not get to you, which is hard to imagine. Not only will your work tend to be sloppy, but you are also more prone to carelessness, and hence accidents.

Chapter 14
Questions
and Answers

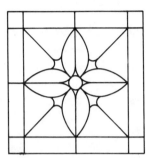

I am often confronted with numerous questions to which answers cannot be found in any book. This chapter presents some of the most common questions asked along with other bits of information and advice that don't seem to fit appropriately in any one category. The questions are broken down first into those that apply to each specific aspect of the craft, and then those that are rather general.

Q. *What is the proper way to number a pattern?*

A. There is no "proper" way. Numbering serves only to correlate the paper pattern pieces to the glass, and later shows where the glass is to be placed in your leaded design. It has no relation to the order in which glass pieces are set; i.e., piece No. 2 would not necessarily be set in after piece No. 1. You could just as easily use any other code, such as A, B, and C, or even symbols. Numbering happens to be best because there is an infinite supply of numbers, and it is a simple system of coding.

Q. *My pattern shears seem to ruin the pattern. They fray the paper along the edges. What's wrong?*

A. You are probably cutting with the entire blade. Take *short cuts* (not *shortcuts*), using the back part of the blades, rather than long cuts using the entire blades. Make sure that the paper is not clogged up between the blades, as this can also produce such a problem.

Q. *What's a good beginning project?*

A. Something very simple. You need not try for beauty in the very first design. Pick something smaller than 30 cm by 30 cm

(about 1 foot square) and use clear window glass. A good rule ⸀
thumb is to begin with a design that contains a few straight lines ᴀɴᴅ
a couple of gentle curves, about four to six pieces in all. This will be
inexpensive and should not take more than three or four hours from
start to finish. It will, at the same time, teach you the basic steps of
leaded-glass construction, and you will in turn have more confidence as you progress to bigger and better things.

GLASS CUTTING

Q. *I'm using a metal-handled cutter, but I can not seem to get a
good hold on it. My hand slips. Any suggestions?*

A. If you are using a No. 2 cutter try a Diamantor. The wooden
handle on these cutters affords a better grip. If you are using a
Fletcher No. 7 or No. 9, try wrapping the handle with masking
tape.

Q. *Should I push the cutter away from me or draw it back toward
me when I cut glass?*

A. You will find it easiest to push the cutter away from you
when you are cutting to a pattern, and to draw it toward you if you
are cutting straight lines.

Q. *How far from the edge of the glass do I begin the score? How
far at the end of the score?*

A. Start your score line about 3 mm (⅛ inch) from the glass
edge—less if you can do it without chipping the glass by applying
too much pressure. You should end the score at the edge of the
glass or as close to it as you can come. Keep in mind, however, that
this takes practice and control. In the beginning, it is permissible to
allow the cutter to run off the edge of the glass. Make sure you are
cutting on a padded surface, as described in Chapter 5.

Q. *Does it hurt the cutter to go off the edge of the glass?*

A. Yes, it does. If it happens too frequently or if it hits the
cutting surface hard, it will put flat spots and nicks in the wheel.
Once you have had a little practice throw away the cutter you used
for your first projects; it will, no doubt, have been niched.

Q. *How long will a glass cutter last? How can you tell when it's
no longer good.*

A. The length of time a cutter lasts depends on several
variables: the amount of damage to the cutter, whether or not it
was used properly, and simply the passage time. Generally, one
glass cutter, if used correctly and kept well lubricated, should last
you through three or four projects. This means that it was used to
cut the right glass for its intended purpose, was not dropped or

banged around, and was not used to go over score lines more than once. If you have doubts about its cutting ability, do not hesitate to replace the cutter. You can compare the way your cutter cuts to the way a new cutter does, on the same type of glass and the same kind of cut. If there is a marked difference in the cuts made, throw the old cutter away. If you are losing quite a few cuts that should otherwise break, it is best to replace the cutter. They are so cheap that it does not make sense not to.

Q. *I think I missed some spots on my score. Can I just go over the line again?*

A. Never, never, never! This will ruin the cutter in one whack, and you probably will not get the piece anyway. If you can see the place you have missed and it is fairly large, you may go back and score the piece in that place only.

Another alternative is to turn the glass over and make the same cut in the same place, but on the other side of the glass. Obviously this will only work on glass that is smooth on both sides, such as antique and clear window glass. Do not try this on cathedral or opalescent glass. Once you have made this score, break the piece out. It's generally better to simply recut the piece or fill in the spaces that weren't scored than to rely on this method.

Q. *My glass won't break on the score line. I can barely see the score, either. What's happening?*

A. From your description, you probably are not applying enough pressure to the cutter. You need a firm pressure; just as important, the pressure must be steady all the way across (not intermittently light and heavy).

It is also possible that you are not using the correct cutter for the type of glass you are cutting. This problem usually occurs with opalescent glass, which is one of the hardest (in terms of density, not cutting ease) to cut. You should use a Fletcher No 7 or No. 9 for straight lines and gentle curves. Be sure that you oil the cutter before each score.

Q. *Why can't I just buy a No. 9 and use it on the softer glasses too, instead of having different cutters?*

A. Because Nos. 7 and 9 have harder steel wheels than those designed for the soft glasses (No. 2 and Diamantor), they should be used only for the hard glasses. Using them on softer glass will result in too deep of a score line, which will have the same effect as one not deep enough, with the result that the piece will probably not break on the score.

Q. *Are carbide cutters good? Can't you use them on all types of glass?*

A. Carbide cutters are good, and they can be used for all the glasses. Their normal lifespan is about six times that of a regular cutter. What you must realize, though, is that while you can cut any kind of glass with a carbide cutter, the pressures you use will be distinctly different. You would not use the same amount of pressure to cut an antique glass (soft) that you would use on an opalescent (hard). It takes time to master these different pressures. Beginning students usually start off with either too much or too little pressure, and use the same amount consistently without regard to what kind of glass they are using. It is important to learn how and when to apply more or less pressure.

Q. *I've gone through a full meter of opalescent glass without getting the piece I wanted. My friend says that opalescent glass is very difficult to cut. Is it, or am I doing something wrong?*

A. There could be a number of solutions to your problem. First check the size (number) of the cutter you are using and whether you are applying enough pressure to get a good score line. Can you see the score? Do you hear it being made? Are there skips in it where the cutter did not score? Opalescent glass is generally a bit tougher than the other glasses, but it should not give you this much of a problem. For the most part, cutting opalescents ranges from easy to difficult, the latter being representative of only a handful of these glasses.

Q. *Is glass with a texture on one side, such as opalescent ripple-back, harder to cut? Does the ripple control the way in which the glass will break?*

A. No to both questions.

Q. *When I make a score, little chips of glass pop off of the line. Also, the glass does not always break the way I wanted it to. What's wrong?*

A. You are using too much pressure, which causes the score line to be too deep. Ease up a little.

Q. *I made a score on a piece of glass and the glass popped apart by itself. What happened?*

A. Some glasses are not cooled properly during the annealing process. This sets up tensions in the glass. Then, when a score is made, the stress causes the glass to separate by itself with a little pinging noise. Sometimes it breaks along the score line, but often it runs across the entire sheet.

Q. *I had to do a lot of grozing on the glass for my first project. Consequently, I took out some rather large chips. Will these show in the finished work?*

A. Unfortunately, they will if the lead does not cover them. Don't attempt to really "bite" when you groze; just take small "nibbles." Any chips along the edges will show up as dark spots in the window, regardless of the color of the glass.

Q. *Will it make a difference if the piece of glass is just a little bit bigger than the pattern?*

A. If the glass is just a little bit bigger, why not groze the little bit away, so that the piece is the right size? It *will* make a difference when the pieces are being put together, especially if the other pieces are, likewise, just a little bit bigger.

Q. *Is there any way I can smooth the edges down without using the grozing pliers?*

A. For very small bits and slivers that you sometimes have along the glass edge, a carborundum stone works well, although it should not be used in place of grozing. Move the stone along the glass at a slight angle in one direction only, never "scrub" straight back and forth. Do this gently, and do not drag the stone back toward yourself.

Q. *Is a grinding wheel a good thing to have for glass work?*

A. A small electric grinding wheel is manufactured expressly for use in stained glass, although it is not really necessary for making flat panels and windows. It finds its place more in Tiffany-style lamp-making, where sometimes hundreds of pieces must be cut and where exactness is most essential. They are not particularly expensive, but you should not need them.

Grinding wheels, belts, and sanders are sometimes used as a substitute for accurate cutting. Do not let yourself fall into this habit. The same goes for excessive grozing. By the time you have finished one or two fairsized projects, you should be fairly accurate with cutting and should not need to do a lot of grozing.

Q. *I have trouble holding the pattern still on the glass while I cut around it. What can help?*

A. Mostly time and practice. You might try some of that stick glue that you buy in the five-and-dime. This has an advantage over tape, which seems to make the glass slightly bigger all around when it's cut. If you use glue, of course, you will have extra cleanup work to do. Do practice cutting to a pattern without such aids. In the long run, it will save you a lot of time.

LEADING

Q. *What kind of border lead should I use for a small piece that is to be hung in a window?*

A. The best lead would be a U-shaped border. This has only one channel and the other side presents a flat face. The 6 mm (¼ inch) size is most commonly used, although it is by no means the only one available. For a neater appearance, miter (cut at a 45-degree angle) the corners where the leads meet instead of butt-joining them.

Q. *When is the Y-shaped border used?*

A. Y-shaped lead may be used in place of U lead in a free-hanging piece, although it is more commonly used in panels that are to be installed in metal or wood window sashes. It is also used for panels that are framed. The "tail" of the Y is hidden by the wood molding or putty and only the face is then exposed.

Q. *What is the best way to lead a glass border around a panel? Should I cut the length of the border in lead?*

A. The best way to get a uniformly sized border (one that does not undulate, but is straight as it should be) is to cut the long piece of lead that is to hold the border in. This is illustrated in 14-1. Cut the smaller pieces that form the breaks in the border as you set each piece of glass in. It is important to strive for the straightest lines possible on borders and similar areas. Crooked, irregular, or bumpy, bulging lead lines in borders especially are most noticeable and disturbing.

Q. *How much shorter than the glass should I cut each lead?*

A. This will vary depending on what size lead you are using. You must cut the lead short enough so that the lead running by it is firmly against the glass, but not so short that you have a gap between the leads. For instance, if you are using a 6 mm lead, you would cut the piece about 3 mm or so shorter than the edge of the glass. Do not overlook this factor. If you do not cut the leads short enough, the next piece of glass and lead will not seat properly. This not only looks sloppy, but it makes the panel weaker, and probably bigger somewhere.

Q. *My first panel came out square, but it also gained about 2 cm. What happened?*

A. You are lucky that it at least came out square. Since it was your first project, I can only guess that your glass cutting is the culprit. Other possibilities are that the glass was not seated properly in the lead. This must be done after each glass piece is set in. Be sure also that the glass is really in the channel and not hanging up on the underside of the lead.

Unless the piece was meant to go into an existing opening or a frame that has already been made to its smaller, original dimen-

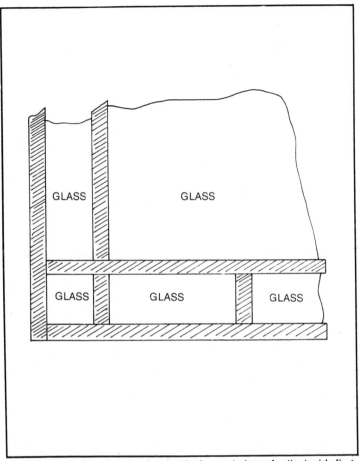

Fig. 14-1. To lead a glass border, cut the longest pieces for the inside first. Then cut and fit the shorter leads.

sions, I would say to leave it as it is. Concentrate on accurate cutting and take the time to groze down any edges that do not match up to the pattern. Be sure that the pieces are tight in the channel when you lead them in.

If you must make the panel smaller, you can do so by removing one of the border leads and trimming the pieces of glass off as much as is needed. How to do this is explained in Chapter 19.

Q. *How can I keep my lead from twisting?*

A. A good way is to begin with straight lead. After you have stretched it, run a lathekin along the channels to open them up and straighten out the lead. Then, before you actually use the lead, run the lathekin through it again. This will eliminate any noticeable bends.

Q. *How is lead measured, and does the size of the channel itself vary?*

A. Lead is measured across the top or "face." See the explanation given in Chapter 2. The channel of the lead does not usually vary significantly in size. The standard size is 3 mm (⅛ inch) since this is also the standard glass thickness. There are specialty leads available with "high hearts" and with wider channels to accommodate a thick glass and with narrower channels. Again, for the most part, these are specialty leads and are used mostly in professional studios for jobs requiring such leads. The lead generally sold in stained-glass shops will be of the standard channel width.

SOLDERING

Q. *My solder joints are bumpy and sharp. What am I doing wrong?*

A. The most likely source of your problem is that the iron is too cold. Let it heat up a little more.

Q. *Is there any way to fix those kinds of joints so they don't look so ragged?*

A. Quite easily, as a matter of fact. Let your iron heat to the proper soldering temperature. Set the tip of the iron down on the lumpy joint for a second or two and then pick the iron up. The joint should have smoothed out under the correct heat. Do not apply more solder during this process; you don't want a big joint, just a neat one.

Q. *I know my iron is too hot because I've burned up a few leads. How can I tell if it's this hot before I burn the leads?*

A. This takes a bit of feel for the soldering process, which I assure you will come with a little more time and practice. For now, however, test the iron as it is heating up on a piece of scrap lead by touching the solder to the tip. As soon as the solder melts easily, you are ready to solder. Once you begin soldering, keep going. Go from one joint to the next without too much hesitation. Test the heat of the iron periodically on a piece of scrap lead. If it begins to melt lead, unplug the iron, but keep on soldering until the iron noticeably cools. Don't fuss too long over one joint. If you cannot seem to get it right, go on to the next and come back to the skipped one later.

Q. *My soldering iron seems slow to heat up and sluggish when soldering. Is the iron going bad? I just bought it.*

170

A. While the iron could be defective, this is not too likely. There are a few other things you check first before replacing the iron. Check the tip of the iron. A frequent cause of this problem is a dirty or corroded tip. Remember to wipe the iron on a damp sponge frequently as you solder. This removes grime and oxides that hamper its effectiveness.

If there are pits or uneven spots on the tip, file and retin the tip before further soldering. This alone often makes a vast improvement in a soldering iron's ability.

If the problem persists, check to see that the tip is tightly seated in the shaft of the iron and that the setscrew is not loose. Tighten it with a small screwdriver if necessary. Also check the small screws on the handle of the iron.

If you have done all this and the iron is still not performing adequately, take it back to the dealer you bought it from and ask him to repair or replace it.

Q. *My solder doesn't flow on the lead joints; in fact, it barely sticks to them. I end up with little globs instead of flat joints.*

A. This is probably happening because you have not fluxed the joints before soldering. Solder will not adhere to joints that have not been properly fluxed. Many students forget this step, as elementary as it is. If this is the problem, apply the flux to the globs you already have and set the iron down on them. This will usually be sufficient to flatten them out some. Do not use more solder.

If you have fluxed the joints and the problem persists, you most likely have a buildup of oxidation and residue on the leads. This will have to be removed before flux and solder are used. Scrub each joint with a small wire brush, apply flux immediately, and solder.

Q. *I have heard about filing solder joints. What is this and why is it done?*

A. Filing a solder joint is just as it sounds: the solder joints are filed down. This is done mostly when the soldering itself was not done properly, usually with a too-cold iron. If you master the soldering technique as described in previous chapters, you should not need to file joints.

Q. *How much chance is there of cracking a piece of glass during soldering?*

A. Not all that much, actually. In soldering lead, the iron never comes in direct contact with the glass. Neither does so much heat accumulate at one spot that this becomes a major risk. Naturally, you should be careful, but it is not a common occurrence.

171

Q. *Is there any way to take solder off once it's on? I think I used too much.*

A. The best way around this is not to use so much, of course. For an average-size lead joint, you really should not need more than about 3 to 6 mm (⅛ to ¼ inch) of wire solder. Bigger is not better in soldering.

To remove extra solder, about the only thing you can do is try to "flick" the solder off of the joint. This is done by dragging the iron across the solder until you have got a little blob of it to one side of the joint. Then, with an up-and-out movement, lift the solder off of the joint and with the iron flick it off the tip. Aim at the floor, not the surroundings.

Q. *If solder gets on the glass, will the glass break?*

A. Usually not, but solder should not be allowed to get on the glass in large blobs. Small pieces are inevitable, and these can be picked or scraped off when you are cleaning the finished work.

Chapter 15
Copper-Foil
Technique

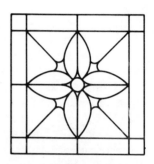

There are two commonly used methods of holding glass together in a stained-glass work. One method, leading of glass has already been discussed at length; other method is called copper foiling.

In the copper-foil technique the glass is cut to a pattern; the edges of each piece are wrapped with copper foil. The wrapped pieces are laid next to each other and soldered together.

It is thought by some that Tiffany devised this technique in his search for a lighter and stronger method of building his now priceless lampshades. Others credit the invention to John La Farge, Tiffany's contemporary, and still others believe that its use was practiced in a cruder form long before either of these two men discovered and used the technique. Whoever the credit belongs to, there is no doubt that the copper-foil method of glass working has opened more doors to creativity and stretched many of the limits imposed by leading.

Using the copper-foil technique can be advantageous because of its lightness, in terms of both physical weight and appearance. A delicate line can be achieved readily in copper foil without diminishing the piece's strength. When it is done properly, the stained glass is actually stronger than an exact copy that has been leaded with came. It is also ideal for small pieces of glass, as it looks lighter, more delicate than lead came and is easier to handle during construction. Small glass pieces leaded with came would most likely be obliterated by the heavier lead line.

It does, however, have drawbacks. For one thing it is very time-consuming to wrap each piece of glass with foil. Glass cutting is another problem: it must be exact. It is most important that the pieces fit together tightly and without gaps, for any mistakes made will show in the finished product and could conceivably also alter the dimensions of the piece. There is no came to overlap the edges and conceal defects.

A great deal of solder is also required—far more than with lead came. This is not as insignificant a consideration as it might seem when you consider that the price of solder is about $14 per kilogram ($7 per pound) and rising. An average lampshade could take as much as 2 kilograms of solder!

I am often asked which is more difficult, leading or copper foiling. Even though there are those who will assure you that one or the other is easier, I personally feel that it is more of a question of the individual's preference and the amount of effort he or she is willing to exert. Both methods are relatively simple processes. Both look equally dismal when done poorly, just as both look good with good craftsmanship. Copper foiling, as I've said, requires more care and patience in cutting glass and more time in construction.

Try both. You will probably want to anyway. You will quickly see for yourself the advantages and disadvantages of each method. You will also more than likely quickly develop your own preference for one technique over the other. This is fine, for at least you will have knowledge of both and may want to choose between the two for different projects.

For some reason copper coiling is usually given sketchy mention in how-to books, but there is really quite a bit to know about it and its uses and techniques.

MATERIALS

Beginners often start with the copper-foil method because for simple projects they can get started with a minimum of supplies. There is no glazing to be done so the small cost and messiness of that job is eliminated.

If you are planning to do it right, however, you should invest in most of the tools and materials needed for leading, as well as a few additional ones. Following is a list of specific materials required for copper-foil work.

For Pattern Making
pattern paper
cartoon paper
pattern shears for copper foil

For Preparation
glass cutters
cutting oil
glass pliers
grozing pliers
Carborundum file (optional)
For Assembly
copper foil
leading nails
work board or table
small Popsicle stick
For Soldering
50/50 or 60/40 solid-core wire solder
soldering iron
soldering flux for copper foil
patina (optional)

As you can see, you will need much the same tools for cutting and soldering though some are different and deserve special mentions.

Pattern shears are necessary for copper foil work, just as they are for leading; however, since the glass pieces, when wrapped with foil, are to meet flush against each other, there is naturally a much smaller gap between the abutted pieces than that allowed for the lead heart. The size of this allowance in copper-foil work sounds almost minute—1mm (1/32 inch)—but, as with leading, it does add up and must be accounted for. If you are only planning to do small things, such as suncatchers to hang in your window, use regular scissors and you may forgo the use of pattern shears, but for small window like and larger panels use pattern shears specially made for copper-foil work. They cost the same as lead shears: the best imported ones are about $20; the lesser-quality Korean shears are about half that price.

Copper foil is thin tape with an adhesive backing that adheres it to the glass. It is sold in rolls containing, on the average, 30 to 35 meters. Since it is used in many different capacities, it comes in a variety of widths. The thinnest is 5 mm (3/16 inch), which is thin indeed and barely covers the edge of the glass. The largest size generally available is about 2.5 cm (1 inch), although even wider foil may be special-ordered. The same most commonly used size is 6 mm (¼ inch) as it overlaps the glass edge sufficiently, but not so much that it looks bulky, and it is fairly easy to work with. A roll of

6-mm foil will cost about $4, which is not bad since it goes a long way.

Because copper oxidizes, the foil is sold in a plastic bag and should be returned to the bag after each use. Make sure the bag is tied or closed in some manner to keep air out and reduce oxidation, which will make soldering more difficult.

Copper foil is also sold in sheet form for filigree and other decorative work, as well as for those who wish to cut their own strips. Hand cutting sheets into strips is a tedious operation, but the sheets are valuable for making odd sizes and shapes.

Popsicle sticks are used to rub or burnish the foil tightly along the glass edge. Indeed, there are special tools made for this purpose. The most common is a *fid*, a cone-shaped piece of wood with a rounded top about the size of the lathekin used in leading. If you want to buy one of these, fine, but Popsicle sticks work very well, I've found, as do lathekins and other pieces of smooth wood. Really, you can use just about anything as long as it has a smooth surface.

Copper-foil flux has more of an acid-base than the oleic acid used for lead. Unfortunately, it is not widely sold, and you may have to make your own. Combine one part hydrochloric acid to seven parts glycerine. Mix well and store in plastic jars or jugs.

An alternative flux can be made by mixing 75 ml (2 ½ ounces) zinc chloride, 30 ml (1 ounce) ammonium chloride, and 180 ml (6 ounces) water. If you want to apply a patina or copper sulfate to the soldered areas, you must clean this flux off well or it will change the coloring of the solder.

Oleic acid is often used for copper-foil work, but although it works, it does not remove oxidation from the copper foil, as does the acid flux upon application. This means that with oleic acid the solder will not flow properly or as well, and the solder will tend to skip over areas of heavier oxidation. If you can not find a place to buy copper-foil flux, make some. You will get much better results.

PATTERN MAKING

The pattern for a foil project is made and drawn up just as it is for leaded work. Make three copies—the working drawing, the cartoon itself, and the pattern. Number each piece on all three copies in the same manner followed for leading.

Then lay the cartoon and working copy aside and cut out the pattern with copper-foil pattern shears. Cut directly down the center of the line.

GLASS CUTTING

Although there are no truly different techniques involved in cutting glass for copper foiling, it is of utmost importance that accuracy be maintained and that the glass edges are as smooth as possible. Any gaps between the pieces will be filled with solder, so it looks much better if there are as few gaps as possible. In addition, the entire panel will grow, just as in leading, if the pieces are slightly larger than the pattern.

Cut the glass exactly to the pattern piece. Check it on all sides agains the pattern to make certain that the glass does not hang over the edge of the paper and that the paper does not extend beyond the glass. All pieces should be checked in this way. Remove any overhanging glass by grozing. If the piece is too small, recut it. In foiling, there is not much room for error.

Because the foil adheres right to the edge of the glass, it will also conform to the contour of that edge. If you have done quite a bit of grozing, the rough edge will be more difficult to foil. Any pieces with large chips or very ragged edges should be recut.

A handy tool to have, while not absolutely necessary, is a Carborundum file. This is a lightweight stone file about 20 to 25 cm (8 to 10 inches) long. Its use is covered in Chapter 4. Carborundum stones are excellent for smoothing rough glass edges and removing stubborn glass bits that will not yield to grozing pliers.

Cut all of your glass before you begin foiling. Lay the pieces out on the working copy. As the pieces lie next to each other, you can get a pretty good idea of how they will fit after they have been foiled, for the gap between them at this stage is not as large as it is when laying out a panel to be leaded up.

FOILING THE GLASS

Wrapping glass in foil can be rather pleasant; it is somewhat similar to knitting and crocheting in that you can take glass pieces and foil anywhere and do it anywhere—with a minimum of fuss. It is not a very messy activity, and you can even (after some practice) foil, watch television, and chew gum all at the same time.

Naturally, the first time you wrap glass you will want to pay rather close attention to what you are doing, but it's easy to get the hang of it. All you will need is the glass, the foil, and your Popsicle stick.

Clean each piece of glass before you begin foiling. This is most important. Because you used oil in cutting the glass, the edges still retain oil residue, despite the fact that you may not see or feel it. Do not settle for a quick wipe with a dry cloth; use glass cleaner and do a good, thorough job. It will make a noticeable difference in how well your copper-foil tape adheres to the glass.

Begin foiling by peeling back a little of the protective covering from the back of the foil. This will expose the adhesive side of the foil tape. Holding the glass piece in one hand, press the tape along one of its edges (Fig. 15-1). The glass edge should be positioned in the center of the tape. The tape should overhang equally on both sides of the glass edge. The two cut edges of the foil should also be aligned. This is a most important point. If the glass is not centered on the tape and one edge of tape overlaps the glass more than the other, the final leaded line will be bulkier, and noticeably so, on one side, especially if it is the only one out of whack.

It should stick firmly. From this point, simply rotate the piece in your hand, continue pressing the tape around all edges. When you get back to the starting point, overlap the tape about 6 mm or so

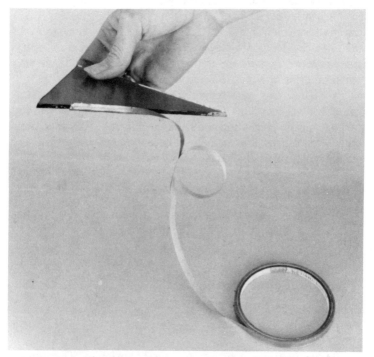

Fig. 15-1. To wrap the glass with foil, hold the glass in one hand, press the tape along the glass's edge. It should stick firmly.

Fig. 15-2. The wrapped glass. The foil has been burnished firmly against the glass's surface.

(¼ inch). Then tear or cut off the tape from the roll. Do not peel the covering off more than about 3 to 5 cm (an inch or two) of tape at a time. It is easy to pull it away as you work and will result in a lot less tangles and crimps.

Once the tape has been wrapped completely around all exposed edges of the glass, begin pressing it down tightly over the top and bottom of each side of the glass. The best tool for this is your very own fingers; just run them along the tape overhang, pressing it to the glass as you go.

Once the piece is wrapped (Fig. 15-2), the next step is to burnish it to secure it tightly to the glass. First burnish the outside edge with the Popsicle stick. Get this firmly against the glass edge. By doing the outside edge first, you will insure that the overlapping edges of the foil will lie flat along the glass and not come away from it.

When you have done the outer edge lay the piece on a flat surface and burnish each of the overlapping edges of tape. Do remember to do both. You will notice immediately how much tighter and neater the foil looks after this process, so don't skip it.

SETTING THE PIECES

Putting together a copper-foil panel is similar to leading one, but there are a few more problems; primarily, you will have difficulty keeping the pieces in place after they are laid out and set against each other.

To assemble your panel you will need a work table or board like that used for leading, with the same kind of right-angle corner made from lath strips. Have your working copy and glass—all wrapped in foil and burnished—nearby.

Begin by setting in the first piece; set in your next piece, making sure that the edges meet well. Hold the pieces together with leading nails. Use buffers, or small pieces of cut lead, between the glass and each nail. While not absolutely necessary, because the foil does provide some protection, you will find that buffers add a bit more stability to the work in progress and provide the best safety precaution against chipped or broken glass.

This process is continued with as many pieces as possible. In some designs, those having mostly large pieces for instance, it is possible to lay the entire panel without any problem. For panels made of smaller pieces, however, you will eventually notice that the glass will start to rise in some area. Hopefully, you will see this beginning to occur and catch it just in time before the pieces pop out of place.

This occurs because as the pieces are set in and held in place with nails, tension mounts between them. The nails keep them from pushing outward, so the only direction available is upward and outward. This is very frustrating, especially if you put all the pieces back together and it happens again. It makes you want to take a hammer to the whole thing.

To avoid this problem, small areas of the panel are built or assembled together. They are then soldered in a few places, called tack-soldering, to hold them in place. In this manner, pieces can be removed, adjusted, or whatever, easily and without major surgery. Use this method only when your project is large, made up of small pieces, or is not fitting properly as you work on it.

If you can construct the panel without tack-soldering, so much the better. If there are any dimensional mistakes with the finished panel, they can then be corrected very simply.

TACK-SOLDERING

Tack-soldering means that the pieces are lightly "tacked" together, usually only at each joint (Fig. 15-3). Very little solder is used.

As noted, it is used to hold pieces together temporarily and is not intended to be a solid bond. If you were to solder the pieces together along all foiled edges at this stage, you would have quite a

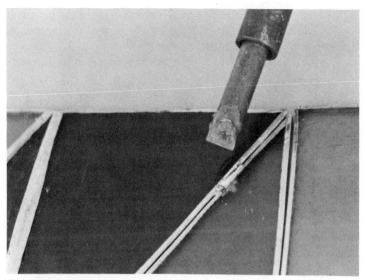
Fig. 15-3. Tack-soldering in selected spots holds the pieces in place.

bit of work ahead should you find that adjustments are necessary once the work is finished.

First flux all spots (generally the joints) to be tack-soldered. On small-pieced windows, you can stop and tack-solder every six or seven pieces or so. If you have a problem keeping the pieces together in only one area of a larger project, you can tack-solder just in that one area. You can also, if you wish, tack each piece in place as you go along. Keep an eye on the iron, though, if you do this. It should not sit for long periods of time heating up. Just be sure that the pieces are as tight together as they can be.

If you are tacking as you go, you must also be sure that the pieces are in the proper position, or at the right angle, or in whatever position they are to ultimately be. If they aren't, you will end up with the rest of the pieces fitting incorrectly.

Continue building, fitting all pieces tightly and tack-soldering as necessary. When you have finished placing the last pieces, set nails tightly around the outer edges to hold the entire design in place, in the same manner used for leading.

Measure the panel. If it is larger than your pattern, or if one or more of the borner pieces stick out beyond the given perimeter, the time to correct it is now, before you begin the actual soldering.

If it is larger in only one or two places, the best solution is probably to take the pieces out and trim them. This must be done

181

with some care so that you do not disturb the rest of the pieces. If you can, it is wisest to further tack-solder the pieces surrounding the one(s) to come out for adjustment.

If the offending piece itself is tacked in place, you will naturally have to unsolder it to remove it. This is done by placing the iron on the tacked portion long enough for the solder to become liquid again. Once this occurs, you can lift the piece enough so that it will not rebound as the solder cools. If the piece is tightly wedged in, it may be necessary to slip a thin object between the piece and the one adjoining it *at the same time you are melting the solder*. This takes a bit of manual dexterity as well as agility, but it is important that you do this only as the solder becomes molten. The tip of your lead knife will work fine. You must hold it there only for the few seconds it takes for the solder to cool when the iron has been taken away. This way you insure that you have gotten a clean separation of the pieces. You may have to do this in several spots, depending on where the pieces are tacked.

Once you have gotten the piece out, remove the foil from the entire piece. Do not simply tear it off of the edge you are going to trim. You won't be able to get a tight bond of the new foil to the glass without going completely around it.

Remove the old foil. Trim the piece to whatever size necessary along one *edge only*. By trimming more than one edge, you may alter the piece so much that it will not fit properly again. When you are finished trimming, clean the glass well with glass cleaner to remove oil residue and any glue that might still be adhering from the first foiling. Then refoil the piece.

Place the trimmed piece back in the panel and check for fit. Since there is no border lead to cover a slightly irregular edge, it is important that all edges meet evenly.

When you have discerned that all edges are straight and fit well, flux the piece and retack it. You need not use any more solder; simply set the iron down on a spot of solder on one of the adjoining pieces of glass. This little bit will be enough to hold the trimmed piece in once again.

TINNING

Tinning is the process of coating all exposed edges with solder. It is an intermediate step between tack-solder and *beading*, the final soldering stage. Indeed, some skip the tinning stage entirely and proceed right on to the beading. Such people feel that tinning requires extra time, extra solder, and, in general, is not really necessary. On some objects this might be permissible, but, as a rule, I feel it is better to tin the foiled surfaces before beading them.

There are several reasons for this. The first is that it gives a more solid "base" on which to lay a bead of solder. Since beading is not so easy to master (at least in the beginning), the thin coat of solder tinned on bonds the pieces and makes the beading job a little easier.

Also, if there are any areas on the foil that will resist solder (due to dirt, oxidation, oil, or general grime), you will spot them in the tinning process and be able to correct them before you begin beading.

The amount of extra time and solder required by tinning is not really that great. It is a relatively simple and rapid process, and does not require that much extra solder—nothing, in fact, compared to the amount used for beading.

A lot of solder is not necessary for this process; you don't want a thick covering, just a very thin coat.

Tinning is best done when your project is completely assembled and tack-soldered. Plug in the iron. While it is heating up, prepare the foil by applying a thin coat of flux along all foiled edges. When you are finished tinning there will be no copper foil visible, as it will all be covered with solder—so do remember to flux all of the seams.

When the iron has heated, melt a small amount of solder onto the foil. It will not require much. Just start with a small blob somewhere. Set the iron down on this solder and rapidly draw the tip of the iron along the foil. The solder will follow along behind the iron almost like magic, leaving the foil coated (Fig. 15-4). A dab of solder goes a long way. When you need more, melt a bit more onto the foil.

Naturally, you may worry about cracking the glass since the heat from the iron is conducted through the copper to the glass. There is not really much danger of this happening if you remember to keep the iron moving fairly quickly and do not allow it to sit in one spot for very long. Incidentally, if you happen to touch the foiled surface you have just tinned, you will find that it is very hot indeed, so avoid doing so.

Continue tinning until all surfaces are done.

Tinning does not make the project rigid, so do not try to lift or turn it over. You will have to bead one side before you can begin tinning the other side.

Small panels or free-form objects, if you wish, can be carefully turned over and tinned on the other side before final soldering. If you must turn a large panel that has been tinned only, use a board to reduce the chance of the panel flexing and cracking. To turn a panel, you will need a board about 5 cm (2 inches) larger on all sides than the outside perimeter border of the panel. A sheet of 1 to 2 cm (½ to ¾ inch) plywood works best. The thicker the better, because the panel may be quite heavy.

Lay the board parallel to the table edge and slide the panel from the table onto the board. It is probably best to have someone help you with this, so that both the board and the panel are well supported.

Once you have gotten the panel onto the board, place the board back onto the table. Gently begin tilting the board downward, toward the floor. Be sure to hold the panel at its corners so that it does not slide right off in a pile. Continue tilting the board until it is upright, on its edge on the floor, *and the panel is flat against it. Do not allow the panel to tilt or lean without the support of the board right against it at all points.*

Now you definitely need a friend. One person must hold the panel in place with a hand at each corner. Keep it absolutely vertical. This is best accomplished by pulling slightly upward while holding, but not enough to actually pick it up. The other person carefully removes the board and slides it in place on the opposite side, the one that has been tinned. In effect, what you are doing is changing the board from one side of the panel to the other. Move the board up against the panel so that they are intimately against each other.

Now, gripping the panel to the board at the top corners, again begin to slant the top edge of the board downward. Slant it enough so that you can easily grasp the bottom corners of the board and bring them up until you have the whole thing, window and board, flat and held between you and your helper. The untinned surfaces will be on top, facing you. Put the board back on the table and tin the other side. This procedure usually involves a bit of synchronized timing between you and your partner, so get the procedure and any "signals" down pat before you begin. It will save a lot of hollering and crossed lines, and possibly your window.

This method can also be used to turn a large or unwieldy panel that has been leaded and soldered on only one side.

Smaller objects will be fairly rigid after tinning on one side, at least enough to turn them over with some care, but the larger the

Fig. 15-4. Tinning, or covering the foil with a thin, flat coat of solder, will make the final soldering step go more easily.

panel gets, the more difficulty there is in handling it, whether leaded or copper foiled.

Some individuals choose only to tin the foil and leave it at that. There is nothing really wrong with this, especially for very small panels or suncatchers, but it is not strong enough for areas. In addition a good beaded line looks so nice that you probably won't be satisfied with just the tinned surface or "flat bead," as it is sometimes called.

Some people tin each piece of glass before it is put into the panel. Now this *can* be time-consuming. It entails coating all surfaces of the foil—back, front, and edge—with solder before assembly. The advantage seems to be rather dubious from my viewpoint, and I don't feel that tinning taken to these lengths is really called for.

Tinning should be a quick, simple process, done with the least amount of solder possible. A cold or slow iron will not perform well for this, so make sure that your iron is fairly hot, and do remember to keep it moving.

If there are bumps or bulges along the foiled edge, they will show. Any gaps between the pieces will require more solder to fill them in. In beading, more solder is applied over the tinned surfaces, so they will not be as visible as they look to you now. Small flaws may be somewhat masked, but even in beading, large holes or bumps will make a difference in how the solder flows and how it looks when finished.

BEADING

Beading is the process of covering the tinned surfaces with solder to form an even, rounded hump, or bead, of solder. The time to bead is, naturally, after the glass pieces have been completely assembled and tinned. As noted earlier, you do not have to tin the foiled edges, but it does make beading slightly easier.

This step is the one most apt to give you the most problems—at least at the beginning. It takes a bit of control, both with the iron and with the solder (simultaneously, no less!) to get the even and smooth uniformity required to give a good bead. It is not an easy process, but it can be mastered with practice and patience.

Beading provides the primary strength of copper-foiled glass. Merely tinning the foil will not give the rigidity necessary to allow the assembled glass to withstand age and weather. The amount of solder used in beading (and it is considerable) is what supplies this strength; the foil itself is nothing in this respect. Therefore, regardless of whether or not you have tinned your pieces, you should bead them.

To bead, start at the beginning of one tinned line. With the iron close to (but not touching) the foil, feed the solder continu-

Fig. 15-5. Beading the tinned line adds strength to the work.

186

Fig. 15-6. The finished bead should be rounded, even, and smooth.

ously onto the tip of the iron. At the same time, move the iron along the line (Fig. 15-5).

How fast do you move the iron? Well, steadiness and evenness is more important than speed, so move the iron continuously, but probably not what you would call quickly. This is difficult to grasp until you actually see it done or, better yet, do it yourself. By trying it, you will see exactly what happens during this process and what you are doing wrong or right.

Once the beading is begun on a single line, it is best to continue along, following the line however far as you can go without breaking the bead. It is possible, of course, to stop and start a bead, indeed sometimes even necessary, but it is often difficult to rework the broken area sufficiently well to get a uniform look.

Before you begin beading, pull out a good bit of solder from the coil. Leave it attached to the coil, though, as this will make it easier to use and will waste less. Remember to be generous with solder. What you are after is a small, rounded hump along all seams. About 3 mm (⅛ inch) high seems to be an attainable and good-looking bead; certainly you would not want it to be too much larger (Fig. 15-6).

This sounds like a relatively easy process; however, it is not as simple as it sounds, and many beginners give up in disgust after a few unsuccessful attempts. Just as many, however, quickly develop an ease for this technique and can not understand what all the fuss is about. I myself loved the look of foil and of working with it, but struggled for some time with the beading process until I felt confident with it. If you have trouble in the beginning, don't give up. If you have trouble in the beginning, don't give up. There is no magic involved, only practice and experience.

One big pitfall to avoid is a too-hot iron. A cooler iron is best for this, slightly below (but only slightly) the normal soldering range. Obviously, you don't (and can't) work with a cold iron or one that is so cool that it leaves a string of spiked points instead of a rounded surface.

You will have to experiment a bit to determine for yourself exactly what this ideal temperature is, as both people and irons (even when the irons are made by the same company) vary. I can, however, give you some guidelines.

An iron is too hot when the solder bubbles and hisses excessively on contact with the fluxed foil. If you are using acid flux, you will have some hissing, but the bubbling is always a reliable sign. The main indicator, though, is when the solder will not rise to form the bead you want, but stubbornly flattens out. Do you know what happens to it? It is going through to the other side of the piece; you would see it there if you turned the glass pieces over. For this reason, this is the most frequent complaint of beginners.

At too cold a temperature, on the other hand, you will find that the solder settles in little blobs and lumps and all kinds of weird shapes. While in some instances you might want to purposely cultivate this appearance, it is not the effect you are looking for in beading.

You will find that solder obeys quite readily when the iron is at the proper temperature and falls right into line as it should. It does not, except very occasionally, sink down and flatten out. As you feed the solder onto the iron, it in turn flows to the foil and should form a nice bead.

You must remember to feed the solder continuously onto the tip of the iron and to keep the iron moving steadily along. If you move too fast, you will have a smaller, flatter-bead. Moving too slow will produce a fat, laborious-looking one. Beading seems to consist of happy mediums, doesn't it?

Another mistake frequently made is allowing the iron to come in direct contact with the foil. As I've said, it should be very close, maybe 1.5 to 3 mm (1/16 to ⅛ inch) from it, but not right on top of it. This will result in the same problem as attempting to bead with too hot an iron; that is, the solder will flow right on through the seam to the opposite side of the pieces. This is also one of the reasons why exactness is stressed. The tighter the fit of the foiled pieces as they butt up against each other, the less problem you will have with solder running through the gaps.

Reworking a Bead

There comes a time (and it comes for all of us, no matter how good we may be) when you are doing to have to rework a bead you have already made. This usually occurs when, for example, the bead progresses nicely and then all of a sudden flattens out due to too much heat or whatever. Or perhaps you are just not satisfied with the way a particular section of the beading looks.

Reworking means, basically, correcting. It means fixing. It means going back and doing it over. It also means that it is quite possible to mess up what you have already done and are pleased with, since the fixed part must flow into the good part. The good part sometimes melts right away and then *it* requires reworking.

For a flat area, the solution is fairly simple. Get your iron to the right temperature and then flow more solder over this area. You can connect it fairly smoothly to the rest of the bead by applying iron heat to the point where they meet. First see if you can bring the tip of the iron very close to this point. Sometimes the heat radiating from it is enough to melt the solder and make it flow together. If it is not, touch the iron very slightly to the solder—just enough to get it to flow in the manner you wish it to. You may have to play with it a while, but don't simply plunge in and jab the iron down on the solder. *This* is how you make bad what was good to begin with.

For areas that have been beaded but not to your satisfaction, a bit more effort is usually needed. Begin about a centimeter or two before the bad area, and draw the iron very slowly along the solder, through the area you want to correct and into the bead adjoining it by, again, a couple of centimeters or so. Sometimes this alone corrects the problem spot. If there are still rough spots, go back and gently apply the iron to these alone in what can only be described as a slow-motion pecking movement. The iron is applied to the solder and then drawn straight up, not to one side or the other as would seem to be the natural tendency. Do this as much as you need to for the immediate area and then slightly to each side to achieve uniformity in the bead.

Beading *joints* (areas where two or more seams come together) often require the same procedure as reworking a bead, since for at least one of the beaded seams the joint is the end of the line and it often ends in a blob that disrupts the flow of the line. For example, if you have one perfectly beaded seam finished and there is to be another seam that will join it, draw the solder toward the already beaded seam. When you get to the joint, apply an instant of heat from the iron and then pick the iron straight up. Don't try to smear the solder to one side or the other. By lifting the iron off of the solder, then, you should have a smooth, unbroken junction where the two meet. If you do not, repair it in the same manner as that given for reworking. That is, set the iron down lightly on the solder (not all the way through to the foil, please) and then pick it up. I call this "playing with the solder", and sometimes it will take a bit of time and patience before you achieve a satisfactory bead. What you want to avoid at such crossings are large globs of solder contributed by each of the joining beads. If you end up with too much solder, push a bit of it off to the side (onto the glass), and then work with what you have left.

Don't be afraid of breaking the glass; solder in such small quantities is seldom enough to do harm. It will set immediately and can be scraped off with your fingernail when you are done. The only glass I would not do this with are the German antiques, which are often quite thin and delicate.

BORDER TREATMENTS

There are several ways to approach borders for copper-foil pieces. The perimeter can be beaded, for instance, on a free-hanging piece. For installation, the outer edge may be tinned and left as is, as it will not be seen beneath the molding or putty of the frame. A border can also be made of lead, which tends to emphasize the panel as a whole and is used mainly for those destined, again, for hanging.

Round Beading

Probably the most attractive although difficult approach is to bead the perimeter. Remember that you will now be working with a very small area, only one foiled edge, instead of the two together that formed the interior seams in the design. An additional problem is the fact that you are attempting to defy gravity in this type of soldering, and it requires more control than plain beading. However, the look of the finished bead is immensely pleasing and well worth the time and effort involved as it really enhances the entire panel.

It helps, first off, if you have used a slightly wider foil around the edges of your piece. This can be accomplished either by using wider foil around all of the pieces that will form the borders of the window or by wrapping the entire perimeter of the panel with wider foil once the interior lines have been tinned and beaded on one side of the project.

Unless it is intrinsic to the design, you would not want to foil the border pieces in a foil that will appear vastly different from that used within the rest of the panel. If you can, and if you are planning to use this method, try to find a foil only slightly larger than the one used throughout. Something larger than 6 mm (¼ inch) foil seems to work best, though you can try beading with the 6 mm if you like.

The best alternative is to foil all pieces with one size of foil. Assemble the pieces, tacking and tinning as usual. Do not tin the perimeter edges—leave the copper foil showing.

If the piece is small, about 30 cm by 30 cm (12 inches square) or smaller, you can wrap the border at this stage. The assembled glass will probably be rigid enough to handle gently.

Using wider foil, wrap the perimeter edge with one continuous strip, being careful to center the glass edge on the foil and also not to bend or apply excess pressure to the window itself. Lay the wider foil directly over the already foiled edges of the perimeter pieces. The glass and the previously foiled edges must be absolutely free of any flux residues or the foil will not adhere. You can lay the new foil over small tinned areas, but it is wise not to try to place it on an already beaded line. Just as with regular foil, this new addition must be as tight on the glass as possible, without air spaces or lumpy areas. It must also be burnished as with regular foiling.

After the border is wrapped, it can be fluxed and tinned. Any seams that join the border may then be completed by tinning or beading. Run the bead to the edge of the panel; this will also give the new foil extra staying power by making it a part of the rest of the panel. It is now ready to be beaded.

Of the two methods, I recommend beginners wrap exterior pieces with slightly wider foil. The wider foil can be satisfactorily worked into the design if it is given enough thoughtful foresight. You'll likely have less problems with it at first than the second method of wrapping the entire perimeter in wider foil, which will be more easily mastered after you've gained a bit of experience in working with foil.

To bead outer edge, then, tin it on the outside edge and both overlapping edges of the foil. It is vital that you work slowly and carefully now and that you keep your iron fairly cool. Lay a small bead first along the overlapping edge of the foil that is facing you. Use slightly less solder than you did for regular beading or you will have a problem with it running off the edge. When you have completely beaded the perimeter in this manner, turn the panel over and do the opposite side in the same way. You now have the hard part left to do, which is beading the outermost edge.

To do this, you will have to prop the panel up so that it is absolutely vertical and not leaning in either direction at all.

Again, working slowly and with a cool iron, begin beading the edge facing you. In effect, you will be laying solder between the two beads (on the overlapping edges) you have already made. Don't try to rush this process. You will only end up with an erratic border and a headache.

Before you begin beading the perimeter clean all glass and already beaded lines. If the panel should tilt at all to one side or the other, you will very quickly notice that solder is running down the edge and onto the glass. If there is any flux on the beaded panel dow, the solder will stick to it as it falls, and you may end up reworking lines that were fine to begin with. So, clean off all excess flux before starting. If your iron becomes too hot, the solder will run off the edge and fall all over the place.

Continue all perimeter edges in this way.

Flat Beading

A border may also be flat-beaded or tinned and left as is if it is to be installed in a window sash or frame. This is a very simple matter.

The window is beaded out to the edge on all lines, as you would normally do. The perimeter is then fluxed and solder is run around all foiled edges, both the two overlapping and the outermost edge. That's really about all there is to it.

On larger pieces, flat border beads are not strong enough, especially in the border which will absorb more weight and stress than the interior of the piece. Therefore, the size of the piece should also be considered before using this method.

Lead Borders

Lead border came is another way to finish your piece. It finds its best use in pieces that are to be hung indoors or in a fairly sheltered area. There is really no point in using it for panels that are to be installed within frames as the lead will not be visible and, unless you need the additional width of the came (such as panel if your came out too small), the effects of this type of bordering will be lost.

For a lead border, use regular lead came border is used, usually a U lead. Be careful when choosing border lead choose one that is not out of proportion with the scale of the overall design. A 6 mm (¼ inch) U lead is usually about right for most pieces; use 3 mm (⅛ inch) lead for smaller panels. You don't want to use such a heavy lead that it overpowers the delicate feel of the foiling. Likewise, too small a lead on too large a panel will look just as odd and will probably pull away from the edges if the weight of the glass is too much.

Measure and cut the border leads the same as if you were leading the panel. The difference, of course, is that you are adding the lead at the end of construction rather than in the beginning. Mitered corners give added strength. Set the leads onto the piece and hold them in place with leading nails. The came will probably cover the foil entirely.

After all of the leads are in place and before you solder, run a lathekin around each of the edges along the border lead. This will crimp it down so that it hugs the edge of the glass tightly and will also make soldering much smoother by providing a flat area. Since glazing is not done on copper-foiled work, you will have to make the lead very secure along the edges. Puttying would normally firm up this bond but, as I've said, it is not necessary with foiled projects.

When you have all four of the leads in place, heat up the iron. Solder the corners of the lead first. Then proceed to solder each joint where the foiled and beaded seams intersect the lead came. It is important to solder each joint. It not only looks much better, but it gives the lead the added strength of being joined to the foil— which will help keep the lead from pulling away when the piece is hung.

FINISHING

You have now completed, for the most part, the construction of your copper-foiled work. The solder you have lovingly applied is smoothly and roundly beaded, but it's so shiny! Many people prefer this to the darker antiqued look that will develop with time. For those who don't, however, there are chemical compounds available to turn that silver to varying shades of copper, gray, or black.

There are two solutions for this. One is called patina, a liquid formula that colors the solder from a medium gun-metal gray to black. The other, called copper sulfate, is sold in crystals that require mixing. It produces a copper color which, depending on the strength of the solution, can be very light to very intense in color.

Whichever solution you use, it must be applied as soon as possible after construction has been completed. In other words, don't let your work sit around for two or three days or weeks before you return to the job of antiquing the solder. You will be disappointed and frustrated. Oxidation begins building up immediately on the soldered surfaces and will act to resist the patina or copper sulfate. Thus, you will end up with a very splotchy job. Of course, you can always scrub the solder thoroughly before application with a small wire brush, but this tears up the smooth surface of the solder and is a time-consuming and needless job.

Patina

Of the two compounds, patina is the more popular. For this job you will need patina, an applicator of some sort, and a dry rag. A number of eminently suitable applicators can be found in your own household. Possibly the best one I've found is an ordinary sponge. A regular kitchen sponge cut up into "bite-sized" pieces, a couple of centimeters (about an inch) square work well because they are small and can be reused. They also make it possible to apply the patina to the solder without getting much on the glass, a definite advantage since patina is very difficult to remove from glass.

A rival to sponges, and probably tops for getting into hard-to-reach places, is a toothbrush. You can really scrub with this if it's necessary.

Rags, of course, will do in a pinch, but, having tried all three, I much prefer sponges and toothbrushes for even, nonmessy application. You can no doubt find a number of other items that will adapt readily to the purpose at hand.

Whatever you use, be sure to wash it thoroughly after you are done if you intend to use it again. Both patina and copper sulfate are corrosive substances and will corrode the applicator if not cleaned well.

Before beginning, clean the panel well to remove any dirt and flux residue that might interfere with the work of the patina. Be especially mindful to remove the excess flux.

To patina, dip the applicator into the solution, or put the solution into a small squeeze bottle with which you can easily regulate the amount to be used. Run the applicator along one of the beaded seams. It will turn dark instantly as the chemical touches it, but it won't be this dark when you are finished, so don't be deceived. Wait a few seconds and then wipe it off with a dry cloth. Rub or buff slightly as you remove the patina. When you are finished, the solder will probably be medium gray in color.

More rubbing will lighten the color somewhat, although probably not drastically. Be sure to cover the sides of the bead and any crevices where several lines intersect.

If you want to darken the color, apply the patina again in the same manner. Wait a bit longer and then buff it off as before. This is about the only way to darken the color more. Sometimes several applications will be necessary before you have the color you desire.

Always store patina out of the reach of children.

Copper Sulfate

If you desire a brownish, copper-colored effect for the solder instead of the gray-black of patina, then copper sulfate is the compound to use. Since it is sold in powder or crystal form, you will have to make up your own solution. There are quite a few recipes for this, two of which follow. The first is the one I have used, and the second, though only slightly different, is recommended by others. I think the difference is that the second, as it also uses an acid in the solution, may require perhaps fewer applications. Try whichever you wish, as both will undoubtedly give the same final result.

Recipe 1: Dilute 2 teaspoons copper sulfate crystals in 1 cup warm water. Stir well to dissolve all particles.

Recipe 2: Dissolve 2 teaspoons copper sulfate crystals in 1 cup warm water. Add two or three drops of hydrochloric acid. Stir well to dissolve all particles.

Neither recipe calls for elaborate mixing and measuring. In fact, if you are not getting the color you want, add more copper sulfate to the solution to strengthen it. If you do this, make the additions gradually and keep track of how much you have added so that next time you can mix it in the needed proportions.

A word about hydrochloric acid: this is a highly corrosive inorganic acid. It should be used with care. Avoid prolonged contact with the acid and with its fumes. There is no real danger in handling or antiquing with the solution made by recipes, but the full-strength acid by itself is dangerous. My own dislike for handling such chemicals if it can be avoided is why I prefer to use the first solution. A little more elbow grease may need to be applied, but that's all right with me.

Store hydrochloric acid out of the reach of children, and be sure that the bottles are properly labeled.

Before you antique the solder be sure the solder is absolutely clean and free of dirt and flux. The antiquing solution will not "take" otherwise. With an applicator like those used for applying patina, apply the copper sulfate onto the solder. You may have to rub a little more than with the patina.

Wait a few moments and then wipe the copper sulfate solution off with a dry cloth. The solder will probably be a rather light copperish (light by my standards, anyway). Go over all the foiled and soldered lines in this manner. Try to achieve a uniformity in color. Be sure to apply the solution on the sides of the bead as well as on its top.

When you have finished, you may decide you want to make it darker. If you do, apply another coat of solution and let it sit a few moments more. Don't allow the solution to dry on the solder, however. Remove it with a cloth as before.

This is how you can achieve the darker copper coloring you may desire. Copper sulfate does not color the solder as quickly as will patina. While patina may well turn the solder black before you know it, more applications with copper sulfate will produce gradually darkening coppers. Continue application until you achieve a shade you like.

You can, of course, as mentioned, strengthen the solution by adding more copper sulfate crystals to it to reduce the number of applications necessary.

When the piece is completely antiqued, you can leave it as it is or you can buff it so that it takes on a lustrous sheen. To do this, use either 000 steel wool (very fine) so that the surface of the solder does not become scratched and blemished. Or use a soft cloth. You will have to put some time and elbow grease into it, but the effects are well worth the effort.

COMMON PROBLEMS

There are few things that can go so wrong in copper-foil work that you can't get the pieces together at all. Mistakes are generally made in glass-cutting rather than in actual assembly, and as already stressed, the accuracy is most important. Following are questions frequently asked by students on a myriad of small but nonetheless important problems. Knowing these answers and techniques before you begin will help your first and following projects progress more smoothly.

Q. *On foiling pieces of glass with deeply curved cuts, the foil seems to tear along the edges. Will this affect the appearance of the panel, and is there any way I can avoid it?*

A. The stress on the foil tape along deep curves causes this problem since the foil does not really stretch or "give" much, if at all. It will affect the way the project looks because the solder simply will not flow over areas not covered with tape. The best remedy for this problem is patience. Lay the tape along the outer edge as you would normally do. It is when you begin crimping it on the overlap that it begins to tear.

Begin slowly crimping it down, a little at a time. Start at one end and bend the tape slightly toward the glass. Do this all along the edge. Then come back and push it down a little more, doing this along the entire curve as before. Finally, come back and slowly press it tight to the glass. The key is to work slowly and in stages rather than trying to get the tape to accept the curve in one operation.

While this method doesn't work all of the time, it works well enough to be used with confidence.

Q. *If I need to remove some of the foil around a piece can I "patch" it with more tape? Can I reuse old foil?*

A. I have tried to patch a spot with foil, and it usually did not work well; the bond was not very good, either. If you need to patch only a very small area, try it; otherwise it is better to rewrap the entire piece using new foil.

Don't reuse foil. It will probably be wrinkled anyway, but even so, the adhesive will not work properly again.

Q. *There is some kind of green ooze coming out of my foiled seams. Is this from the copper or solder or what? It's very hard to get off.*

A. The green ooze is from the adhesive used on the tape. You must be using foil with a low-melting adhesive; the heat of the iron is melting the adhesive. Unfortunately, it may ooze indefinitely. There is copper foil and then there is copper foil, you see, and even though they *look* alike, they aren't. The best kind of tape to get is one with a high melting point for its adhesive backing.

As you have observed, it is very difficult to remove this ooze from the glass. If it sets up, it will be that much harder, and maybe even impossible. Try first washing the glass with water and a mild soap. When you have done this, use glass cleaner to remove whatever is left. It will take a lot of rubbing as the adhesive will streak onto the surrounding areas if you're not careful.

Q. *I read somewhere that you shouldn't use a corrosive (acid) flux. I've been using a paste flux. Why do you say it's okay, even better, and is there any advantage to it over the paste flux?*

A. Well, this is a matter of personal preference really. Acid flux is better than either paste flux or oleic acid, both of which are used for copper-foil work. The disadvantage is that acid flux will corrode a copper-tipped soldering iron fairly quickly. By corrode, I mean that it will leave small pits and ridges in the tip and will eventually make the normally flat surface of the tip slightly concave. If not taken care of, this condition will progressively worsen until the tip is worthless. To correct the problem file the tip and retin it, as explained in Chapter 9. Filing and retinning can be done numerous times before you will be ready for a new tip.

Acid flux is better, I feel, because it cleans the surfaces of the foil to be soldered, thereby removing dirt and oxidation, which can be a major barrier to good soldering. In addition, it allows the solder to flow much more easily than either paste flux or oleic acid. This is an important point to consider since soldering plays such a large role in foiling.

Paste fluxes are all right for soldering, but they are so messy. It is very difficult to keep them off the glass and, once on, the mess seems to spread.

Oleic acid is also messy and difficult to beep off—and clean off of—glass. It is fine for joint soldering, where only a small area needs to be fluxed; but in copper foiling the entire seam must be soldered, and therefore fluxed. Oleic acid will not remove any oxidation from the foil, which is another problem, and it also will not give as good a flow of solder.

Q. *Can I leave my work exposed for any length of time or will the copper oxidize? It's about halfway soldered.*

A. This is a good question. Once you have begun soldering, it is really best to finish the job. You will find it difficult to solder if you leave it partially done, and this difficulty will increase the longer the project is left unfinished. Even if all of the seams are tinned, you will find beading a frustrating task if the piece is allowed to sit too long. You will need to apply more flux (and here's hoping that you're using the acid based flux) to remove the oxidation on the solder, as it will also oxidize.

If you are planning to patina or antique the solder with copper sulfate solution, you would be wise to solder the piece, clean it well, and start right in on the darkening process. Again, leaving the project between stages will make your job harder when you return to it, whether soldering or antiquing.

If you must leave it for a period of time, cover the entire project with plastic, getting out as much air as possible and tucking the plastic under the edges. This will give a good deal of protection against exposure.

Any areas that oxidize anyway, even after being covered, will have to be scrubbed with a small wire brush. You will be able to find these areas easily, as the solder will not flow on them. Patina or copper sulfate will give a splotchy finish instead of a uniformly colored one, which is the most desirable.

Q. *I can't seem to get an even bead on my foiling. The solder all runs down to the other side of the panel. What am I doing wrong?*

A. Providing you don't have any really large crevices between the pieces, I would say that the iron is too hot for beading. Let it cool some.

Q. *I'm getting lots of bubbles in my solder. During the actual soldering, the molten solder spits and fumes. What's going on?*

A. Either there are large gaps between the pieces which are being filled with solder, your flux is impure, or your iron is much too hot. The sizzling noises could come from any one of these, and so could the bubbles in the solder.

The flux may have been contaminated by dirt or other foreign matter. If so, try a new bottle. By the way, you should use a separate brush for copper-foil flux, not the same one you use for oleic acid. Never mix these brushes as the fluxes will spoil each other.

If the flux is not the problem, I can only deduce that the iron is too hot.

Q. *When I tin the foil, the edges of the copper foil become loose and sometimes even pull away from the glass very easily. How can I prevent this?*

A. First, make sure that each piece is burnished before you tin it. If you remember, this is done by rubbing all the surfaces of the foil with a small stick or similar object. This process makes the tape adhere to the glass as tightly as possible.

The other problem that might be occuring is that the tape is so old that the adhesive is worn and is not performing as it should, though this is not likely. I have kept a roll of foil for over a year without the adhesive losing its effectiveness, although I'm sure that the various qualities of copper foil available are different in this respect.

The most probable cause is, again, that the iron is too hot. Let it cool off some and don't allow it to heat up so much.

Q. *What is the best way to store copper foil?*

A. Copper foil is sold in a sealed plastic bag, and is is best to store it in this manner. A "zip-locking" sandwich bag works ideally.

FREE-FORM DESIGNING

One of the nicest things about copper foiling is that it can be quite spontaneous, thereby increasing its versatility. Small, free-hanging things can be easily and quickly cut, wrapped, and soldered, and you can make half a dozen suncatchers in an evening if you wish, without the complications of patterns, etc. I've filled many short-on-time but long-on-creative urges by putting together a few choice scraps of antique glass or cutting a few simple shapes and foiling them into a simple but pleasing abstract hanging.

All you need to do is to decide what kind of form you want to make. If, for instance, you want to makes a flower such as the one pictured in Fig. 15-7, all you need do is cut, at random, several petals and a center. You can make the edges slightly curved if you wish so that the pieces will conform to each other better. These cuts are all freehand, without a pattern, though you can cut a cardboard template if you wish. Since these are to be free-hanging and of no specific size, you need not worry about patterns, pattern shears, and tight tolerances.

When you have cut the pieces, wrap each one in foil. Burnish the edges so that the foil adheres well to the glass.

Now all you have to do is tack the pieces together, tin the surfaces, and bead them if you wish. On something so small, it is not really necessary to bead the foil. They are very light anyway, so do it either way you wish.

You would be wise, however, to tin each piece of foiled glass separately before tack-soldering them. If the piece is to have irregular edges, such as the flower does, you won't be able to get into tight spots with the iron for tinning. So tin each piece and then lay them out for tacking. Once you have tacked such a piece so that it is held to another, flow enough solder along the seams so that they are joined, with no gaps showing.

If you are doing an abstract piece, you can move the pieces around in different positions before tacking them together. When you have found the one you like best, tack it and finish soldering.

Fig. 15-7. Small free-form pieces can be cut without a pattern and are fun to make.

You can darken the solder with patina or copper sulfate, just as you would for other projects.

Solder on a small loop or a piece of wire and hang with fishing line. They look beautiful—and so easy!

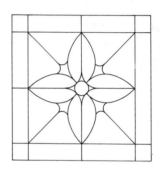

Chapter 16
Three-Dimensional
Designs

One of the most useful applications of copper foil is in designing and creating three-dimensional objects. Probably the most well-known and popular of these is the Tiffany-style lamp, but there are also mny other projects that lend themselves well to this method, including glass boxes and terrariums.

The use of copper foil in three-dimensional projects has several advantages over leading, although both methods can be used. Copper foil, however, gives a more delicate look to the finished item, whatever it may be, so you should consider this fact when deciding what you will make. It is also more flexible than lead, in the sense that curves can be created by using small pieces of glass foiled together. This effect isn't really possible with lead came unless the glass itself is "bent," an advanced technique that is not covered in this book.

The primary advantage of copper-foiling over leading with came is the weight factor. A stained-glass box, for example, that is put together with copper foil will be light as a feather compared to its leaded counterpart. It will also look much lighter, without the heavy lines that lead came imposes.

Tiffany-style lamps demand the use of the foil method almost exclusively. They often contain hundreds of pieces of glass, and to lead all of these would boggle the mind—not to mention the weight of the finished lamp in lead came. Leaded lamps, regardless of style, will almost always begin to sag in a relatively short period of time from their sheer weight. This means that the lead begins to pull away from the glass and vice versa. Pretty soon what you will have is a veritable health hazard to anyone innocently passing under such a lamp.

An exception to this might be a lantern-style lamp that is supported from below by a bracket or a very simple and fairly small straight-panel lamp. This is a lamp formed by several triangular pieces of glass that fan out at varying degrees from the top. There is usually no design to break up these pieces; and if there is, it is pretty simple. Even so, these types of lamps can just as easily be made in the copper-foil technique and will not only look much nicer, but will be much stronger and will resist the unfortunate effects of sagging.

Before you tackle any sort of lamp, however, it is best to start small. Making three-dimensional items in glass is much different than making flat panels and windows, and in some respects you must begin as a beginner once again. Boxes and terrariums are good projects to start with. They are small enough to require little investment in terms of dollars and time, yet they easily show you the different techniques inherent in this manner of glass crafting. You will have the chance to experience these and learn from them before you attempt such a project as a lamp shade, which has its own peculiar problems to be dealt with.

Boxes can be made to serve a number of purposes. Jewelry boxes and letter boxes serve practical functions, but a small collection of different-sizes and different colored boxes makes an attractive coffeetable display. A couple of boxes made with opalescent glass and filled with sand or pebbles make good bookends. There is no end to the uses you can find for them. They also make pleasing and unique gifts.

You can make a stained glass box out of any glass you happen to have around, or you can buy whatever you want to use. It can be all one color or done in alternating colors. With a little more planning, you can also make boxes with a design on the top or even on the sides of the box. Remember that although I say box, it does not necessarily have to have four sides or be square in shape. Hexagonal boxes are very pretty, as are triangular ones. Terrariums are really just larger "boxes," and the same principles apply for both.

I have made boxes using both copper foil and lead came. My first attempts were in lead, and I believe that this fact alone increased the difficulties that arose. The boxes themselves looked bulky and didn't turn out quite like what I had in mind when I began.

There is a lead came available that makes the sharp corners on a box a bit easier to manage. It is sometimes called corner lead or *45-degree* lead, because it has three flanges, as shown in Fig. 16-1. When it is set upright, one piece of glass (or one of the box sides) will fit into one channel and the other side of the box will fit into the other channel. This will make the two pieces sit within the lead, but at the angle needed to form the box shape without stretching the lead or exposing the edges of the glass. If you'd like to try making a leaded box, this is the kind of lead to use.

Although accurate glass-cutting is essential, the kind of pattern-making done for flat patterns in lead or copper foil is necessary only if you plan to include some sort of design in the top or sides of the box. In that case you must treat the box lid just like a small flat panel. For your first three-dimensional project make a simple four-sided box, with all sides measuring the same dimensions without any such design.

First decide what size box you want to make. For illustrative purposes, we'll say that the sides of the box are to be 10 cm (about 4 inches) long and 7.5 cm wide. This will make the finished box, without the top, 7.5 cm deep. Since the principle is the same regardless of size, you may enlarge or decrease these proportions if you wish.

As I've said, there is no pattern made, although a template is used to cut the pieces of the box. A template is like a pattern, but it is usually used when several pieces of glass are to be cut all to the same size. To make a template for the box, draw the size on a piece of pattern paper (this is the heavier paper, not cartoon paper). For this template, draw a rectangular shape measuring 10 cm long and 7.5 cm wide (Fig. 16-2). Make sure that the corners are asolutely

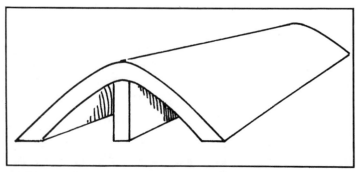

Fig. 16-1. Corner lead, or 45-degree, lead, is used for the corners of boxes and similar objects.

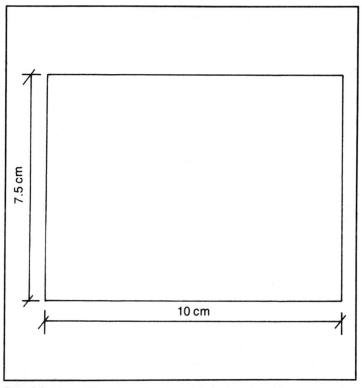

7.5 cm

10 cm

Fig. 16-2. You will have to make a template (or templates) for constructing a box.

square and that the lines are straight. This is not the time for freehand drawing.

Label the top edge. This will help you later when you begin putting the box together. This mark will be transferred to each piece of glass that you cut to it.

Since all four sides of the first box will be the same size, this is the only template you will need to make for now. If, for instance, two of the sides were narrower, you would also have to make a template for the different pieces.

The top and the bottom of the box are also cut to a template, but I've found it better to wait until all four (or however many) sides are cut and put together before making the top and bottom template. Since the dimensions usually change slightly during construction, the top and bottom of the box can be made to the dimensions of the box itself instead of to a template that may or may not be the correct size.

Now you are ready to cut out the template; you may use regular shears. Just cut right on the line and try your best to keep the lines straight.

Once the template is cut, you begin cutting the glass. Cut four pieces for this box, and be sure that you cut exactly to the paper template. Label the top of each piece of glass with either a small piece of masking tape or a glass or China marking pen. It doesn't matter how you make the top just so long as you know where the top is. When you have cut all the pieces, hold them together and set them on edge on a table. *All edges should be even*; if they aren't, groze or recut the ones that don't match up. Recutting them is better because you want a smooth edge. If the edges are not even, the box will not fit together properly and will come out somewhat lopsided. So be forewarned.

Clean the pieces with glass cleaner to remove any excess oil or dirt before you foil them. Foil each piece of the box separately. Be sure that the glass is centered on the foil. When you have wrapped and crimped the foil, don't forget to burnish it with a Popsicle stick or something similar. This will keep the foil as tightly as possible to the glass.

Now we are ready to put the pieces together, the worst part, in the beginning at least, because many people can't figure out how to hold the pieces together, keep them at the correct angle, and still operate a soldering iron and solder. If you're wondering why you weren't born with four hands, I'll let you in on a valuable secret: there is an easy way to do all of this with only two hands! It's probably so simple that it's overlooked.

Basically, what you will do is assemble it as it will look when it's done (without, of course, the top and bottom in place). When the pieces are in place, the box is tack-soldered. If any adjustments in position need to be made, you can do some as you go along, but it's best if you avoid too much bending after you have tacked the box. Since the solder hardens so quickly, any repositioning of the sides of the box may risk pulling the foil away from the glass, which is a no-no.

To assemble the pieces you will need a roll of masking tape. Scotch tape works in a pinch, but it's generally too flimsy and narrow to do the best job.

On your work board, begin setting the pieces up. Make sure that all the tops of the pieces are up (you marked them for this purpose, remember?). Take two of the sides and set them at right angles to each other. Put a piece of tape (about a 5 to 8 cm piece)

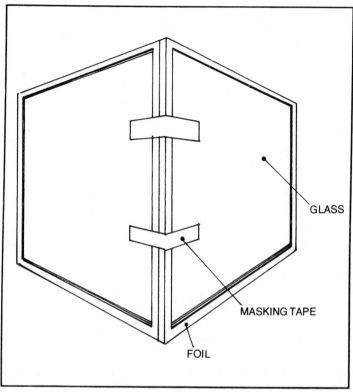

GLASS

MASKING TAPE

FOIL

Fig. 16-3. To set the side pieces in place, two sides are placed upright and held together with tape.

along the inside of the corner, as shown in Fig. 16-3. Now put another along the outside. The tape should be positioned in about the middle of the glass and should overlap on each side by 3 to 5 cm (an inch or two). You may find it easier to use two strips of tape, one on the top and one on the bottom. Either way, after you have taped the two sides together, they should stand by themselves and stay in the position they are set.

Add the third side of the box, again, taping it on the inside first and then on the outside. By taping the inside, you add extra support and help minimize the chances of the whole thing collapsing inward.

Set the fourth and last side of the box against the two open ends. They should match up exactly. If they don't, move them around gently until the two edges meet the edges of the fourth piece. Now tape the outside of this last piece to the two sides, as shown in Fig. 16-4.

The four sides should now create a box shape with all pieces set and held together by tape. The box should be secured well enough that it doesn't wobble excessively or lose its shape when you touch it. It may be necessary at this point to adjust it slightly so that all corners are square. You need not remove the tape to do this; just move the sides slightly until any lopsidedness is corrected.

Also make certain that all the top edges are even all the way around and that the bottom edges are all sitting flat on the table. If you do not do this, you will have a problem similar to that of a table with an uneven leg—it will wobble.

Heat the soldering iron and flux several points along each of the inner and outer corners. Tack-solder these points so that the box is held together by points of solder. Remove the masking tape from the entire box, carefully so as not to disturb the adhesion of the copper foil tape or pull it away from the glass. The box is now standing on its own.

The next step is to tin all the seams. Set the box on one side and tin the two corners facing you; then turn it and do the other two. Don't forget to tin the inner seams, too, and the top and bottom edges of the box.

Now you can either leave the box tinned or bead the seams. If the tinning is done neatly, it can be left as-is and look very nice. Of course, I feel that beading always looks nicer, but it is a little more difficult to lay a neat bead on a three-dimensional project than it is on a flat surface, so it may take some practice. Try it anyway, and if you can't get it to look good, you can always flatten the solder out and just leave the tinned surface.

The main problem with beading such places as corners and other areas that are not flat is gravity. If the box, for instance, is not set exactly at the correct angle, the solder will refuse to bead up and will instead stubbornly roll down the sides of the box. Another pitfall is working with an iron that is too hot. This will cause the solder to flow right through the seams and fall on the inside of the box.

So you will first have to set the box so that the seam to be beaded is as flat as possible. You can use a small cardboard box or a couple of bricks or almost anything that will securely prop the box up from both sides so that the surface to be beaded is straight up.

It is best to begin with an iron that is almost too cool, but still hot enough, of course, to melt the solder. Start melting off small

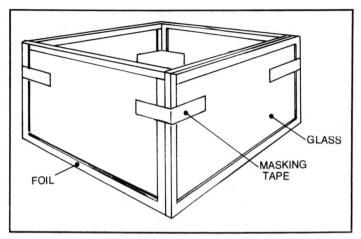

Fig. 16-4. When all four sides are together and held in place with tape, check that the corners are square.

drops of solder along the seam until you have covered it from one end to the other. It will look pretty bumpy at this point.

By the time you have finished this process, the iron will have heated up a little more. Begin at one end of the bead and touch the tip of the iron onto the surface of the solder. The solder will become molten again and should form the beginning of the rounded bead you are after.

To round off this bead, then, here is the basic process. "Dip" the iron into the solder, moving slowly along the length of the seam. Don't try to hurry this; you won't get good results. Work slowly, overlapping each dip into the previous one to get uniformity on the bead. Don't touch the iron all the way through the solder to the foil itself; this will create too much heat and cause the solder to flatten out completely. Just dip into the top surface of the bumpy solder and bring the iron straight up instead of "dragging" it to either side.

When you have finished the bead (Fig. 16-5), clean it well with a soft dry cloth to remove any excess flux. If you don't do this, any solder that may roll off of one of the other beads as you do them will stick to areas where flux residue remains. This usually means that you will have to melt it to get it off, and in the process mess up the beading you have already done.

Turn the box and prop up and bead each corner seam in this manner. If you have trouble getting the solder to bead, and if it is

209

rolling down the sides of the glass, you will have to adjust the angle at which the box is sitting. Remember that if the box is not propped at the correct angle, the solder will not stay where it is supposed to.

When you have all four outer seams beaded, do the inside corner seams. Those that will be inside of the box. Because these will not really be seen, and because it is difficult to bead these seams, it's quite all right to simply tin all interior foiled surfaces, and let it go at that. Be sure that your iron is not super hot and that you do not allow it to remain too long on any one spot. This may cause the heat to melt through the seam and ruin the carefully laid bead on the outer corner.

You now have a box, except, of course, for the top and bottom. The reason both of these are left until the basic shape has been constructed is so that the pieces can be cut to conform exactly with the box, making up for any slight discrepancies in size. Really, no matter how careful you are, this is best left until the box is soldered.

Decide first whether you want the bottom to fit inside the four bottom edges of the box or to cover the edges, thereby adding very slightly to the height of the box. Either way is fine. The only reason for this decision is that, depending on which way you choose, different methods are used to make the proper-sized template.

You will need a piece of pattern paper to make the template. It should be slightly larger—about 2.5 cm (an inch)—than the box on all four sides. You'll also need a very sharp pencil. To make a template to fit inside the bottom edges (in other words, flush with these edges), place the box on the paper and draw around all four sides on the *inside* of the box. Before you remove the box, mark one side of it with a piece of tape or marking pen. Mark the corresponding side on the paper. This will eliminate unnecessary headaches later on when you are trying to figure out how the bottom fits in.

When you lift the box off, you will have the outline of the template to be drawn on the paper. Your bottom must be made slightly smaller than this shape to accommodate the space the foil will take up. The difference will not be much—0.8 mm (1/32 inch) is the exact amount—but this must be taken into account. Small as this allowance may seem, it must be taken into account or the bottom will not slip nicely into place.

You can do this by eye, really. Either cut to the inside of the line or, if you are the very technical type, draw in another line inside the shape, measuring it as you go. Just make sure that you

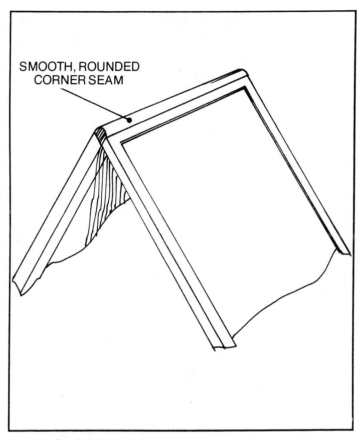

SMOOTH, ROUNDED
CORNER SEAM

Fig. 16-5. Beaded corner seam.

end up with a slightly smaller template than what you have drawn. Don't make it too small, however, or the gaps will have to be filled with solder.

Once the template is drawn and cut out, cut the glass to the template. Be sure, again, to mark the glass to correspond with the marked edge of the template.

Before you foil the glass, set the box over the cut glass to check the fit. If you have cut it correctly, it should just fit inside the bottom edges.

Clean the glass to remove any oil, and then wrap it with foil and burnish all edges.

Again set the box down over the bottom piece. It should fit snugly on all four sides. Be sure you have matched up the marked edges of the box and the bottom glass.

Let your iron heat and, while it is heating, flux all inner surfaces where the bottom and the sides meet. Since the bottom fits flush, there will not be much visible foil on the sides of the box, but you want to create a strong enough bond to enable you to turn the box over without the bottom falling out.

When the iron is hot, tack or tin whatever surfaces you can find. The corners are a must, and are usually easily tacked. Once you have the bottom soldered so that there is no risk of it moving or falling out, turn the box over so that you are looking at the bottom of the bottom.

Flux all bottom surfaces. Using small amounts of solder, tin all the edges and seams where the glass pieces meet. Make the tinning as flat as possible so you don't create uneven edges that will make the box rock. Don't bead these seams for the same reason; besides, it isn't necessary.

If you want the bottom to overlap and cover all bottom edges, the procedure for making the template is slightly different. Place the box on the paper and draw around the *outer* edges with a pencil. Cut this template slightly smaller also, so that, with the addition of the copper foil and the soil, it does not protrude beyond the boxes edges. You may think that this difference will not matter much, but your work will look sloppy and amateurish otherwise.

Soldering is much the same, except you can get right to the bottom of it, if you'll excuse the pun. Turn the box over (on what will be the top) and solder the bottom directly onto the bottom.

Now you can decide if you want to make a hinged top or a loose top that will just sit on the box, or if you want no top at all. Whether or not you hinge the top, you will want the top to fit well and cover all top edges of the box. Make a template for this as you did for the bottom by tracing around the outside of the top of the box. Mark one side as before, and cutting the top slightly smaller to allow for the foil.

For a loose top, simply clean the glass and wrap it. Tin the foil so that it is covered with solder and, voila!—a top is born.

The procedure is the same for a hinged top except, of course, that you need a hinge. Use only brass or copper hinges; small ones can usually be found in larger hardware stores.

Before soldering the hinge on, it must be tinned too. Be sure you use an acid flux. Dip the part of the hinge that is to be soldered into the flux. Coat each part with solder, being careful not to get solder or flux on the movable pin of the hinge, as this will gum up the whole works.

When you have both of the hinge bases tinned, hold them to the foiled glass with a pair of needlenose pliers and apply the iron. The solder that is already on the top edges should be enough to form a tight bond. Repeat this for all parts. A box this size should have two hinges to cut down on stress. Also, needless to say, the hinges will have to be small so that they do not hang over onto the glass, or at least don't overhang too far.

Generally, it's best to leave the lid loose, or device some other means of attaching it to the box. The wear and tear on hinges of any sort will eventually lead to problems, such as the hinge coming loose or the foil pulling away from the glass.

A copper-foiled box is watertight, which no doubt adds to its appeal. Larger boxes can be planted with small plants to make an attractive display. It should be noted, though, that not all plants will grow in such containers because of the lead in the solder. You may have to line such a box with plastic with some holes in it for drainage, but you won't have to worry about leaks.

This box is a very simple, basic experience in three-dimensional work. I strongly recommend that you make one or two of these before attempting larger projects of this nature. You will add to your knowledge as well as to your collection. There are also many ways you can vary the basic pattern. You can add more panels to create a different shape; you can make it taller or shorter or bigger or smaller. You can make one out of different-colored glass, out of one color, or out of clear glass. Experiment and use your imagination!

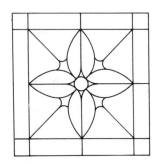

Chapter 17

Working with Mirror

Using stained glass in conjunction with mirror, either for practical or purely decorative purposes, is a unique and effective way of showing off both of them. A few problems unique to working with mirror arise, however.

To begin, you should know that there are many grades of mirror available, ranging from the highest quality to poor quality. You can expect to pay in relation to the kind you are buying; as a general rule, though, mirror is usually cheaper than colored glass.

Buy mirror at a regular glass store if your stained-glass supplier does not carry it (and many do). If you can, stay away from using mirror tiles. These are the kind sold for mirroring your entryway or whatever. They are usually a 30 cm or so square and thinner than the kind of mirror you should be using. They are also usually of somewhat lower quality, which means that they may either give a distorted reflection or that the mirrored backing will peel off too easily. When this happens, you are left with black spots which are plainly visible from the reflective side of the mirror. So be sure that you begin with good-quality mirror.

Mirror is always cut on the shiny, reflective side. To attempt to cut on the back side will ruin the cutter and not do a lot for the mirror, either. It's my opinion that mirror is easy to cut, almost as easy as plain window glass, but I've had a few people tell me that they had really terrible trouble with it. The two important elements are using the correct cutter and getting a good score. Breaking is the same as for other glasses.

The cutter to use for mirror is a No. 2, since mirror is classified as a softer glass. Be sure that the cutter is properly lubricated. Make the score and break it.

Grozing presents a slightly different problem. You must be careful when working with mirror that you do not scratch or chip the backing. This is the main hazard, and the main problem students have. Because of this, any grozing that needs to be done should be carried out with a very light touch. If the edges are very ragged, you might be better off simply to recut the piece rather than risk taking a big chunk out by grozing. Of course, some very small chips may be covered by lead or copper foil, and you don't have to worry about these.

One of the most frequent uses of mirror with stained glass is in a simple hanging mirror. This could range from a mirror bordered on all sides by glass, as shown in Fig. 17-1, to a more elaborate version like the one shown in Fig. 17-2. I prefer copper foiling to leading for constructing mirrors, but either can be used.

The glass most commonly used to accent mirrors is opalescent glass. This is because the mirrors are usually hung flush against a wall where no light can show through them. Antique or semitransparent glass without light coming through them leave a lot to be desired. Opalescents, on the other hand, show color from any vantage point. If lit, either artifically or naturally, the effect is, of course, heightened, but the color will be discernable without benefit of light.

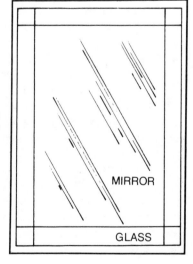

Fig. 17-1. A very pretty mirror can be made by bordering the mirrored glass with colored glass.

MIRROR

GLASS

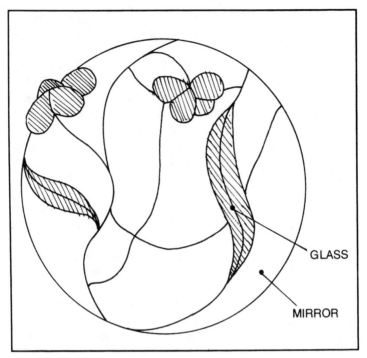

GLASS

MIRROR

Fig. 17-2. A more elaborate mirror design.

Another effective use of mirror is to design the panel you wish to make and do the whole thing in mirror. Geometric designs are especially attractive.

Other items can also be made out of mirror. Boxes, small lantern reflectors, and many other projects can be created with mirror alone or in combination with colored glass.

Whether you use lead or copper foil to put your mirror together, take special care when you begin soldering. Remember to remove any flux that gets onto the backing of the mirror (don't worry about the shiny side). If it is allowed to remain there, it will gradually eat away the backing, again leaving ugly black patches wherever the flux was left. The oleic acid will have a slower action than the copper-foil flux, but either will have this effect. So be sure to observe this rule and follow it diligently. Also be careful during soldering. When you are soldering the back of the mirror, the intense heat from the iron can cause the backing to blister and peel off. For this reason, try to confine your soldering to the smallest areas possible. Do not allow the iron to come in direct contact with the back of the mirror.

Chapter 18
Lamps

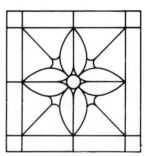

Who doesn't love the beauty of a well-crafted glass lampshade? Bits of colored glass are at their best as they sparkle and shine in the light from the lamp. Even when unlit, a stained-glass shade is a beautiful piece of art. A stained glass lamp provides color and accent to any room.

Because making a lampshade is an art in itself, you should wait until you have confidently mastered the techniques of working flat in glass before you begin a lampshade.

This chapter deals primarily with lamp construction and will show you how to make a lamp with straight plain panels using the copper-foil technique. If you wish, you can alter the directions to make the lamp in leaded came instead. Designing lampshades and making the molds used in their construction is not covered, since they are far more advanced undertakings.

As with starting out in any new area, it is best to start simply. The panel-lamp instructions provided will give you the satisfaction of finishing a project in a relatively short period of time. If you have no use for such a lamp and really hanker for a more ornate one (such as the Tiffany style described under Types of Lamps), at least choose a design that is fairly simple and free of too much intricacy. Lamps with designs and many pieces of glass take much more time than plain paneled ones; I know of one very intricate lamp that took 18 months to complete. Two or four months for a simpler design is not unreasonable.

TYPES OF LAMPS

Lamp building is fun, though frustrating at times. It takes more time probably than any other project you might undertake. Lamps come in all shapes and sizes, from small patio lanterns to desk and table lamps to hanging swags.

The simplest style to make is a *straight-paneled* lamp. These are made up of several triangular pieces of glass. No design breaks up the shade's panels, which can be very narrow or wide at the bottom, tapering toward the top. Each panel is the same size. Straight-paneled lamps are fairly easy to construct and do not take as much time as most other lamps. You can see the results of your efforts in a day or two, depending on how much time you devote at each working session.

Tiffany-style lamps—named after Louise Commfort Tiffany, the man who brought the copper-foil method to popular use—are probably the most time-consuming to make. They are made of many small pieces of glass, often in intricate designs, each piece individually wrapped with copper foil and soldered.

Tiffany's lamps were constructed of glass made in his own glassworks. The glass had unique textures and delicate shadings that cannot be duplicated today. His lamps were often extremely intricate and today are worth thousands of dollars.

A *story lamp* is a combination of the straight-paneled lamp and the Tiffany-style shade. It has plain panels that make up the upper part of the shade and a patterned border of skirt around the bottom.

There are also small *lantern-type* shades, which usually stand only a few inches tall. they can be a lamp in themselves, or they can be constructed to fit inside a metal base, such as a wrought iron lantern.

LEAD CAME VS COPPER-FOIL

Lamps can be constructed with either lead came or with copper foil. The differences between the two are in appearance, strength, and weight. In general, I feel that any lampshade that can be made in lead came can be done better in copper foil. The following guidelines will help you determine which method is best for you.

Generally, a copper-foiled lamp will be more delicate looking than a leaded one, since the soldered foil lines are not so wide or so heavy looking as lead came. A 5 mm (3/16 inch) foil is recommended for Tiffany-type shades, which have many small pieces. It is very narrow and must be wrapped carefully, as it is barely larger than the thickness of the glass, but the final results are stunning.

Lead is used mostly for plain straight-panelled lamps. In shades with small pieces of glass, such as in Tiffany lamps, lead came looks much too heavy and cumbersome. It is also not feasible to work with lead in such shades as leading small pieces of glass, even in flat panels, can be frustrating.

Straight-panelled lamps can also be made with copper foil, which I feel produces a more attractive appearance.

Another element to consider is the weight of the lamp, which is directly related to the strength of the finished glass shade. A stained glass lampshade, whether foiled or leaded, is considerably heavy. A foiled shade, though, will be the lighter of the two. Eventually, with leaded shades, the weight of the hanging glass will begin to pull the lead away from the glass, a process known as *sagging*. If this condition isn't corrected, the lamp will sag more and more, and you may soon have a real safety hazard on your hands. The only way to correct this problem, unfortunately, is to take the lamp apart and relead it.

Copper foil does not present this problem. Most foiled shades are reinforced, which adds, of course, to their durability. However, even if they were not, there is much less danger of the glass separating from the foil than there is with leaded glass.

The bulk of the weight in foiled shades, especially in the Tiffany-style, is not the glass itself, but the solder that such a lamp requires. Much more solder is used in foiled lamps because of the beading involved. In fact, the amount of solder needed is about the only drawback to copper-foiled lamps; a good-size Tiffany shade will easily use a couple of kilograms of solder, and this alone represents a fair investment.

GLASSES TO USE

The most commonly used glass for stained glass lampshades is opalescent, and for good reason. Although you may think the pure colors of antique glass will look pretty with the lamp's light showing them off, this is not, unfortunately, always or even often the case. Any type of glass with a high degree of transparency will allow too much light to pass through; this creates a hot spot; the bane of all glass shades. All you will see when you look at such a shade is the very visible lightbulb growing through and creating an obnoxious glare.

Now, this fact does not seem to faze some people, because I have seen lamps constructed of antique and cathedral glasses. Even cathedral, when used alone, produces this hot spot effect to some degree, although not as markedly as antique or other clear glasses.

If you want to use some of these glasses because of their colors in your lamp, there is no reason you can not do so; as long as you use them with discretion. For instance, a straight-panelled lamp might have a skirt or lower border of antique or cathedral glass. This is quite permissible because the skirt of the lamp will be below the light bulb, not in the path of most light emanating from it, so the light will be deflected. Touches of the more transparent glasses in an otherwise opalescent shade add color and interest, but it is wise to remember not to use such glass in large areas or in places where the bulb will shine directly through.

Opalescent glass being more dense and opaque, does not present this problem. Light is diffused; not transmitted through it. Even when the lamp is not lit, the color of opalescent glass remains fairly true. Unlike transparent glasses that seem to go flat or black without benefit of light, opalescent glass remains bright and interesting.

LAMP PROJECT

This lamp design is only one of a vast array of sizes and shapes of lamps, but it is easy (as easy goes) to make, and is a good project for a first lamp.

The size of the lamp is 28 cm (11 inches) high, which is one way to measure a lamp. The other way is to measure the diameter, usually of the bottom, which in this case is 30.5 cm (12 inches). The top diameter is 5 cm (2 inches). The lamp has 12 sides or *panels*, and all panels are the same size.

The pattern for the lamp's panels is given in Fig. 18-1. Make a *template* of this pattern by tracing Fig. 18-2 onto pattern paper. You will need only one template, since all panels are the same size.

This lamp is designed to be constructed in the copper-foil technique, although, because of its simplicity, it is the type of shade that you will also sometimes see leaded. You will, I believe, have a better-looking lampshade if you use copper foil. I recommend 6 mm (¼ inch) at the very widest, and 5 mm (3/16 inch) foil if you are careful and can do a good job of both cutting and wrapping the glass. Foil this narrow does not leave any room for error in either step.

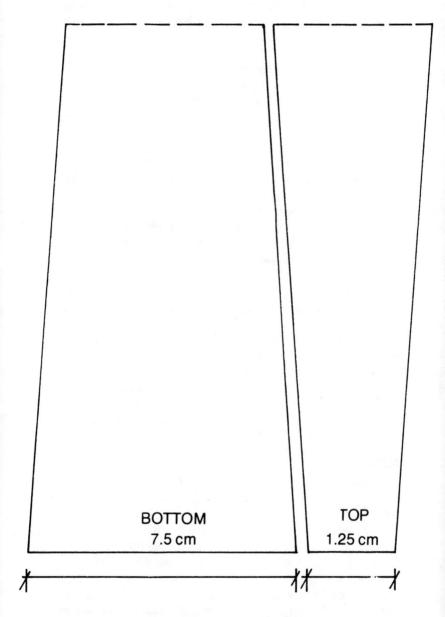

BOTTOM
7.5 cm

TOP
1.25 cm

Fig. 18-1. Pattern for lamp panel drawn to full size. Make a template from this by tracing the two parts, joined at the broken line, onto pattern paper. The pattern measures 28 cm in height. You will need to cut 12 glass panels from your template.

221

When cutting glass for a lampshade, carefully consider how to cut the pieces most effectively—that is how to get the greatest number of pieces from the lease amount of glass—since lamps can require quite a bit of glass. In a straight-paneled lamp, such as the one shown here, the problem is easily solved. Figure 18-2 illustrates the ideal way to layout the pieces on your glass to seriously cut down on glass waste. Cut one piece of glass to the template; then reverse the template (turn it 180 degrees) and cut the next piece, and so on.

You should be able to cut about four panels from one 30 cm by 30 cm piece of glass, and you will need 12 panels in all. You can make the lamp from a single color of glass, or you can use two or three different colors of glass by alternating every other or every third panel in a different color.

Cutting glass for a lamp is the same as for flat panels, naturally. You want to be sure that the cuts are accurate and that the edges of the glass are as smooth as possible. Check your template periodically for fraying edges. This sometimes occurs when many panels are being cut from one template, and it may be necessary to make another template, depending on what kind of pattern paper you are using. Just be sure, if you need to do this, that the templates are exactly the same size! It might be a wise idea to make two in the beginning; it is easier to match them up for identical size when they are unused and unfrayed.

Once the pieces are all cut, wrap them with foil, as described in Chapter 15. Remember to burnish all edges with the Popsicle stick after wrapping so that the foil is as tight to the glass as possible. Now you are ready to begin assembly of the shade.

Assembly

A lampshade such as this is built mostly flat. By that, I mean that it need not be supported in its eventual position as it is being constructed; it is put together flat on a table and then lifted gradually into position when all pieces are set together and taped.

Begin by nailing some kind of wooden stop to your work board. This will provide a solid edge against which to start laying the glass pieces. Set one piece of glass against this stop (Fig. 18-3) and hold it firmly in place with nails at top and bottom. Set the next panel against the first and hold the second securely with nails as well. Continue this process until you have set all 12 panels in place (Fig. 18-4). The space that is left between the last panel and the first determines the angle at which the lamp will form its final

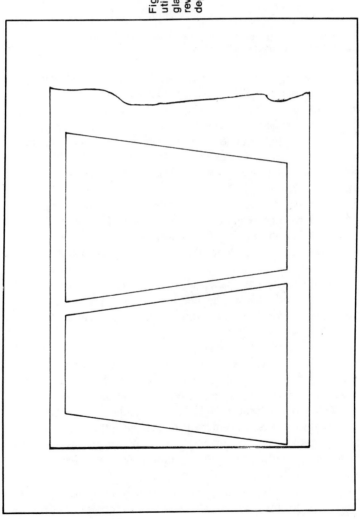

Fig. 18-2. To cut panels in glass utilizing the greatest amount of glass and cutting down on waste; reverse the template (turn it 180 degrees) for each panel.

Fig. 18-3. The first panel of the lamp is set against a wood stop and held in place at top and bottom with nails.

shape. The larger the gap, the sharper the angle. If you had no gap at all, you might as well have made a stained glass Frisbee, because the lamp will not rise to become a shade.

When you have positioned all the panels, then, is the time to check that the top and bottom edges align as they should and that there are no huge holes or gaps between the panels. From this point, you will have to work a little more slowly—and more carefully, too.

With masking tape, tape each piece securely to its adjoining panels. Don't scrimp on the tape here because for a short time at least, it will be about all that is holding the lamp together while you maneuver it and tack-solder. Tape it at the top and bottom and in between for good measure.

When you have the panels taped together, plug in the iron and remove the nails that are holding the pieces in place. Flux each panel somewhere at the top and bottom of each seam in preparation for tacking.

Now you're ready to begin pulling it together. Very slowly and *very* carefully, holding as many of the panels as you can by their upper edges, begin lifting the whole thing up off of the board. Move it gently until the two open edges meet and the panels form a complete circular form (Fig. 18-5). The shade will be somewhat wobbly at this stage, so remembr to keep the bottom edges on the table or work surface and to move slowly. When you have the open edges meeting (the gap is closed), tape these two edges securely also.

The lamp may or may not stand on its own at this point, depending on how liberal you have been with the tape. If it seems

224

too risky, you will have to hold it steady with one hand and begin tacking with the other—just as difficult as it sounds.

Melt off some solder with the iron and touch the iron to the points you have fluxed. If you alternate panels as you tack, you will be able to let go of the shade a little sooner. Tack every other seam, top and bottom; then the shade should be secure enough to stand by

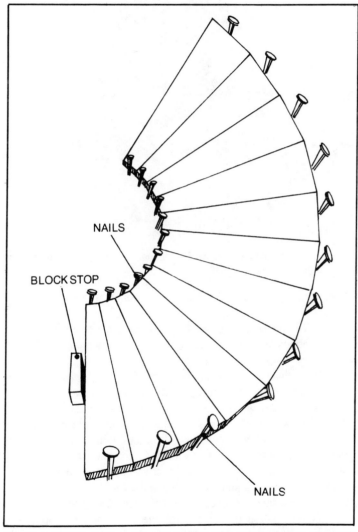

NAILS

BLOCK STOP

NAILS

Fig. 18-4. All 12 panels, each wrapped in foil, are set flat on the work surface.

Fig. 18-5. The lamp taking shape. Each panel is held in place with masking tape until after it is tack-soldered.

itself while you tack the remaining points. You are now halfway home.

Once you have the shade tack-soldered, the rest of the procedure is about the same as for copper foiling other objects. Tin all seams, both inside and out.

Lampshades are almost always reinforced, at least when they are properly made. On straight-panel lamps such as this one, the process is fairly simple. Lengths of copper wire are cut and soldered along the inner seams of the lamp. You need reinforce only every other panel, so you will need six reinforcing wires instead of twelve. Straighten the wire as much as you can; then lay a piece along one seam. You can bead directly over the wire so that it is completely covered and not at all visible. Skip the next seam and reinforce the succeeding one until you have all six pieces soldered in. Remember that this is done on the *inside* of the lamp.

Now take another length of wire and bend it to fit around the top opening of the lamp, as in Fig. 18-6. Turn the shade upside-down so that is rests on its uppermost edge. Working inside the shade, solder the wire along the inside rim of the top opening so that it touches all reinforcing wires along the seams. Bead this reinforcement also.

Now you are ready to begin beading the outer seams of the lamp, just as you have done in other copper foil work. You will need to prop the shade securely between two heavy objects or in a box so that each seam is as level as possible as you bead it. Trying to bead the lamp just as it sits upright is a frustrating prospect as all of the solder will run down the glass; so find something that will keep the lamp held at the correct angle for soldering.

When all soldering is completed, treat the solder with copper sulfate solution or patina, as discussed in Chapter 15.

Wiring

Now that you have the shade, you will need to know how to wire. For this particular lamp, you can either use the vase-cap or the bridge method.

Electrical wiring and lamp parts are available at hardware stores and; better yet, a lighting-fixture store, which have more of a specialized selection. Take the lampshade with you, if at all possible, when you go to buy parts, so that you are sure of obtaining pieces that fit properly.

Figure 18-7 shows a *vase cap*. This is actually comprised of two vase caps, one inside the top of the lamp and another larger one

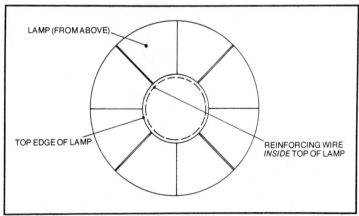

Fig. 18-6. The lampshade, as viewed from above. Copper reinforcing wire (broken line) is soldered inside the top opening (solid black line) and down every other inside seam.

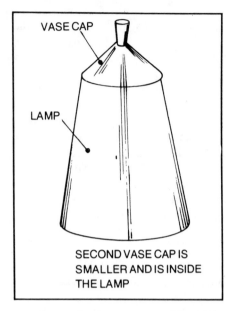

Fig. 18-7. A vase cap can be used for wiring the lamp.

on the outside. The lamp parts hold them together as illustrated in Fig. 18-8. Alternatively, you can solder one vase cap directly to the shade, providing the cap is made of solid brass or solid copper. Use a copper-foil flux for this. The cap *must* be solid brass or solid copper, or it will not take the solder.

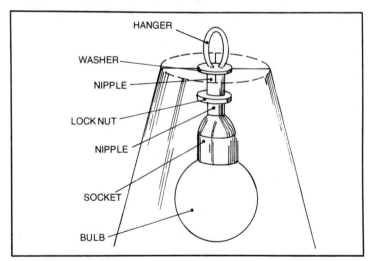

Fig. 18-8. Lamp parts needed for wiring a lamp. They go between the two vase caps.

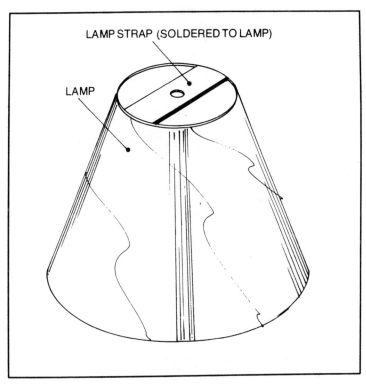

LAMP STRAP (SOLDERED TO LAMP)

LAMP

Fig. 18-9. In place of a vase cap you can use a bridge or lamp strap.

A *bridge* may also be used. This is sometimes called a lamp strap, and a slightly different version that works on the same principle is called a *spider*. Both versions are made of metal and designed to span the entire opening of the lamp's top, as shown in Figs. 18-9 and 18-10. Solder the bridge or spider directly to the lamp and screw the fittings through the hole in the middle.

It is a simple process to wire the lamp in this way, and the fittings often come with their own instructions.

The best kind of bulb to use in a stained-glass shade is a globe type, which diffuses the light over a larger surface. Regular light-bulbs, though, may also be used. The idea is to eliminate as much glare and light intensity as possible.

FORMS

Domed lamps, such as those made by Louis Comfort Tiffany, are usually designed and constructed on a *form*, a solid object or

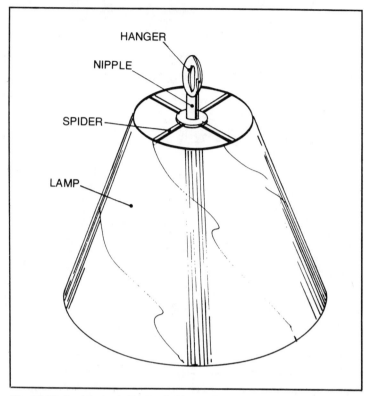

HANGER

NIPPLE

SPIDER

LAMP

Fig. 18-10. A spider is similar to a bridge and is also used for wiring a lamp.

mold made in the shape of a lampshade. In the past, each lampmaker had to make his own form. Wood and plaster were most often used for this purpose. Hardwood molds are still considered the best but are quite expensive, sometimes costing hundreds of dollars. The advent of Styrofoam and Styrofoam lamp forms has no doubt been a real boon to stained-glass lamp construction, and there is today a broad selection of styles and shapes from which to choose.

To design a domed lamp, the design is drawn directly on the form. The pattern for each glass piece is traced directly off of the form. When all glass pieces have been cut and foiled, they are nailed or pinned directly to the form for soldering.

If you wish to make a domed lamp but do not want to design your own, or do not feel you have the skill to do so, you can buy a kit containing a form and design. Many kits contain forms that are only a portion or slice of the whole lampshade. The form may have one or two pieces, depending on the lamp design. A repeating design usually has only one piece; nonrepeating designs may have two. What you will get is a form, a pattern for cutting and assembling the glass pieces, a set of instructions, and a chart telling you how much glass to buy. All you need to do is cut out and number the pattern pieces, cut the glass, and assemble and solder the pieces. For a repeat design you solder the pieces in units or sections; when all the sections are completed; they are soldered together to form the whole lampshade.

Most forms represent one-sixth of the entire shade, for lamps that have six repeats, but molds for one-quarter (for shades with only four repeats) and one-third (for shades with only three repeats) can also be purchased.

These Styrofoam forms are economical, lightweight, and make constructing a domed lamp more pleasure than pain.

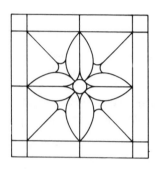

Chapter 19
Repair

There comes a time in every glass artist's history when something will need to be repaired. Careless handling, small children, and accidents are always a threat, and it is good to know how to go about the job of repairing before the need arises. As with other tasks, there is a right way and a wrong way, and I've seen too many people tackle the job in the wrong way.

For the most part, anything that is broken can be fixed, one way or another. Naturally, there are special problems in leaded glass because all of the pieces fit together something like a jigsaw puzzle. To get to one piece, you usually have to disturb quite a few others.

There are basically three methods of repair. One is actually just a means of hiding the break. The other two involve removal of the broken piece(s) in one of two ways. They are more painstaking to make but produce better results. The choice between which method to use is dependent on how bad the break is, how noticeable it is, and where the piece to be repaired is located in the overall design. No repair is easy to make, especially the first time you attempt them. Hopefully you will not need to practice them often.

HIDING THE BREAK

This method of repairs involves adding a new leaded line and is actually the easiest repair to use. It must be used with utmost discretion because it involves altering the design of your stained glass, even if only minutely. Done poorly, it can ruin the continuity of the design and draw attention to itself.

There are two general rules to observe. One is that the break in the glass should be very small to begin with, or at least not immediately noticeable. No gaping holes or shattered pieces here, please. Second, it can be used on large areas only if the leaded line added does not appear to be stuck in after the fact. It is, of course, but it should blend so well in the design that no one but you will ever know (and don't tell them, either!). Figures 19-1 and 19-2 illustrate this point. You must consider how the added lead line is going to appear. If it will be unobtrusive to the design, fine; then use this method. If it is going to look obvious, you should remove the piece for repairs. You will learn the importance of the factor better after you understand what is involved in the process. This method is something like piecing lead during stained-glass construction. The glass itself is not removed.

First clean the surrounding glass areas and leads and make sure they are absolutely free of putty and other debris.

Cut a piece of lead long enough to span the break. Use the same lead type as you used in the original construction. With your lead knife, cut away the entire face on one side of the lead so that you now have a thin strip of lead. Lay this piece over the break and

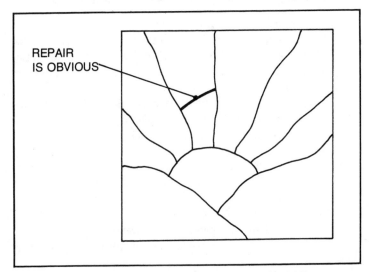

REPAIR IS OBVIOUS

Fig. 19-1. This is a very poor and obvious use of lead to hide or cover a break.

REPAIRED HERE

Fig. 19-2. This is the kind of design in which broken glass can effectively be hidden with additional lead. The repair will never be noticed.

determine if and how it needs to be bent to conform to the break and still look natural. Figure 19-3 shows a piece of cracked glass. Figure 19-4 shows the lead that will be used to repair it. Notice how the one piece of lead is bent so that it will cover the crack when it is laid over the break.

When you have all this figured out, lay the lead back over the crack, position it for the last time, and plug in your iron. Flux both ends of the lead piece where it meets the adjoining leads. When the iron is hot, solder the piece in place just as if you were soldering any other lead joint. You will probably have to hold one end of the piece down while you solder the opposite and so that the iron does not pick up the lead.

Do this on both sides of the glass; don't get lazy and forget about the second side. Remember, you want to make the repair low-profile, so turn the project over and hide the crack on the other side.

After you have completed this step, take a small fingerful of putty and "glaze" the lead line. Just push the putty in and around the

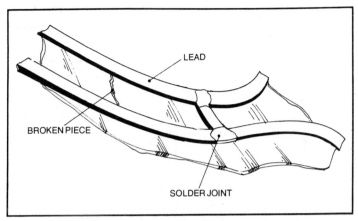

Fig. 19-3. This break can be repaired by hiding or covering it.

lead—on both sides. Apply a tiny bit of whiting and then clean it up. It should now look fully integrated into the design.

In a symmetrical design, say one with a traditional design that repeats itself, it is necessary to add the same lead to each identical point in the design, whether the glass in that area is broken or not (Fig. 19-5).

As you can see, this does sound fairly simple, and it is if you keep in mind that it is not a suitable solution for all problems. Actually, its use is limited to rather few situations, at least if you want to do a professional job.

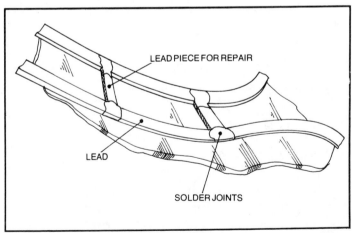

Fig. 19-4. Bend the face portion of lead came to conform to the general break line, place it over the break and solder it where it meets other leads.

Fig. 19-5. Even when the break is only one on side of a symmetrical design, the opposite side should also be patched so that the lines are balanced.

REPLACING BROKEN GLASS

In many cases removing glass is like pulling teeth: it is not easy or even fun to do, but it can be necessary. There are two ways to remove and replace broken or cracked pieces of glass. One way involves cutting or splitting the lead face away from—but not completely off of—the heart and peeling it back. This is done only to the lead that surrounds the broken glass, and only the broken glass is removed. The other way involves completely cutting through the lead heart and removing whole pieces of lead. In this method you usually must remove several pieces of lead and glass—not just the piece that is broken.

The determining factor in choosing which method to use is the location of the broken piece in the overall design. If it is, say, a piece of the border, or toward the outer edge of the design, it is always best to remove it by cutting completely through the lead and removing several pieces of glass to get to the broken one. If the piece is in the very center of the design, you would have to remove quite a few pieces to get to it, so you would want to cut and peel back the lead to remove and replace only the broken piece. Usually the broken piece falls somewhere between the outside edges and the center of the design, and you will have to depend on your own judgement.

Removing Lead and Glass

Although this method often entails removing and replacing several pieces of lead and glass, it is often easier to do. For illustrative purposes, let's say you want to remove a piece of glass that has been broken, and it lies just inside the border glass of the design, as illustrated in Fig. 19-6. The numbered piece next to it

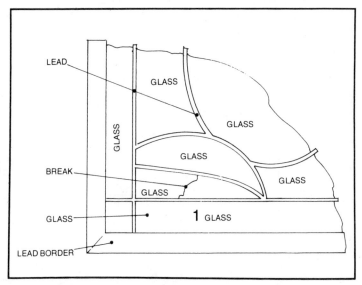

Fig. 19-6. Remove piece 1 so that you can get to and remove the broken piece.

represents the other piece that will have to be removed in order to replace the broken one.

For this process you will need a small saw—like a jeweler's saw or a small hacksaw—a putty knife, and a pair of small wire cutters (not the garden variety).

Set the panel against some sort of brace. The L-shaped lath strips you used to build the panel works fine. Turn the panel so that the area you will be working on is close to you.

Make the initial cuts with the saw as shown by the arrows in Fig. 19-7. You may be able to use your lead knife if you have used a thin border lead, but most heavier border leads require the use of a saw.

Since you do not want to repair any more pieces than necessary, you must be very careful not to place any undue pressure on the glass itself; which could cause other glass pieces to break. Do not lift it up while you are sawing or cutting. Keep the panel flat on the table and cut as much as you can. For the border lead, you can pull the panel slightly off of the table edge to get at the underside.

You can also "unsolder" joints if that will make the job easier. It often does, especially when the solder joints are large or have a

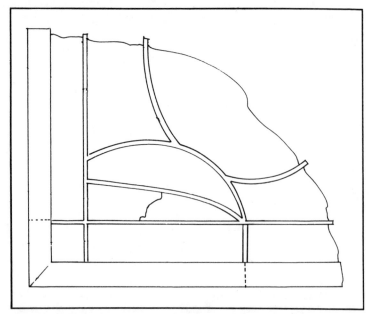

Fig. 19-7. The two broken lines indicate where the border lead must be cut so that you can remove the border piece of glass to get to the broken one.

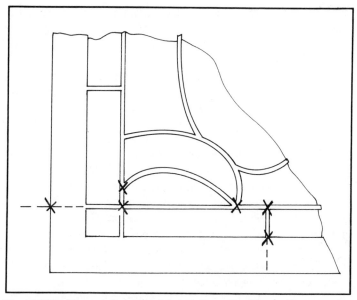

Fig. 19-8. The X's mark the solder joints that must be thoroughly severed to the lead heart.

lot of solder on them and the saw won't cut through easily. To unsolder joints, simply heat up the iron and set it down on the joint until the solder flows. At this point, wiggle the blade of your lead knife in between the two leads. This must be done when the solder is still molten, so you will have to apply the heat of the iron and separate the leads at the same time. Don't worry about saving these leads. They'll be cut away and replaced anyway, so it doesn't really matter if you burn them up.

Make the cuts on the border first. If you are going to unsolder the joints, do so now or else cut through them with the saw until you can see the heart of the lead. Remember that the panel is still soldered on the other side, so don't start pulling and prying yet. Cut through all lead joints on the pieces to be removed (Fig. 19-8) to free the surrounding pieces. Now you must turn the panel over and do the same on the other side.

Once all of the solder joints are cut through, you can begin wiggling the border lead until it pulls free. Remove the border piece of glass.

At this point you must be careful, especially if you will be removing many pieces. As you remove each piece, scrape the old putty off the edges of the glass with your putty knife and lay them down in the exact order in which they fit together. Don't just pile them up somewhere, especially if the pieces are similar in shape or size. If you don't lay them in order, you are quite apt to be completely at a loss when it comes time to begin putting the panel back together again.

To remove the inner pieces, pull the lead away from the glass enough to get the wire cutters in to cut it. From this point you should be able to cut a little and wiggle a little until you can get the glass pieces out. Cut the leads back as far as you can. Try to cut them almost to a lead joint so that, when you begin leading the panel again, the joining will not look too obvious.

When you get to the broken piece, cut it out and remove it. Cut a new piece of glass to match it and then lay it with the others.

Before you begin leading back up, be sure that all the straggling leads are cut back to the nearest lead joint. Then clean out any putty you can see remaining in the exposed channels of the lead.

To begin releading, set in the first piece (the replacement for the one that was broken,) and hold it in with a nail and a buffer lead, just as you did in panel construction. Lead it in, making sure that the new lead smoothly meets the end of the old lead. Set the remaining pieces in the same manner.

When you get to the border, cut a length of border lead that will fit snugly against the open edge; the cut ends should meet smoothly. You must strive for a neat job here especially, or it will look like a real mess.

When you have the border in place, flux and solder the joints. Turn the panel over and solder the reverse side, too. Now all you need to do is glaze both sides of the repaired area.

Splitting and Peeling Lead

This method is used mostly for repair of difficult areas, though it is also satisfactory for small breaks and most other types of damage. It requires cutting face of the lead (the part you can see) away from the heart until the glass can be worked free. The piece is then replaced and the lead repaired. If this method is used conscientiously and correctly, the repair should not be visible. A sloppy job will make the repaired area even more noticeable, so take your time.

To split the lead, you will need to use something such as a putty knife, although a lead knife works best for me. You will also need some epoxy glue.

To begin, cut through the face of the lead near one of the solder joints surrounding the broken piece. Remember not to put

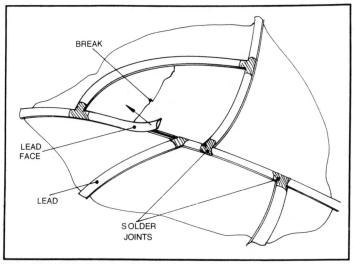

BREAK

LEAD
FACE

LEAD

SOLDER
JOINTS

Fig. 19-9. For stripping the lead face, cut through the solder joint and slide your knife under the face of the lead along the top surface of the glass. Peel back the lead face as you go.

too much pressure on the glass as you will be cutting right on top of it; you don't want to break any more pieces. The face of the lead is cut away by forcing the blade of the knife along the heart of the lead (Fig. 19-9). The face should come away in one piece; if you cut through it, it will be difficult to repair, so go slowly. Make sure as you are pulling the lead away that you keep it as free of bends and kinks as you possibly can, because these will show up later when you begin to repair the lead.

You must cut all of the leads that surround and hold the broken piece. When you get to the end of each lead, bend it slightly away from the glass and leave it attached. *Do not cut it off.*

When you have stripped all the leads, you will be able to see the edges of the glass (Fig. 19-10). If the panel has been glazed, remove as much putty as possible with a nail or other small sharp object.

Begin working the broken glass free of the lead channel. Sometimes it is easy to remove, but sometimes it requires a bit of patience and gentle prodding to get it out. Try not to mar or crimp the remainder of the lead. When you get the glass out, you will have a hole in the panel. Clean any remaining putty out of all the channels. Now cut the replacement piece of glass.

You will probably have to exercise more care getting the new piece back in than you did in getting the old one out, so you must go

241

slowly and not force anything. Trim a little of the glass if you need to, but don't try to push and shove it in.

This is only half the battle. Now you must replace the lead. Before you begin, take the lead face and carefully begin laying it down so that it covers the heart of the lead and the edges of the glass. It should look just as it did before you cut it away. Smooth it down so that it lays flat without bumps.

Once you have determined that it is going to go back smoothly, mix up some epoxy. Spread it with a narrow object on the underside of the lead face and on the exposed lead heart. Follow the directions provided on the epoxy tube for bonding. Don't, however, let it get spread around on the glass.

Lay the face of the lead back over the glass, pressing gently but firmly at small intervals.

When you have finished gluing the leads in place, you will need to resolder the connecting points of the lead. When the glue is quite dry and the lead face is securely in place, you will also have to go back and spot-putty the repaired area. Now all should be back to normal.

CORRECTING OVERALL SIZE

Sometimes it becomes necessary to alter a panel's size because it either comes out too large or too small. Fortunately, this is usually detected before you solder the panel together if you have been taking measurements all along, and you should be. In this case, it is simple to correct, although it does detract from the sense of accomplishment (at least momentarily) and sometimes from the design, too, although not too often.

First check that the glass is tight in the lead channels, if you have tapped and prodded and pushed, and the panel still refuses to shrink that last half-centimeter or so, the only thing you can do is trim it to fit.

To do this, you must remove the border lead on the too-large side and take out all of the pieces of glass there. Trim the pieces to the correct size and then replace them in their position, making sure they are tight in the lead. Replace the lead border and *check the measurement all the way across* to be certain that the border is even. When you have determined that it is, you can go ahead and solder the panel together.

If the panel is too small, you have one or two options, depending on how small or large the difference is. If it is very slight, 1.5 cm to 3cm say you can probably remedy the problem by loosening

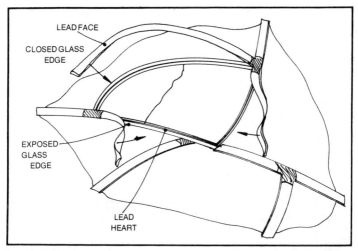

LEAD FACE

CLOSED GLASS EDGE

EXPOSED GLASS EDGE

LEAD HEART

Fig. 19-10. All leads surrounding the broken piece have been stripped back to the solder joints, but not severed off. The edges of the broken piece of glass are fully exposed.

the border lead and a few of the pieces of glass that are in it. At no time, however, should you loosen the pieces so much that the edges of the glass show or rattle alarmingly. This method is only useful for small discrepancies in fit.

For anything more drastic, you will need to remove the border lead and the pieces of glass that lie along that edge. Recut them, making each piece slightly larger to enlarge the panel to its correct measurement. When this is done, replace the pieces as before, seat them well in the lead, and put the border lead back on.

To shrink or enlarge a panel that has already been soldered, there is obviously a little more work involved. Basically, the process is the same as for removing a broken piece of glass. The major operation involved is unsoldering the border lead. It can be cut off if the panel is small, but, of course, you will have to replace it with a new piece of lead, as you will when you unsolder the old lead also. Don't try to reuse border leads that are removed—they will forever look shoddy.

To unsolder a joint, you need only place the iron on the joint until the solder becomes molten. At this point, quickly wedge something sharp and narrow (the blade of your lead knife works well for this) between the two leads so that a clean separation of the leads is accomplished before the solder sets (which is very quickly). You must separate them while the solder is still molten, which means keeping the iron on the joint while you separate the leads.

243

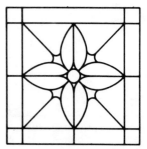

Bibliography

Duval, Jean Jacques. *Working in Stained Glass*. New York: Thomas Y. Crowell Co., 1972.

French, Jennie. *Glass-Works*: The Copper Foil Technique of Stained Glass. New York: Van Nostrand Reinhold Camp 1974.

Hill, Hill, and Halberstadt. *Stained Glass: Music for the Eye*. Oakland: Scrimshaw Press, 1976.

Isenberg, Anita and Seymour. *How to Work in Stained Glass*. Pennsylvania: Chilton Book Co., 1972.

Quagliata, Narcissus. *Stained Glass from Mind to Light*. San Francisco: Mattole Press, 1976.

Rentiens, Patrick R. *The Technique of Stained Glass*. New York: Watson-Guptil Publications, 1967.

Tiffany, Louis C. *Rebel in Glass*. New York: Crown Publishers, 1964.

Index

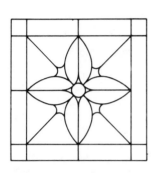

A fascinating intro
to leaded glass design and construction!

All About Stained Glass

by Nancy Walke

Have you ever admired a stained-glass window or leaded glass lamp? Wished that you, too, could turn bits of colored glass and lead into decorative designs? Thought it would be too difficult a craft to learn? If so, here's the book you've been waiting for!

Here are all the practical and creative how-to's of leaded stained glass work. Everything you need to know to make windows, mobiles, and even lamps is covered; from an explanation of the tools and materials you'll need to construction techniques and directions for making actual projects. You will discover that stained glass means more than just one type of colored glass. It means antique, cathedral, opalescent, flashed, slab, beveled, and faceted glass, and much more.

You'll learn about the tools of the glass-working trade and how to use them. There are details on shears, cutters, special glass pliers, knives, soldering irons, glazing compounds, and more. Then you'll get a thorough grounding in the five stages involved in making a stained glass window: pattern making, glass cutting, leading, soldering, and glazing. How to brace and reinforce your work and how to install it are covered along with how-to's for hanging small panels and frame-making.

Because you're bound to have questions as you get more involved in your stained glass project, the author has included a special chapter, written in question-and-answer format, that deals with both general and special problems that may be encountered.

Using copper foil, rather than lead came, to fasten your glass segments together, safety tips, how to make three-dimensional objects such as stained glass lamps and boxes, how to repair damaged pieces, and much more are all discussed.

Anyone who has ever wanted to learn how to make stained glass as well as the glass craftsman who is looking for new design tips and techniques will find just what they're searching for in this complete guide to the art!

Nancy Walke is a magazine editor and free-lance writer who has had extensive experience designing and making a variety of stained glass objects from windows to lamps and accessories.